Dutch Dwellings

DUTCH DWELLINGS

The Architecture of Housing
by Dick van Gameren

PARK BOOKS

Table of Contents

6 Introduction

1 The House
10 Doors, Stairs, and Streets

2 The Ensemble
42 Palaces and Projects

3 The Plan
66 Patterns and Models

4 The People
110 Cooperation and Customisation

5 Space and Material
128 Seven Elements of Housing Design
130 I The Street and the Square
150 II The Courtyard and the Patio
170 III The Park and the Garden
182 IV The Hall
196 V The Fireplace
202 VI The Wall
212 VII The Roof

6 A Catalogue of Projects
226 Apartments
280 Terraced Housing
292 Individual Houses
312 Studies and Master Plans
315 Eleven Facades

7 Appendix
330 Glossary
331 Bibliography
334 Image credits
335 Acknowledgements/ The author

6 Introduction

1 Windows and bricks, Talmalaan, Utrecht (D28).
2 *The Little Street*, view of a canal house in Delft, painting by Johannes Vermeer,
   around 1658 (Rijksmuseum Amsterdam).
3 *The Courtyard of a House in Delft*, painting by Pieter de Hooch, 1658 (National Gallery London).
4 Sketch of canal houses in Amsterdam by Steen Eiler Rasmussen.
5 The open view, Talmalaan, Utrecht (D28).

Introduction

The design of housing is again at the centre of attention of both architectural practice and education. In the last decade, the global issues of growing urban inequality directly connected to the lack of affordable housing and the disastrous consequences of climate change have become more urgent than ever. The ongoing rapid urbanisation has made the question of how to design and build housing that keeps our cities accessible, affordable, and inclusive a key issue in today's societal and political debate.

Whether these urgent challenges will lead to a radical change in the architecture of housing is difficult to predict. The house is for most of us a place of permanence, the place where one wants to find a quiet niche away from the rapidly changing outside world. A house is a place where people can connect to their roots, and consequently, for many, requires an architecture that is familiar and firmly anchored in time and space.

After a period where customisation and individuality in housing design took centre stage, calls for standardisation and prefabrication have returned. The dichotomy between customisation and standardisation has been a constant element in the debate on the architecture and production of housing for more than 100 years, as has been the discussion on tradition versus innovation. Looking back on these debates in the past, one can, however, conclude that standardisation often led to an outcome with a short lifespan, and that the design of housing is more characterised by the persistence of existing patterns than by an acceptance of new ideas and innovations.

The architecture of housing today still appears to be closely linked to traditional patterns, in terms of both space and material. It is not difficult to see a direct connection between Dutch houses of today, characterised by a narrow frontage, a brick facade, and generous windows with open curtains that afford a view to the interior,[Fig.1] and the domestic scenes of seventeenth-century paintings by the Delft masters Johannes Vermeer and Pieter de Hooch.[Fig.2,3] One of the most lucid writers on architecture in the last century, Steen Eiler Rasmussen, dedicated a small book, simply titled *On Amsterdam and Delft*,[Fig.4] to what he identified as the curiously modern aspects of historic Dutch townhouses, with their clear colours, lightweight construction, and extremely large window openings, culminating in those masterful paintings of everyday life in light-filled interiors.

2

3

Introduction

4

Where do these patterns come from, how did they evolve over time, and what are the main spatial and material aspects of designing housing today? By understanding these things, we can start thinking about an architecture of housing that addresses the necessities of today and of the future.

These questions on the essence of the architecture of housing are investigated in a series of essays and by looking at a collection of around forty built projects designed by the author. Looking at the projects, the sequence of space from public to private is addressed: starting from the street, the public space; then moving through the in-between spaces of courtyards, gardens, and halls; before arriving at the private heart of the house, the fireplace. Next, the wall and the roof as the material elements of the inhabited space are explored. This is followed by a documentation of the projects as a catalogue of housing typologies. Detailed sections of selected projects illustrate typical construction methods. The main focus is on affordable housing; more than half of the documented projects have been built as social housing, commissioned by housing corporations.

In the preceding chapters the projects are placed in the larger perspective of Dutch housing design, exploring how housing in the Netherlands developed over time, and how this had a defining impact on the author's work. The texts seek to trace the elements that characterise Dutch housing design, starting off with centuries-old traditions of building, and continuing with the major changes that have happened since the start of the twentieth century, when architects became involved in housing design and production. Dutch housing design gained a worldwide reputation in the last 100 years, thanks to architects such as Hendrik Petrus Berlage, Michel De Klerk, Michiel Brinkman, Willem van Tijen, Gerrit Rietveld, Jaap Bakema, and many others, but also due to politicians, housing corporations, and other agencies that recognised the importance of good and affordable housing. The essays investigate the relation between the private interior and the public exterior, how housing in large numbers connects to the city or landscape as a whole, the position and plan of the individual dwelling, and finally the roles of those who commission the housing project, and those who live in it.

Connecting long lines of development over time with the author's projects of today, this publication tries to give insight into what the crucial aspects of housing design are, and to define the characteristics of Dutch dwellings.[Fig.5] The book looks to illustrate what the architecture of housing needs to address in order to make spaces that afford its residents both privacy and community, spaces that can become a valued and indispensable part of their everyday lives. Housing design can and must make a key contribution to the realisation of an 'open society', as Bakema called it, or, in today's terms of sustainable development, to making our cities and settlements inclusive, safe, resilient, and sustainable.

1 The House
Doors, Stairs, and Streets

The House

Cities are shaped by buildings. Residential buildings are the main fabric of the city. The way in which the city's housing takes up open space, creates new private space, and at the same time defines public space has seen dramatic changes in the last 100 years. These changes are clearly visible in how the relation between the private interior and the public exterior was shaped. The visual and functional connections of the two have determined the way Dutch housing and Dutch cities evolved over time, and remain today a fundamental part of housing design.

> Our historic cities of today are a monument of our social history, a memorial, however, from which the unattractive parts of our history, of the life of our ancestors, have been erased.
>
> Auke van der Woud, *Koninkrijk vol sloppen*

Doors, Stairs, and Streets

Auke van der Woud, an architectural historian, published a book in 2010 titled *Koninkrijk vol sloppen* ('Kingdom full of slums'). The book gives a remarkable insight into Dutch cities at the end of the nineteenth century, demonstrating that at that time places such as Amsterdam and Rotterdam were full of overcrowded and dilapidated buildings with thousands living in slum-like conditions.[Fig. 1, 2]

Over the eighteenth and nineteenth centuries, many individual townhouses were subdivided. A typical seventeenth-century house, built to accommodate just one family and their business, would have been converted into an apartment building. Many families were compelled to live in a single room or even in basements, in very humid conditions, lacking adequate sunlight and ventilation, and with poor sanitation. The cheerful and bright domestic scenes of seventeenth-century paintings were an image of distant times.[Fig. 3]

As elsewhere in Europe, the urban population in nineteenth-century Netherlands was growing. Those migrating from the countryside to the cities to find work had to find a place to live within the mostly seventeenth-century borders of the cities, as Dutch military laws prohibited cities from expanding beyond their fortifications. Only when these laws were abolished in the second half of the nineteenth century could cities start to expand and build new housing for their growing populations.[Fig. 4]

Comparing a map showing the built areas of Holland, the western part of the Netherlands, in 1880 with a similar map from today, one notices a staggering increase of the built-up area. This change can largely be attributed to a continuous and massive production of new housing in the twentieth century.[Fig. 5] Obviously, the growth can be explained by the need to eradicate the overcrowding of the historical cities and by the growth of the population from roughly six million people to about seventeen million today. However, the increase of the built area is to a larger extent due to the increasing amount of occupied residential space per inhabitant. In around 1900, a family – then on average composed of five people – would have a residence with an average floor area of 40 square metres, or 8 square metres per person. At the end of the twentieth century the figures changed to an average family of only two and a half people living in 90 square metres – almost 40 square metres per person, a five-fold increase.

The historic centre of Amsterdam still today shows the way Dutch cities and their houses were built for many centuries. Famous is the seventeenth-century expansion, which saw the development of concentric rings of canals divided by a system of radial streets and secondary canals. Within this clearly defined structure, the built fabric still today consists of individual houses, built side by side to form completely closed urban blocks.[Fig. 9, 10]

The traditional Dutch townhouse has several identifying characteristics: the house has a narrow frontage, usually from 4 to 6 metres wide. At the same time, the house is deep, varying from 10 to more than 20 metres. The height can range from two to five floors, always covered by a steeply pitched roof with the ridge perpendicular to the street.[Fig. 6]

There are obviously rational reasons for the linear plot arrangements and the method of constructing these houses. The conditions of the soil in Holland, more marshland than readily buildable land, required an initial collective effort to create streets above water level and build canals to operate as the drainage system to keep the feet of the citizens dry. Building narrow and deep houses allowed the streets to accommodate an optimal number of houses. The availability of building materials played another crucial role. The scarcity of larger wooden beams for construction purposes was a key factor, as already during the Middle Ages most of the trees in the Netherlands had been felled. Larger wooden construction material had to be expensively imported, so it was mainly used for churches, public buildings, and ships. Therefore, to economically engineer wall-to-wall wooden floors, housebuilders were limited to spans of 4 or 5 metres.

This span size is remarkably still the prevalent one in housing construction, although wood and brick as structural materials have been replaced by concrete. Just as persistent is the tradition of building houses with

14　The House

Dichte bebouwing in de Amsterdamsche Jordaan, inmiddels gesaneerd.

Amsterdam, Jordaan, Lindengracht.
Inmiddels gesaneerd.

Amsterdam, Jordaan, Suikerbakkersgang.
Inmiddels gesaneerd.

2

4

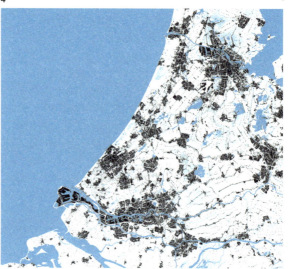

5

3

15 Doors, Stairs, and Streets

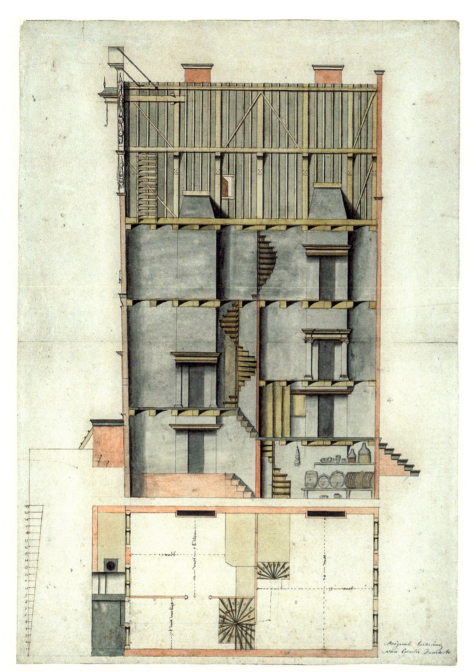

6a

6b

1 Zwarte Bijlsteeg in Amsterdam, 1920.
2 Overcrowding and dilapidated housing in the working-class area Jordaan, Amsterdam, around 1900.
3 Damp, dark basement dwelling on the Zeedijk, Amsterdam, 1913.
4 Built-up areas in the western part of the Netherlands in 1880.
5 Built-up areas in the western part of the Netherlands in 2000.
6 Section, plan, and facade of a typical Amsterdam townhouse, drawing by Cornelis Danckerts, 1678.

16 The House

7 The wooden structural elements of an Amsterdam townhouse, drawing by Cornelis Danckerts, 1678.
8 Two Amsterdam townhouses with wooden frame structure in lower part of the front facade. Doors, some open or half open, lead to the half-sunken basement, the ground floor, and the upper floors.

load-bearing side walls. The dominance of a structural layout with load-bearing partition walls perpendicular to the street facade is clearly connected to the shape of the Dutch house (narrow width, long depth). The most efficient way to build was to combine load-bearing with partition walls, meaning the side walls and the necessary wooden pile foundations were shared with the neighbouring houses. It also made it possible to create very open facades as the facade is only an infill, like a twentieth-century curtain wall facade. In the relatively cold and dark Dutch climate, large window openings are a necessity to bring the desired daylight into the deep houses. Compared with what was customary elsewhere, the facades were built in reverse order. First, a carpenter would position the window frames, on a temporary structure if necessary, and then the bricklayer would fill in what remained open with bricks.[Fig. 7] The large window and door frames, which in many houses dating from the seventeenth century or even earlier span the whole facade at the street level, also had a structural role, carrying the brickwork of the upper floors, a remnant of the earlier fully wooden townhouse structures.[Fig. 8] This way of building remains common today, as facades continue to be constructed as an infill after the main structure is finished.

In around 1880, when cities could finally expand beyond their fortifications, speculative builders took control. They built cheap and fast, endless repetitions of a multifamily house type that was firmly rooted in the centuries-old building traditions. This so-called revolution building did not involve architects, nor any significant city planning. Existing land parcellations, often characterised by a system of small, parallel ditches leading to larger and more widely distanced canals, would simply be transformed into a grid-like pattern of streets. Thus, the size of building blocks was a result of the existing polder land patterns.[Fig. 11, 12]

The new housing areas were as repetitive as the polders. Series of identical housing blocks were erected along seemingly never-ending streets. The street facades showed a clear articulation of the repetition of what was in essence still the typical townhouse of the historic cities, again built with brick load-bearing partition walls and wooden floors. The big difference, however, was that while the old canal houses were built to be single-family homes, the new houses were built for more than one family. The buildings were subdivided; either into four flats, running from front to back, one on each of the four floors, or into a total of eight apartments, two back-to-back per floor. (The buildings' maximum height was four floors, as limited by structural brick walls with a thickness of only one brick, and wooden floor beams.) The units were accessed by a steep and narrow shared internal stair, following the same patterns as in the older townhouses.[Fig. 13]

Although clearly an improvement compared to the overcrowded old townhouses that had turned into squalid tenement buildings, the quality of the units, especially those occupying only half a floor, was questionable. In these units, beds were positioned in alcoves, which were dark spaces without daylight or ventilation. The urban structure resulting from these constructions was also problematic. The block size depended on the old patterns of ditches, often resulting in very narrow inner courts inside the closed building blocks, and overall a monotonous urban fabric.[Fig. 14]

There was an ever-louder debate at the turn of the century on the way the cities had been extended and how the working class was housed, resulting in the Dutch Parliament passing the Housing Law, or Woningwet, which had been proposed by the liberal minister Goeman Borgesius. Passed in 1901 and implemented one year later, the Housing Law was to have a huge impact on how housing in the Netherlands was to be planned, financed, designed, and built.[Fig. 15]

The new law introduced a series of measures to improve the quality of housing and urban planning. Firstly, it laid out a set of regulations establishing minimum qualitative and quantitative requirements for newly built housing. Secondly, it required cities of more than 10,000 inhabitants to make and approve urban extension plans. Both elements of the law meant that architects and urban designers from that point forward had a crucial role

18 The House

9   Map of Amsterdam from 1844, showing no change or growth since 1680.
10 Aerial view of the historic centre of Amsterdam.
11 Map of Amsterdam from around 1920, showing the early urban extensions following the existing land patterns, and the contours of Berlage's Amsterdam South expansion plan.
12 Aerial view of speculative housing in De Pijp, Amsterdam, from the end of the nineteenth century.
13 Speculative housing in Tullensstraat, Amsterdam.
14 The narrow inner courtyard of a speculative housing block in Govert Flinckstraat, Amsterdam.
15 'Dear man, that is very spicy food indeed!': a cartoon from 1901 in which a woman, personifying the Dutch parliament, is presented by minister Goeman Borgesius with the new Housing Law.
16 Diagram showing the location of toilets (*privaat*) in the Jordaan neighbourhood, from a 1920 survey of the area's living conditions. Most dwellings had either a toilet accessed from the kitchen area or no toilet at all.

19 Doors, Stairs, and Streets

13

14

Eerste Kamer (tot Mr. Goeman Borgesius): „Maar goeie man, wat een gepeperde kost! En dat nogal nu ik zoo weinig tijd heb!"
(*De Amsterdammer* (Groene) 9 Juni 1901)

15

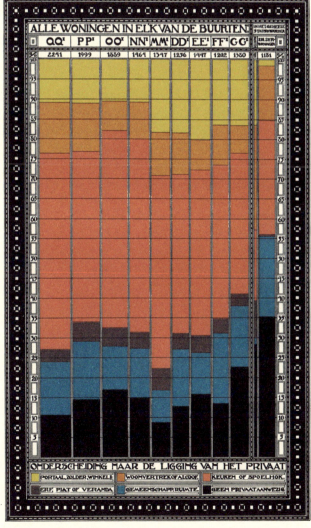

16

to play in the design and formal approval of projects. Other equally important elements were the powers given to local governments to redevelop slum areas and uninhabitable dwellings,[Fig. 16] the creation of design committees to advise on all building applications, and a new system for financing housing that created the possibility for private groups to start non-profit housing corporations.

The book *De Woningwet 1902–1929* was a commemorative publication accompanying an exhibition in Amsterdam that celebrated the twenty-fifth anniversary of the Housing Law, documenting its far-reaching impact on Dutch urban planning, housing design, and production. Looking at the first housing projects developed after the introduction of the new law, it is clear that the designs continued the practices that had evolved over centuries. The construction methods follow the structure of load-bearing side walls of bricks and small wall-to-wall spans, combined with relatively large window openings in the facades.[Fig. 17] What is, however, immediately visible is the architectural intervention. Projects no longer simply repeated the articulation of the standard single, subdivided house, but were instead trying to make the repetitive unit part of a larger composition, paying special attention to what had remained until then completely ignored, the question of how to design the corners of the urban blocks. This first phase of housing design by architects is called the 'rational phase'. Pioneers of housing design, architects such as Jan Ernst van der Pek, Jaap Klinkhamer, and Hendrik Petrus Berlage, introduced a new architecture, one that was efficient, economical, and made use of traditional building methods.[Fig. 18]

Architects began to explore the issue of accessing the individual units. While four-storey apartment blocks were seen as essential to the affordability of housing in urban areas, the shared internal staircase was considered as one of the most unsuccessful components. It affected the privacy of the units and disconnected the dwelling from the street. A residence's connection to the street, in particular, was considered essential to the character of the traditional Dutch house, both in urban and in rural conditions. An (half-)opened front door, expansive ground-floor fenestrations, and a *stoep*, or privately owned strip of pavement in front of the house, created the characteristic threshold and open connection between the street and the house, as depicted by Vermeer, De Hooch, and other seventeenth-century Dutch masters.

Architects tried to come up with alternatives to the narrow shared wooden staircase. Perhaps the best-known example of this effort to reconnect the house directly to the street is the Justus van Effen housing project in Spangen, Rotterdam, designed by architect Michiel Brinkman in around 1920.[Fig. 19] Within a still-traditional structure of four storeys with load-bearing brick walls and floor spans of 4 metres, Brinkman proposed an inventive section. Ground-floor units with two 4-metre bays had direct access to a central courtyard. On top of these units were similar ones, each of which had an individual stairway leading to a front door on the ground level. On top of each bay of these two units was a maisonette unit, only one bay wide but two storeys tall, resulting in a more-or-less traditional 4-metre-wide terraced house with the bedrooms on a second level.[Fig. 20] The maisonettes could be reached by a wide, partly cantilevered concrete gallery, accessed by generous shared staircases and two large elevators. This design allowed for each residence to have its own front door to an outside street, and therefore to receive the then-customary delivery of the daily necessities, such as bread, milk, and other groceries. In other words, it restored the direct connection between the public and the private spheres.

The Spangen block was the first social housing project utilising the access deck, or gallery, typology in the Netherlands. The generous width of the access deck turned it into a veritable street, where people met and children played, as period photography shows. The idea of the 'street in the air' was enthusiastically embraced by many architects after the Second World War, among them the members of the Team 10 group. Indeed, they cited Brinkman's Spangen block as a reference for their own designs. [Fig. 21]

Doors, Stairs, and Streets

It is interesting to note that the three largest cities in the Netherlands all developed their own solutions to the question of how to connect the individual stacked unit to the street. The Hague had introduced even before the Housing Law some specific building rules that were extended later in the Municipal Building Regulations as required by the new law. One of these early rules was the requirement of a direct connection between the front door and public space. This rule was created to abolish a common problem in The Hague: for decades, clusters of tiny courtyard houses, often in a back-to-back typology, had been constructed in the inner courtyards of building blocks. These courtyards, *hofjes*, built by speculative builders to house the urban poor, turned into what contemporaries considered to be overcrowded slums, breeding grounds of anti-social behaviour and criminality, and sources of infection owing to their lack of any proper sanitation.[Fig. 22]

By establishing a rule that all front doors had to face a public street, the construction of these courtyard houses inside building blocks became impossible.

The rule also prevented the construction of apartments with internal shared staircases. This led to some interesting typological experiments and finally to the creation of a specific type of access called *het Haagse Portiek*, which would eventually be employed in other cities as well.[Fig. 23] Typically, the *Haagse Portiek* buildings would have three floors. The ground-floor units had their own front door to the street, and an open, generous stone staircase (as prescribed in the municipal regulations for fire safety) would connect the street with the front doors of the units on the first and second floors. The second-floor units had their front doors on the first floor with an internal staircase.

The development of housing design in Amsterdam took a different turn. After the city's rationalist period (the first phase of post-Housing Law housing design as exemplified by Klinkhamer's early housing and by Berlage's housing on Javastraat in Amsterdam East), a group of upcoming architects, known as the Amsterdam School, focussed more on the exterior architectural expression and less on the development of plans and interior qualities. The by-then acclaimed architect and urban planner Berlage introduced a new design approach to planning new extensions of the city with his scheme for Amsterdam South. In his final 1915 master plan, the grid-like urban structures resulting from the old land parcellations employed from 1880 to 1910 were replaced with a much more formal and rather monumental urban composition of wide boulevards. In between these main arteries, patterns of smaller streets, squares, and green pocket parks were bound together in a larger frame-work of new canals. The plan resulted in eventful sequences of clearly articulated urban spaces and can be considered as the most successful extension plan of twentieth-century Amsterdam, having remained almost completely unchanged in its 100 years of existence.[Fig. 24]

The architectural projects had to follow the proposed urban structure. The large and often irregularly shaped closed building blocks defined the open spaces of the plan. Street corners, nodes such as squares, and the points of bifurcation of the main boulevards had to be articulated by the building blocks. Each individual architectural project had to become part of the urban composition, contributing to the precisely defined continuous street facades.[Fig. 25]

The architects of the Amsterdam School were masters at designing facades that could express the intentions of the urban plan. They developed a unique expressionist brick architecture. The most talented exponents of the Amsterdam School – architects Piet Kramer, Joan van der Mey, and probably the most famous of all, Michel de Klerk – contributed several projects to the extension.

Remarkably, their best-known and most expressive projects were for social housing, commissioned by the Amsterdam housing corporations. For almost all of the twentieth century, Amsterdam was governed by social-democrat city councils for whom the creation of social housing was a key policy. The ideal was to create social housing for the working class as, or even more, beautiful than the

22　The House

17

18

19

20

21

23　Doors, Stairs, and Streets

22

23

17　One of the first housing projects built under the new Housing Law. Van Beuningenstraat in Amsterdam, design by Van der Pek.
18　Javastraat in Amsterdam, design by Berlage.
19　Perspective with view into the collective courtyard of the Spangen housing project in Rotterdam, design by Brinkman.
20　The Spangen project, as built.
21　Early view of the 'street life' on the upper access deck of the Spangen project.
22　The courtyard housing for the poor in The Hague.
23　Typical example of a housing block with a *Haagse Portiek*.

24 The House

24

25

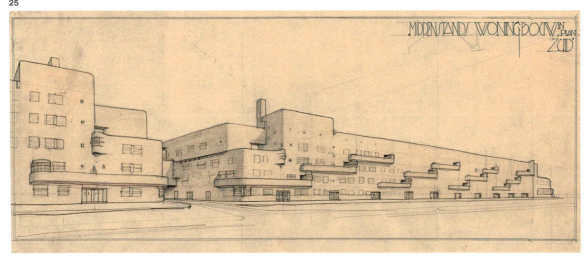

26

25 Doors, Stairs, and Streets

27

28

29

30

31

24 Berlage's Amsterdam South extension plan, 1915.
25 Aerial view of the eastern part of Berlage's extension plan looking towards the River Amstel, as built in the 1920s and 1930s.
26 Sketch of De Klerk's design for housing on the Vrijheidslaan, Amsterdam South.
27 The built result of De Klerk's design, showing the corner shops at the back.
28 Typical Amsterdam housing block, with front doors to the ground-floor units, doors leading to the upper-floor units, and corner shops. Design by Gulden and Geldmaker.
29 Middle-class *boven-benedenwoningen* in Amsterdam South, designed in the office of Eduard Cuypers.
30 Housing on the Churchilllaan, with a repetition of clusters of six front doors. Facade design by Van der Mey.
31 Collage by Alfred Boeken, ridiculing the architecture of Amsterdam South; the caption states: 'Success show: "a laugh and a tear", Facade Parade.'

housing for higher-income groups. These high ideals resulted in facades designed with as much architectural imagination as striking craftmanship.[Fig. 26]

Clear examples of this approach are De Klerk's projects in Amsterdam South for the Dageraad and for the buildings along the Vrijheidslaan, one of the main boulevards. The project on the Vrijheidslaan is characterised by a very strong sculptural monolithic expression with horizontal bands of balconies that end in semicircular bay windows, thus emphasising the speed of movement on the boulevard. The street corners were further articulated with curving corner shop pavilions growing out of the main volume.[Fig. 27] The plans were traditional, and the buildings were still built in the centuries-old way, with brick structural partition walls and wooden floors. The plans were provided by the builders, or other, more anonymous architects. The architects whose names were connected to the projects were often only hired to design the facades. Their ambition to create rather grandiose compositions, emphasising the sculptural possibilities of brick building and articulation of the corners, was often realised at the expense of the interior quality of the dwellings. Criticism started to grow quite soon.

The block on the Vrijheidslaan, with facades designed by De Klerk, is a typical example. The architect's idea to emphasise the mass, the solidity of the built brick volume, led to a design with high and small windows, which were very much against the Dutch desire to have ample daylight and a strong visual connection between the private and the public space. The residents started to complain. So, only a few years after construction, the private company that commissioned the project decided to make some changes, enlarging the windows and lowering the parapet of the balconies along the Vrijheidslaan.

Some Amsterdam architects and builders concerned with the quality of the housing production tried to address the issue of the shared staircase. A local building regulation stated that a maximum of only six apartments could be entered via one staircase, meaning that in most housing projects only the ground-floor units had their own front door on the street while the three upper floors were accessed via a collective staircase.[Fig. 28] Architects looked for solutions where more units would have their own street-facing front doors, thereby avoiding the shared stair. A typical solution for middle-class housing was the *boven-benedenwoningen* type, consisting of two maisonette units, one on top of the other, each with its own front door.[Fig. 29]

The single-floor units in Amsterdam's four-storey buildings, largely used by lower-income residents, required more complex solutions for each house to have its own front door. A layout with six front doors in a row was often adopted, which implied a rather intricate interior disposition of stairs. The ground-floor unit obviously had its front door, next to which was the private front door opening to stairs leading to the first-floor unit. The second- and third-floor units had one shared staircase for both units, which was also accessible for the two lower units to reach the attic, which contained storage spaces for each apartment. Mirroring this layout resulted in a repeated sequence of two, four, and six front doors facing the street, known as the 'door-batteries'.[Fig. 30]

After some early experiments, the ideas and designs of a new generation of Dutch architects and urban planners became more and more prominent. Influenced by architects such as Le Corbusier in France and Walter Gropius in Germany, and encouraged by Dutch front-runners in the CIAM like the urbanist Cornelis van Eesteren, architects started to advocate for a new approach to housing design based on an equal and abundant provision of daylight and ventilation in all housing units, putting the rationality and quality of the housing first, rather than designing the housing block within a formal urban structure. A fierce debate about housing design was initiated by two groups of progressive architects organised in two associations – De Opbouw in Rotterdam and De Acht in Amsterdam – and brought to a wider public in their collective journal called *De 8 en Opbouw*. They argued against housing as built in Amsterdam South, stating that this was *schortjes woningbouw*, or apron housing, resulting in a 'circus parade' that only cared for the design of the street facade.Fig. 31 The modernists stood for the quality of the house itself, the quality and functionality of the plan, the flexibility in room use throughout the day, the amount of daylight, ventilation, and so on. Around 1930 this new modernist, or functionalist (a term preferred by the Dutch), movement gained more and more momentum and resulted in a drastic shift in housing production and design.

A crucial moment in this shift was the 1932 publication of *Praeadvies Organische Woonwijk in Open Bebouwing* ('Preliminary advice for an organic residential neighbourhood in an open building structure'), drawn up by *De 8 en Opbouw* and written by, among others, Van Eesteren and Willem van Tijen. It advocated an 'organic' structure for housing neighbourhoods, which meant a clear and logical connection between the area's green spaces and the city's system of green spaces, a thoughtful orientation of all dwellings in relation to sun and wind, the avoidance of closed building blocks, and the avoidance of positioning dwellings along the main traffic routes.Fig. 32

In 1936, the municipality of Amsterdam organised a competition called Prijsvraag voor Goedkoope Arbeiderswoningen (Competition for Affordable Housing for the Working Class). A subsequent book containing the results of the competition shows that the idea of the closed perimeter blocks with the complex corner solutions and the very expressive facades was gone, replaced with an almost manic focus on rationality.Fig. 33

Discussions on the access systems and the avoidance of shared stairs disappeared, as a central shared staircase was evidently the most economic and rational solution. One can still clearly see this moment of change in housing design in an area called Landlust, in the western part of Amsterdam. What was planned to be another housing area with Berlagian closed perimeter blocks was radically transformed by the city planners by opening the block structure. The narrow end parts of the long rectilinear blocks were left open, to be closed only with single-storey shops or simply with a fence. This resulted in a series of long, parallel free-standing slabs of housing, avoiding all complexities of corner units, and giving each unit the same amount of daylight and sun. With this rather simple adaptation, suddenly a completely new urban structure arrived. The perimeter block where the inside courtyard of the block was not visible from the street dissolved. The courtyard was transformed into a collective space accessible to all the people living there, visible from the public street. An issue of the *De 8 en Opbouw* magazine from 1935 was entirely dedicated to the merits of the Landlust project.Fig. 34

The housing blocks themselves were still built with brick load-bearing walls and wooden floors. However, the appearance of balconies on the best sunlit side irrespective of the position towards a street or the inner courtyard introduced a new architecture of housing. The balcony changed from a utility space that was not seen from the street into a dominant element in the architectural expression of housing design. With a seemingly minor intervention in the urban structure, a completely new way of thinking about and building housing in the city took off.Fig. 35

Simultaneous with the Landlust project in Amsterdam, a more radical innovation was realised in Rotterdam. The Bergpolderflat, finished in 1934 and designed by Willem van Tijen, who would become one of the main protagonists of Dutch post-war housing design, abandoned all long-standing conventions of housing design. Nine floors of identical apartments were accessed by open galleries, which were mirrored on the other side of the building to serve as private balconies. The load-bearing structure was made of steel.Fig. 36 Facades and interior partitions were made as transparent as possible with windows in the exterior stretching from partition wall to partition wall. The facades were designed with the most lightweight, open infill possible. Brick as a material was conspicuously absent.Fig. 37 There was an intention to provide collective amenities, such as a kindergarten, to compensate for the minimal space inside the dwelling units. However, in practice, only a laundry room and a shop next to the entrance hall were part of the final construction.Fig. 38

The House

32

33

34

32 Cover collage of the study of De 8 en Opbouw promoting 'An organic residential neighbourhood in an open building structure'.
33 Cover of a publication on the results of a competition for affordable working-class housing organised by the Amsterdam Municipality.
34 Cover of *De 8 en Opbouw* magazine devoted to the Landlust project in Amsterdam West.
35 The Landlust project, design by Merkelbach and Karsten.
36 The steel structure of the Rotterdam Bergpolderflat, design by Van Tijen.
37 The Bergpolderflat, with shops in the entrance pavilion.
38 Interior of a dwelling in the Bergpolderflat.

29 Doors, Stairs, and Streets

35

37

36

38

The House

The days of the ubiquitous closed perimeter blocks with awkward interior solutions and units without cross ventilation were gone. Twenty years after Berlage's monumental Amsterdam South expansion plan, the municipal planning office led by Cornelis van Eesteren presented a radical new extension plan, called the Algemene Uitbreidingsplan van Amsterdam (General Extension Plan, AUP). The AUP was characterised by a spacious framework of green spaces and wide roads with clusters of free-standing housing blocks. Fig. 39

A few years after the AUP was introduced, the Nazis invaded the Netherlands, leading to a period of stagnation. When the war ended in 1945, the country faced a major housing crisis. Some cities had been severely damaged and the population after the war started to grow drastically, in the baby boom era. This resulted in a period when the country's economy had to be built up again, and an enormous need for affordable housing had to be addressed.

A group of architects, who, before the war, were all on the frontline of modernism, were now collected in Groep 32 and had created a counterplan for the AUP project. They proposed a return to what they saw as the Amsterdam traditions of urban planning and published an extensive study. The design proposed a new concentric ring of canals, and a monumental ordering of the housing in large, meandering and complex octagonal superblocks. The project was published in 1946 in the book *Bouwen in Amsterdam*, but was never seriously considered by the city, and it remained a design on paper only. Fig. 40

The post-war construction of the Western Garden Cities according to the 1935 AUP resulted in vast residential areas that were, in terms of housing types and architecture, extremely monotonous. The closed building blocks of earlier times were replaced by geometrical configurations of free-standing housing blocks in larger repetitive clusters, creating a series of new residential neighbourhoods. One architect would design a cluster of three or four blocks, called a *wooneenheid* (residential unit), that would be repeated eight or nine times, and then another architect would design another cluster, again to be repeated to form another neighbourhood. Fig. 41, 42

Though the repetitive character can be understood in part as the result of the scarcity of material and money after the war, it can also be seen as a reflection of Dutch society at that moment. The idea of the multicultural globalised society, which is now very strong in a city like Amsterdam, would arrive only thirty years later. The Western Garden Cities were built for a very homogeneous population. In order to make the housing affordable, almost all the projects were built as social housing by the Amsterdam housing corporations, resulting in the remarkable fact that more than half of the Amsterdam housing stock is still today social housing taken care of by housing corporations. Fig. 43

With financial means limited and the demand for housing enormous, new industrial building methods were gradually introduced, finally abandoning the old modes of construction. The brick load-bearing walls became a thing of the past, and new and experimental methods of concrete construction and pre-fabrication were introduced. The first phases of new buildings focussed still very much on four-storey buildings with apartments accessed via a shared central staircase (this type of building is called a *portiekflat*). The modest building height obviated the need for a lift. In later building phases during the 1960s, lifts became a more common element, and the gallery access system in blocks of more than four storeys became more and more the standard.

To increase annual housing production, large-scale projects designed using industrial building methods became increasingly dominant. This development continued till the early 1970s. Despite the increased use of large-scale, industrial-style projects, the Dutch continued to debate how mass housing – characterised by shared staircases and anonymous and endless access galleries – did not conform with the way most people wanted to live.

The architect Jaap Bakema introduced the idea of a split-level section where apartments were accessed via clusters of front doors on internal corridors with daylight coming in from

Doors, Stairs, and Streets

both ends, allowing the shared corridor to serve as an interior street. The apartments would continue over or under the corridor, giving free views to both sides of the building unhindered by external access galleries.[Fig. 44]

A very interesting experimental housing project from this period in Amsterdam relates directly to the 1920 project in Spangen in Rotterdam. This project, Het Breed, was designed by Frans van Gool, who was very productive in designing housing in the post-war period. Het Breed (1962–1968), located in the northern part of Amsterdam,[Fig. 45] proposed a configuration of long meandering blocks of five floors with spacious single-floor apartments. The units on the ground and first floors have their own front door at the ground level, opening onto an open, covered arcade. The apartments on the three upper levels can all be reached from an internal but open gallery, or as Team 10 coined it, 'a street in the air'.[Fig. 46] These streets were connected from block to block by so-called aero-bridges, which were covered steel bridges identical to those introduced at that time at Schiphol Airport to connect planes to the piers. By connecting the access galleries, a second continuous network of 'streets' was created on the third floor of the project. Another interesting aspect of the project was how full advantage was taken of the concrete structure to create completely glazed facades between the load-bearing walls.

The peak of large-scale, industrial housing production was the development of the new housing neighbourhoods in the south-east of Amsterdam in the 1960s. The large urban extension, called Bijlmermeer, was built with a range of industrial systems. The most dominant elements were big meandering blocks of flats standing in a continuous, expansive, and green car-free space – the ultimate modernist dream, as expressed in Le Corbusier's pre-war visions of the Ville Radieuse.[Fig. 47] The project proposed, in accordance with the earlier CIAM manifestos, a complete separation of functions and of traffic modes: roads for cars were all elevated, the ground level was dedicated to pedestrians and cyclists, and then, on a third level of connectivity built 10 metres above ground, elevated railway lines connected the area to the centre of Amsterdam.

What was planned as the ideal city failed. Many of the intended collective amenities inside the housing structures were not realised, and the proposed building height was augmented with two extra floors, adding to the anonymity of the housing blocks.[Fig. 48] A few years after its construction, serious social and technical problems started to appear; now, only forty years after the project's construction, more than 75 per cent of the development has been demolished and replaced with other housing. One of the major issues of the project was the disconnection of the private from the public and collective space. The vast green, in-between spaces lacked any connection with the housing, as the residents moved from the elevated roads via the parking garages to the endless access galleries, never touching ground. So, the separation of the house and the city, the radical disappearance of a connection between the front door and the street, and the anonymity of the endless repetition of identical units created a living environment that was unloved, neglected, and eventually a highly problematic and unsafe housing enclave.

The reaction to this failure of the large-scale, industrial housing production was to move (back) to the most radically different housing type possible. The subsequent dominant housing type was not the apartment building, but instead the terraced house, in a suburban setting, with a strong individual articulation. Instead of expressing the large-scale, industrial construction methods in an architecture of repetition and uniformity, architects turned again to more traditional housing types and to bricks, articulating the individual house with a strong emphasis on the connection of the house to the street. It was the period of *het woonerf* – commonly referred to as 'cauliflower estates' by the Dutch.[Fig. 49] They can be characterised as fractal-like structures with meandering streets where cars are forced to slow down, front yards where you can park your car, and back gardens that lead to labyrinthine collective green spaces. One of the most interesting examples is de

32   The House

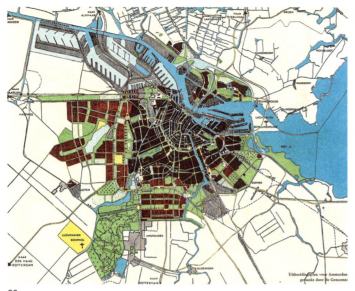

39

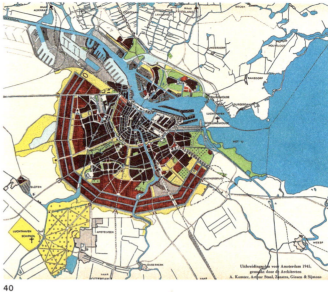

40

41

42

43

39 The 1935 extension plan for Amsterdam.
40 The 1945 alternative extension plan, design by members of Groep 32.
41 The detailed post-war design for the Western Garden Cities, the main part of the 1935 extension plan.
42 Model of the final design of the Western Garden Cities.
43 The Zuidwestkwadrant neighbourhood of Osdorp, the most western part of the Western Garden Cities.
44 The Elvira flat in Delft, design by Bakema, with a split-level layout of units wrapped around an internal corridor, as indicated by the windows in the side facade.
45 Het Breed in Amsterdam North, design by Van Gool.
46 Het Breed's fourth-storey deck, giving access to three floors of units. Aero-bridges connect the different blocks.
47 Construction of honeycomb blocks in Bijlmermeer, the Amsterdam South-East extension plan, 1970.
48 Sketches for the Bijlmermeer housing, showing the intended but never realised collective amenities on the lower two levels.

33 Doors, Stairs, and Streets

44

45

46

48

47

Krekenbuurt in Zwolle, designed by architect Benno Stegeman, who built similar projects in different suburban developments in the Netherlands.

A major drawback of this kind of planning is that these neighbourhoods never became part of the city, as they are isolated, introverted enclaves with little to no public interface.[Fig. 50] Nevertheless, these low-rise suburban housing developments were and still are successful because they offered a clear way to get back to the tradition of living in a house on the ground with your own front door on the street. Over time, many of these low-rise developments turned into endless suburban neighbourhoods, eating up the rural areas between the large cities, either as extensions of these cities, as new towns, or as *groeistad* (villages turned into new residential towns).

These developments remained the dominant development type through the 1980s and were given a new impulse in the 1990s with the Dutch government's Vinex policy.

D29 A typical example of the Vinex programme is the residential development near The Hague, called Ypenburg, which is at first glance an endless sea of suburban housing. However, attempts to create neighbourhoods with a distinctly different character were probably more successful here than in many other similar developments. <u>Deelplan 1</u>, designed in 1996, had to make a contrast with other parts of Ypenburg where the individual expression of the dwellings was the basic principle. Large continuous roofs bind the clusters of terraced houses together in one overall composition, creating the idea of a garden city with a relatively high-density urban character, in which the expression of the open and collective space is the dominant feature.[Fig. 51]

The result of these suburban building booms was an exodus of the middle class, which was escaping the post-war housing areas of the cities to find the suburban idyll of an individual house with a garden and a front door connected to the street. As such, the only people left living in the larger cities were those who could afford to live in what were seen as attractive, mostly pre-war, areas, and those who could only afford to live in areas with slowly degrading, post-war social housing.

Cities had to start looking for possibilities to build new middle-class housing within the often already fully built-up municipal boundaries. In Amsterdam this became a political issue as the city sought to prevent the loss of a middle-class population and to address the threat of the post-war developments turning into low-income enclaves with an amalgamation of social problems, as could be seen in the *banlieues* of Paris. The Amsterdam Municipality started to look at ways to create new housing for new families within the existing city in higher densities than the suburban projects. Two main strategies were employed: the redevelopment of former industrial areas, that is brownfield development; and a radical redevelopment of the post-war housing neighbourhoods. These strategies are in keeping with Auke van der Woud's statement: 'If the Dutch have a national cult today, then it is one of reconstructing and renovating, of cleaning up and replacing' (*Koninkrijk vol sloppen*). One of the best examples of the first approach is Amsterdam's Eastern Docklands, a harbour area that by the 1980s was completely abandoned as its activities had moved westward towards the North Sea to newly developed larger docks and industrial sites.[Fig. 52]

The district was developed in sections, with very different and even contrasting master plans for each harbour pier. Interestingly, all plans reintroduce, in different ways, more or less traditional urban patterns.[Fig. 53] Jo Coenen's master plan for the KNSM Island revived the Berlagian idea of large and monumental closed courtyard blocks lining a central boulevard. Some of the architecture within the plan brought back elements from the Amsterdam School, such as the beautifully crafted wooden entrances of Hans Kollhoff's Piraeus building. Sjoerd Soeter's plan for Java Eiland reintroduced the concept of the individual canal house. The former harbour pier was cut into fragments by excavating small canals that were then lined with canal houses designed by young architects.

D32 Remarkably, the canal houses had to be built as one project, using the industrial building methods developed in the 1970s. Within the restrictions imposed by the building system, it was, however, possible to build a series of houses with very different interior layouts and facades. The five-storey house on two of the new canals shares a lot of characteristics with the historic Dutch townhouse. This new canal house is narrow, about 4.5 metres wide, 12 metres deep, and five floors high.^{Fig. 54}

For the third master plan, designed for the piers called Borneo Eiland and Sporenburg, urban planner Adriaan Geuze of West 8 made a more extreme design decision. He proposed a series of long, parallel closed perimeter blocks made up of three-storey townhouses, bringing back the direct relationship, via the front door, between the house and the street. However, in order to achieve the required densities in a plan largely consisting of three-storey townhouses, he had to introduce some very large apartment buildings that stand out like cathedrals in a city of small houses. Therefore, although considered an example of experimental design, the concept of the project was very traditional in that it created an urban environment dominated by individual townhouses that are directly connected to the narrow streets and quays.

The ideas for Borneo Eiland were taken to their extreme at the Scheepstimmermanstraat. Here individual plots were offered to those interested to have their own house designed and built individually, outside of a larger development. This returns to habits last seen when the historic centres of the Dutch cities were built centuries ago. This idea of an individually commissioned and built house was completely lost in Amsterdam where, from the end of the nineteenth century, housing was built in large projects either by housing corporations or private developers. This new – but also old – way of development opened many eyes. The resulting diversity was enthusiastically received, and similar projects were and still are initiated in many cities in the Netherlands.

D36 In the house designed for the Scheepstimmermanstraat the challenges of this project became clear, both in the process of building and in the design itself. The plot for the house was just 3.8 metres wide, and 16 metres deep. It was decided to make the two narrow facades out of timber window frames only, maximising the light that enters the house. In the heart of the house additional daylight is introduced by means of two small light wells.^{Fig. 55}

The redevelopment of the former harbour district proved successful, and indeed managed to keep middle-class families with children in the city. The city decided to continue the development of similar new residential neighbourhoods, characterised by relatively high-density plans (relative to Dutch habits) compensated by the presence of open water. One new development was IJburg, a new district built in the open waters east of Amsterdam, following a centuries-old tradition of building city districts on new land. Although based on different design principles, the creation of IJburg followed the ideas developed by Bakema in the 1960s in his Pampus scheme (see p. 53).

The first large IJburg Eiland to be built was Haveneiland (Harbour Island). The island's street grid created building blocks with an unusual depth. This, when combined with the required density, meant it was necessary to build houses in the inner courtyards as well, thus creating an intricate system of accessible courtyards and inner streets within the very rational grid.^{Fig. 56, 57}

D12 In the first social housing built on the island – Blok 23B1 – these urban principles led to an L-shaped block in which both terraced housing and apartments are reached by interior streets carved out of the main building mass. The streets, partly open, partly covered, give access to the front doors of the housing units. The old idea of a street in the air was reinterpreted

36　　　The House

49

50

51　　　　　　　　　　　　　　　　↑ D29

52

53

37   Doors, Stairs, and Streets

54 ↑ D32

55 ↑ D36

56

57 ↑ D12

58 ↑ D12

49 Krekenpad in Zwolle, a typical low-rise *woonerf* project, design by Benno Stegeman.
50 Krekenpad in the 1970s.
51 Ypenburg Vinex area between Delft and The Hague (D29).
52 Aerial view of the Amsterdam Eastern Docklands.
53 The Eastern Docklands transformed into a residential area.
    From left to right: Borneo Eiland, Sporenburg, KNSM Eiland with Java Eiland behind.
54 Canal on Java Eiland (D32).
55 Individual houses on Borneo Eiland (D36).
56 Plan of IJburg with detailed design for Haveneiland.
57 Haveneiland being built; in the centre, Blok 23B1 (D12).
58 Inner street on Haveneiland, Blok 23B1 (D12).

as a street on the roof. The top apartments were built as maisonettes, with front doors accessed from an uncovered, open deck. Birch trees planted on the deck enhanced the idea of a street.^{Fig. 58}

The second strategy to keep middle-class families in the city was the redevelopment of post-war neighbourhoods. This initiative took off in the 1990s and focussed very much on the Western Garden Cities, the built outcome of the 1935 AUP extension plan. Built more than forty years earlier, the houses there were considered too small for the standards of the time and technically outdated. But, in addition to obsolete housing conditions, another driver for redevelopment was a social and political one.^{Fig. 59, 60}

As these areas had a large stock of cheap social housing, there was a large concentration of low-income residents, often with migrant backgrounds. The municipality of Amsterdam feared that these areas would turn into a ghetto and decided to start a social engineering programme through building engineering. It initiated an expansive campaign to demolish a large part of the existing housing and rebuild it with higher densities and a more mixed programme, aiming to attract higher-income groups and increase the viability of the languishing shops and schools.

Housing corporations stepped in and started projects by replacing their properties with new housing while tripling the former densities. Two-thirds of the new housing was sold on the commercial market to subsidise the one-third of the new housing that would remain social.

D10 D07 The project in Osdorp on the Nierkerkestraat and the project near Delflandplein in Slotervaart were both based on this strategy. The project on the Nierkerkestraat is part of one of the more radical projects of the Western Garden Cities renewal, as almost the entire Zuidwestkwadrant neighbourhood of Osdorp was rebuilt.^{Fig. 61} Although the city wanted to have less public open space, the generous presence of open space in these areas, with now an abundance of mature greenery, is probably the most valuable legacy of the 1935 design for the Western Garden Cities. Following the original open urban structure, the Nierkerkestraat project was designed not as a closed perimeter block, like many of the other interventions in the area, but as a cluster of free-standing volumes, closing off the in-between space as a collective garden for the residents. The five built volumes all open towards the surrounding streets with large entrance halls giving access to the apartments on the upper levels. The ground-floor apartments connect to the streets with 4.5-metre-high spaces, an open work- or living space in between the street and the other more private spaces of the unit.^{Fig. 62}

For the project near Delflandplein, the municipality also required a minimisation of open green spaces and the creation of a closed inner courtyard. This courtyard was made visible from the street through large double-height openings and entrance lobbies. The building replaced three existing clusters, or *wooneenheden*, of social housing, all with small apartments of around 60 square metres. The new building reflects the much more diverse composition of today's urban population of Amsterdam. Units vary from one-room studios for residents with special needs to six-room maisonettes for large migrant families.^{Fig. 63} This variation in types and sizes was accommodated in the standard system of industrial housing production, utilising a concrete 'tunnel' system with a 5.4-metre floor span between load-bearing partition walls where walls and floor were cast in one go. This system was used in many of the illustrated projects, as wide-ranging as the Java canal houses, the Nierkerkestraat housing, and the IJburg block.

Even more radical than the renewal of the Western Garden Cities was the transformation of the Bijlmermeer. What was the ultimately unsuccessful effort to build the Ville Radieuse of Amsterdam has been changed in the last thirty years into an amazing collage of low-rise terraced housing enclaves à la Vinex, new apartment towers, and closed building blocks.

D13   The project on the Karspeldreef did not replace one of the large original honeycomb structures, but instead the parking garage that served two of them. The elevated road that once bordered the garage has been brought back to ground level. The project contains a mix of social facilities, shelter and accommodation for homeless people, apartments, and terraced houses. The green space that surrounded the original buildings but was not connected to them, is now directly accessed from the terraced houses and from the central collective courtyard via a large open gate.[Fig. 67]

A final project that demonstrates the qualities new developments can bring into the existing urban fabric is the Funenpark on the edge of Amsterdam's historic centre. The Funen project is built on the site of a former industrial area that was used for decades as a railway depot.[Fig. 65] The main idea of Frits van Dongen's master plan was the creation of an inner city; a green, car-free neighbourhood comprising small and large distinctly different buildings with an almost endless variety of housing types. This proved to be a successful strategy.

Looking back at the past 120 years of Dutch housing history, one can see that those neighbourhoods that were planned with one solution, one type of housing, in the end were never successful and had a very limited life span. Society changes and the needs and requirements of people change. A single dominant type in a residential neighbourhood means that people need to move to another, different place if their situation or demands change. The housing of such neighbourhoods increasingly lacks variety over time, and therefore these areas become less attractive places in which to live.

D03   The project for a six-floor residential building in the heart of the Funenpark shows even on the scale of the building itself a mix of types and sizes. It was commissioned by a housing corporation that wanted a combination of larger family units and small apartments for singles and couples in one building of only twenty-two units. The ground and first floors contain maisonettes for families. These units can be considered townhouses, with their own private front doors leading directly to the surrounding green space. As an in-between layer of this sandwich building, two floors contain small one- and two-bedroom apartments. On the top floor, there is another open-air space, with an enclosed square with a tree and small alleys leading away from the square. The square and alleys lead to the front doors of six free-standing two-storey houses. The client saw this as the realisation of an ultimate dream – living in the middle of Amsterdam in a free-standing house, realised as social housing.[Fig. 66] The free-standing position of these rooftop maisonettes creates the rare possibility of having daylight access in one's house from all sides. The windows have been positioned in such a way that there is no privacy issue between the houses. The curtains don't need to be drawn, once more creating the open domestic atmosphere we know from the seventeenth-century Dutch paintings of everyday life.[Fig. 64]

The principle of mixing, of a rich differentiation in housing categories, types, and sizes, proves to be a crucial aspect in creating a new neighbourhood that can, once the residents move in, become part of the city as a whole. Another aspect demonstrated in the Funenpark is the importance of maximising contact between dwellings and the publicly accessible spaces in between. The building rules of the Funenpark master plan demanded a maximisation of the number of front doors on the ground-floor level, leading to direct social control of the open space, which, in this central location in Amsterdam, is a condition for creating a safe public space. It proves how one of the oldest characteristics of urban housing in the Netherlands – the open connection between the interior of the house and the outside public space – remains a key element of housing and urban design.

40 The House

59

60

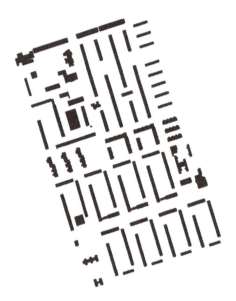

61

62 ↑ D10

63 ↑ D07

41 Doors, Stairs, and Streets

64 ↑ D03

65

66 ↑ D03

67 ↑ D13

59 Interior of model dwelling in the Western Garden Cities, 1956.
60 The same dwelling in 2000. The *portiekflat*, designed by Merkelbach and Elling in collaboration with Mart Stam, was demolished in 2001.
61 Zuidwestkwadrant, Osdorp, Western Garden Cities. Figure-ground diagrams for 1880 and 2020. Most of the original housing has been demolished; some blocks have been renovated.
62 Zuidwestkwadrant, Nierkerkecomplex (D10).
63 Slotervaart, Western Garden Cities, Noordstrook Delflandplein (D07).
64 The interior of a rooftop maisonette (D03).
65 Aerial view of the Funen area. In the centre, late-nineteenth-century speculative housing and, to the right, the former storage and expedition buildings.
66 The new Funenpark project, to the right (D03).
67 Karspeldreef in the former Bijlmermeer. The elevated road has been returned to ground level, the original parking garages and shopping centre replaced by new housing (D13).

2 The Ensemble Palaces and Projects

The Ensemble

Het paleis van de toekomst zal ongetwijfeld gevormd worden door alle huizen samen van de vele mensen die erin wonen (The palace of the future will without doubt be shaped by all dwellings together of the many people that live in them).

Jaap Bakema, inaugural speech, Delft University of Technology, Department of Architecture, 1964

Palaces and Projects

When architects started to be involved in housing design on a larger scale, moving away from the individual house to the creation of larger ensembles, they were looking for precedents of something that didn't exist yet. In this chapter the search for a model for clusters of housing, for the ensemble, that accommodates different groups of society, includes amenities and services, and therefore creates an architecture of community, is explored in the Dutch context and in a wider perspective. Diocletian's Palace in Split, a Roman palace turned into a city, emerges as a recurring source of inspiration. Projects designed by architects based on the ideas represented by the palace and its growth and change over time have resulted in a number of remarkable and innovative developments.[Fig. 2]

> I was fond of wandering about the Adelphi, a mysterious place with those dark arches.

Charles Dickens, the great English novelist of the nineteenth century, was one of the first writers to make urban life as the scene of social relations a central theme of his work. The Adelphi, an exceptional and pioneering design for a collective housing ensemble in London, appears several times in his work. It is 'a mysterious place' in his semi-autobiographical novel *David Copperfield*; and, in *Little Dorrit*, it is a place of unexpected quiet in the heart of London: 'there is always, to this day, a sudden pause in that place to the roar of the great thoroughfare'.

The Adelphi was the result of a daring, and almost failed, undertaking of the four Adam brothers; one a banker, three of them architects. They designed, developed, and built the Adelphi project as speculative housing, a grand ensemble on the banks of the River Thames around 1769. A major inspiration for the project was Diocletian's Palace in Split, which Robert Adam, one of the brothers, visited in 1758 on his grand tour of Europe; he later published a set of plans and views that he had painstakingly recorded and measured in situ. His interest was in the original building, but at the time of his visit, the enormous structure of the Roman palace had already been changed by generations of inhabitants into a city of monuments, churches, working places, and dwellings.[Fig. 3]

The Adam brothers designed a new palace on the banks of the Thames, built of houses and workplaces. It was the first building project in London to face the river. Until then, the riverbanks had been a backyard of the city, lined with warehouses, wharves, and decaying homes alongside the stinking mudflats of the tidal river. In the Adelphi project, the difference in level between the riverbank and the city was compensated by a series of vaulted streets, passages, and cellars set on the bank; these formed the podium for an ensemble of houses, accessed via a second system of streets on the podium level. In the centre of the podium was a closed building block with twenty-four townhouses. The eleven most prominent houses in the block, facing the river, were set back in relation to the substructure, creating an open space initially known as the Royal Terrace and later as Adelphi Terrace. (This is the first known use of the English term 'terrace' to denote a row of houses.)[Fig. 4] The substructure and superstructure homes and streets formed a coherent whole. An arcade along the riverfront and openings in the sides of the podium gave access to the twilight world of the lower streets and cellars.[Fig. 5] A section of the plan is almost a diagram of urban life, an underworld for storage and traffic, populated by workers and eventually the homeless. The two basement floors of the houses on top penetrate into these cellars. These basements were the domain of the servants of the middle-class families living in the upper part of the houses.[Fig. 6, 7]

Despite the design's ingenuity, Adelphi Terrace faced from the beginning many problems. The revolutionary development of densely clustered houses in a palatial composition, on top of working spaces and storage, was difficult to sell. The cellars proved hard to rent for they flooded at high tide. In Dickens's times, they were used as stores for wine and coal. The arched roads between the cellars were always publicly accessible and became a notorious hideout for thieves and the homeless.

46 The Ensemble

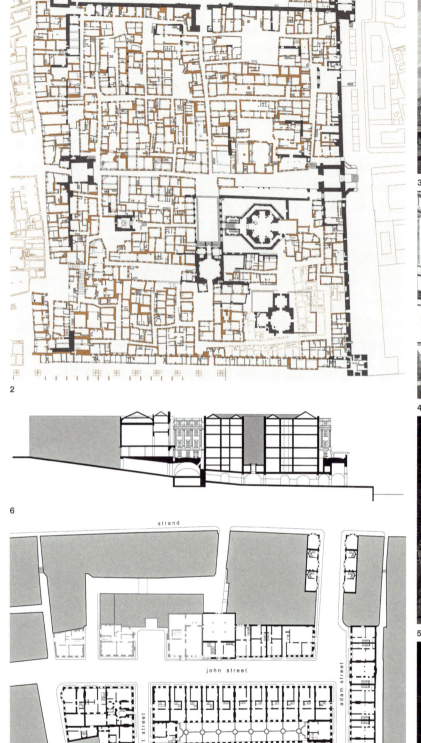

2

6

7

3

4

5

8

47 Palaces and Projects

9

10

11

1 Arch leading into the courtyard of Het Schip in the Spaarndammerbuurt, design by De Klerk.
2 Plan of Diocletian's Palace in Spoleto. In black, the surviving parts of the original Roman palace.
3 Engraving of Diocletian's Palace, seen from the sea, by Robert Adam. Published in 1764.
4 Engraving of the Adelphi project in London, seen from the River Thames, design by the Adam brothers.
5 The subterranean roads and storage cellars of the Adelphi.
6 Section of the Adelphi: to the left the Strand, to the right the Thames.
7 Plan of the deck level of the Adelphi, connected to the Strand.
8 The Adelphi in the first quarter of the twentieth century, before demolition of the central terrace of townhouses.
9 Perspective drawing of Het Schip, Spaarndammerbuurt, Amsterdam, design by De Klerk.
10 Aerial view of western part of the Spaarndammerbuurt, built according to the urban superblock design by Van der Mey from 1914.
11 Plan of the Spaarndammerbuurt; in black, the Zaanhof, the Zaandammerhof, and the projects of Michel de Klerk around the Spaarndammerplantsoen.

The expansion of Victorian London and the necessary sanitary improvements brought fundamental changes to the project and its surroundings. Construction of the Victoria Embankment separated the Adelphi from its river frontage.[Fig. 8] Eventually, in 1936, the entire central block was demolished to make way for a large office complex. Only parts of the terraces of houses that were built on the sides and at the back of the central block survive, together with fragments of the still publicly accessible arched roads underneath. Time took over the Adelphi, as it did Diocletian's Palace, but it was less friendly and much more destructive in London.

The urban squalor and misery of the living conditions of the working class in nineteenth-century cities, so vividly depicted by Dickens, led all over Europe to philanthropic attempts to create good housing for those who couldn't afford it. Only around the turn of the twentieth century did national and local governments start to take care of the problem as well.

In the Netherlands, the introduction of the Woningwet, the Housing Law, in 1901 was a turning point, and the construction of affordable housing commissioned by the cities themselves or by housing corporations became a dominant contribution to urban development in the twentieth century. One of the most impressive efforts in the century's early decades was the design and construction of the second part of the Spaarndammerbuurt in Amsterdam. It is most famous for the Eigen Haard housing block, better known by its nickname Het Schip (The Ship), designed by Michel de Klerk for a housing corporation.[Fig. 9]

Het Schip forms part of a larger ensemble of social housing, designed and built between 1914 and 1921. A number of leading architects, all actively engaged in the new production of housing made possible by the 1901 Woningwet, contributed to the project. The Eigen Haard housing corporation asked architect Joan van der Mey, one of the founders of the Amsterdam School movement, to redesign the street plan for the second half of the Spaarndammerbuurt, a large working-class extension of Amsterdam close to the port and railway yards. Until then, new housing areas were planned in keeping with the patterns of speculative nineteenth-century housing neighbourhoods, following the old land parcellations, resulting in long, narrow, repetitive building blocks.

Van der Mey, instead, proposed a series of superblocks – large, continuous, and often irregularly shaped structures that gave access via gates and small side streets to a second inner ring of housing around large public green spaces. In between the outer and inner ring were private gardens for the ground-floor units, collective gardens for all residents, and playgrounds for the schools integrated in the blocks.[Fig. 10, 11] The result was a remarkable sequence of irregularly shaped streets, courtyards, and squares, all connected to one another. The housing units themselves were based on the then-customary typologies. The brick load-bearing structures and wooden floor and roof construction followed centuries-old traditional building methods.

De Klerk's design for Het Schip fits neatly into the larger composition, with the famous cigar-shaped tower on the longitudinal axis of the neighbouring, much larger Zaanhof. Compared to the other projects, the building is relatively small, filling a rather awkward triangular space between the larger superblocks and the railway yard south of the neighbourhood.[Fig. 12] Like the other superblocks, Het Schip also contained some services, including a post office at the sharp end of the triangle, and a school building already existing halfway down the block was integrated in the project. The small, publicly accessible courtyard behind the post office can be considered a synthesis of the aesthetic and social ambitions of the development as a whole. It was published in many period publications and applauded as possibly the most beautiful space created in social housing at the time. However, critical voices were also heard, commenting on the expense needed for the creation of this 'palace for the working class'.[Fig. 1, 13, 14]

The adjacent Zaanhof was designed by three architects. The outer ring of the superblock was designed by architects Tjeerd Kuipers and Arnold Ingwersen and is based on the standard typology of four floors of apartments with shared internal staircases.

The large, covered porches that give access to the inner garden court are flanked by towers and corner shops on the ground floor, creating the image of a small medieval town. The inner ring, designed by Herman Walenkamp, has a smaller-scale appearance, with three-storey buildings with a *boven-benedenhuis* typology and a school building. The architecture is reminiscent of earlier English Arts and Crafts housing design.[Fig.15] The next superblock, with a highly irregular and complex shape, the Zaandammerhof, was designed by architect Karel de Bazel. Here both the outer ring and the inner ring are built using one typology, the standard type of four floors of apartments with internal access.[Fig.16] The connections between the outer ring and the inner ring are developed as small side streets, not as 'city' gates. A large school is integrated in the inner ring. The closed courtyards between the two rings are designed as collective gardens for the residents, the spacious central court as a publicly accessible square with playgrounds.

State involvement in improving the housing for the working class became visible all over Europe and reached a climax with the large-scale housing programme implemented by the city of Vienna in the 1920s after the end of the First World War and the collapse of the Austro-Hungarian Empire. High levels of working-class unemployment were combined with wretched living conditions, generally regarded as the worst in Europe. The city's social-democratic council initiated a programme to build good, affordable housing for the impoverished working classes, financed by the revenue from newly introduced municipal taxes. From 1923 onward, many building projects were completed, producing a total of 64,000 dwellings. Rents were extremely low, being based solely on a contribution towards maintenance, thus reducing the cost of living for residents. The programme is mostly associated with the Karl-Marx-Hof, a 1,100-metre-long building with two large collective courtyards and a central part with huge gates. The building, nicknamed Ringstrasse des Proletariats, turned from a palace for the working class into a workers' bastion when besieged by fascist troops during the 1934 February Revolution, the tragic ending of the socialist period.

The first projects of the programme, built in the 1920s, were not closed, fortress-like enclaves. Although designed as a coherent whole, their ensembles still endeavoured to mesh with the surrounding urban structure. These *Gemeindebauten* (municipal buildings) created a new transitional space that overturned traditional relations between public and private, outside and inside. The masters of this approach were two of Otto Wagner's pupils, Heinrich Schmid and Hermann Aichinger, who were responsible for a substantial proportion of the building programme. An exemplary work is the Rabenhof, constructed in several phases between 1925 and 1929, on the site of former army barracks and several slums.[Fig.17] The Rabenhof is an urban superblock, fitted with great care into the surrounding urban structure yet whose distinctive spatial structure creates an open egalitarian enclave in the city. In one single grand gesture, the complex links a series of courts connected by gates, superpositioned on an existing street pattern into a network of unparalleled spaciousness. The misery and inequality of the nineteenth-century city, with its closed building blocks where poor housing for those with little means was hidden in inaccessible courtyards behind the decorated facades of the middle-class apartments facing the public streets, were mercilessly exposed by the new collective housing.[Fig.18-20]

The Rabenhof project also contains a large number of amenities for residents, including a theatre, a laundry and bath house, sociomedical facilities, a kindergarten, a library, and thirty-eight shops. The project's building components combine to define a precisely designed, interlocking network of passages, gangways, squares, and courtyards.[Fig.21] It originally accommodated 1,097 dwellings. Despite the wide variety in the form and position of the linked building components, the dwellings are all almost identical and configured in the same pattern. A total of seventy-six staircases provide access to three dwellings per floor: two double-aspect dwellings with three rooms and one single-aspect dwelling with two rooms.

50   The Ensemble

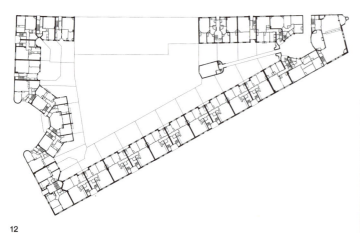

12

13

15

16

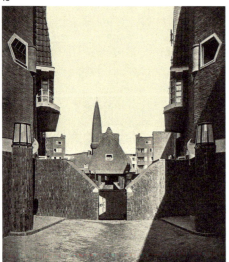

14

12 Ground-floor plan of Het Schip, with the post office in the sharp corner to the right. The white contour shows the existing school building that was integrated by De Klerk in his design.
13 Drawing of the collective courtyard in Het Schip, looking towards the post office, as published in *Wendingen*.
14 The courtyard of Het Schip looking west towards the collective meeting hall.
15 The Zaanhof, inner ring of the superblock, design by Walenkamp.
16 The central courtyard with the original playground of the Zaandammerhof, design by De Bazel.
17 Plan of the Rabenhof in Vienna, showing its insertion within the existing city, design by Schmid and Aichinger.
18 Rabenhof, view of the arched gate over the Rabengasse. To the right, the front square of the theatre.
19 Rabenhof, the Rabengasse seen from the south.
20 A collective courtyard, Rabenhof.
21 'Nolli' plan of the Rabenhof, indicating all collective amenities and collective entrances.
22 Tafuri's *Vienna Rossa* study, showing the Karl-Marx-Hof.

Palaces and Projects

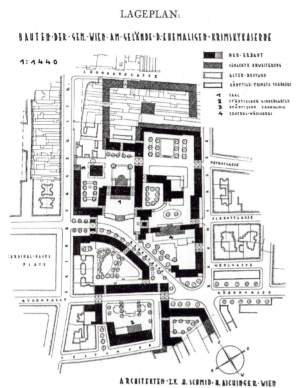

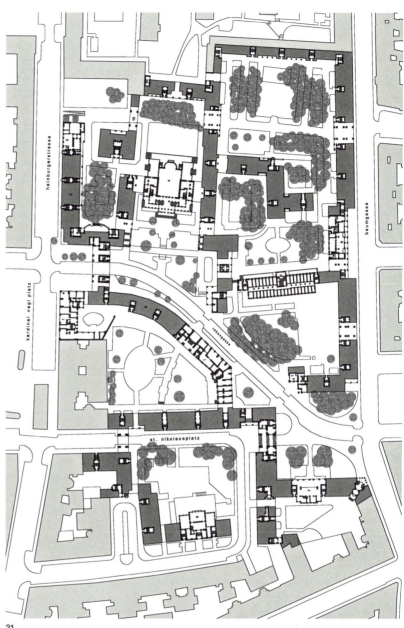

17

18

19

20

21

22

The Ensemble

This progressive programme of social and cultural services was not necessarily translated into a new architecture. The architecture and construction methods of the Viennese *Gemeindebauten* tended to be traditional and labour intensive, thus creating many jobs for those unemployed after the end of the war and the collapse of the empire. Designs were generally planned on the basis of open space and connections to the surroundings; the resulting building mass was then filled with the standard types of dwellings, which were all directly connected to the surrounding city, but were positioned within the project without regard for orientation to sunlight or to the city itself.

Of the many studies of this unique building programme, Manfredo Tafuri's *Vienna Rossa* is perhaps the best known.[Fig. 22] Tafuri described the projects as a conflict between technique, ideology, and form, and hopelessly regressive from a typological point of view. One could address the same criticism to the Amsterdam School housing of the same period. The Viennese and Amsterdam projects were in many respects the opposite to what was happening from the 1920s in neighbouring Germany. Many German housing experiments focussed on the development of new construction methods, and the design of the most efficient plans, either in terms of economy or in terms of functionality and flexibility. Adolf Rading introduced the idea of *Typisierung*, while Walter Gropius tried to formulate scientific evidence of the advantages of high-rise buildings and their linear repetitive ordering. To realise these ideas, the designers looked for open spaces, outside the existing city, a tabula rasa in pastoral landscapes.

It was Le Corbusier, working in France, who took this utopian project to its most extreme manifestations. His Plan Voisin turned even large parts of the centre of Paris into a clean slate for towers and meandering slabs in an endless green space.[Fig. 24] The Unité d'Habitation in Marseille was the most complete realisation, between 1945 and 1950, of his ideas for collective housing and resulted in a vertical garden city, a self-sufficient community, with shops, kindergarten, and other amenities inside the building itself. The residents live in splendid isolation from the city and from one another, in beautifully designed and acoustically separated apartments.[Fig. 23]

The post-war housing needs led to a frenzied search for new models for collective housing throughout Europe. The modernist planners had taken over, and projects like the Viennese Höfe and the Amsterdam School urban ensembles appeared now as images from a distant past. The Dutch architect Jaap Bakema, an active member of Team 10 and already involved in the 1941 study for housing in post-war Rotterdam, worked with an almost missionary zeal over thirty years on the development of the optimum models for housing. He saw housing as the vital element of his vision for a new, open post-war society. In a fascinating series of lectures on Dutch television in 1962, he explained his ideas, later published as *Van stoel tot stad* ('From threshold to town'). [Fig. 25]

Bakema proposed open, geometrical configurations of linear housing blocks, creating long perspectives into the flat, open Dutch landscape. Each grouping could be repeated to form larger compositions, showing many parallels to the aesthetics of the pre-war Dutch De Stijl movement.[Fig. 26] A single cluster, referred to in Dutch as a *wooneenheid* (residential unit), contained a series of different housing types, high- and low-rise, that accommodated dwellings for all stages of life. There were dwellings for couples and singles, small and large families, and the elderly, all together forming the still-homogeneous Dutch society. Over some years, the designs for groupings became more expressive and finally the individual blocks grew together into large sculptural structures that positioned themselves in existing cities or untouched landscapes, on land and on water.

A comprehensive realisation of these ideas can be found in the industrial town of Eindhoven, where Bakema was invited by a collective of individuals employed by the Philips factories to create a design for a new urban neighbourhood with a variety of dwelling types that the clients were unable to find in the existing city.[Fig. 27] The design for 't Hool started

Palaces and Projects

in 1962; the last part was finished in 1972. *De wooneenheden* (visual units) were developed into a large composition of 500 dwellings, mirrored once to create a new neighbourhood of more than 1,000 units. The large ensemble was subdivided by means of a series of private, collective, and public open green spaces. A tower and linear apartment blocks close the ensemble to the north, serving as a town wall between the city and the open land.

Bakema proposed fourteen different housing types, for all types of households and incomes. The result was a built catalogue of housing types with an unprecedented variety. The *groeiwoning* (growing house) type, which afforded the inhabitants to change and extend their house over time, deserves special mention. The notion of 'growth and change' became a driving factor in Bakema's designs. He saw this idea as a fundamental requirement for urbanisation, writing in *Forum* magazine (1962): 'The individual should decide himself on changes in the environment where he lives in order to consider them as his own.'

To illustrate his idea of urban appropriation, Bakema used the example of Diocletian's Palace. As an editor of *Forum*, then the voice of the Dutch structuralist movement, Bakema devoted an issue in 1962 to the palace he had visited during one of his tours of Europe, like Robert Adam did 200 years earlier. Bakema published extensive documentation in plans, sketches, and photography of the palace-turned-town.[Fig. 29] At the end of the *Forum* issue, he drew parallels with Kenzo Tange's metabolistic scheme for Tokyo and Le Corbusier's OBUS project in Algiers, before ending with his own sketches for the *groeiwoningen* in 't Hool.[Fig. 28] Bakema saw the palace in Split as a direct model for urban planning, the creation of a structure or framework that could be adapted to the desires of the people inhabiting that structure.

Besides the idea of growth and change, Bakema also explored the transitional element as a design theme. In his high-rise projects, the elevated street became the main element of transition between the apartment and the city. This street was first introduced as an internal corridor in his prototypical project for the Interbau 1957 in Berlin. In 't Hool, the short corridors of the Berlin project were developed into a network of elevated streets, wide access galleries connected by bridges, spanning the gaps between the blocks.

Another *Forum* issue, in 1965, was again devoted to a single project, this time Bakema's proposal Stad op Pampus, a study for an extension of Amsterdam towards the east, to be built in the open water of the IJ river. Bakema presented the project in *Forum* as 'a contribution towards the solution of the approaching total urbanisation of the Netherlands'.[Fig. 30] It was an alternative to the usual concentric expansions and the ultimate consequence and continuation of his investigations into residential clusters. The main idea of the Pampus plan, a project for 350,000 inhabitants, was to connect the city with nature, so that 'town-dwellers can live in the country'. A central infrastructural axis connects a series of artificial islands; there are clusters of housing on each island, with high-rise buildings positioned near the axis, and low-rise housing towards the edges of the open water. The repetitive linear layout culminates in a denser end point at the fourth cluster of islands, where huge linear structures, *woonwanden* (housing walls), define a continuous spine as the centre of what is essentially a new town of 200,000 residents. The housing units in the *woonwanden* were accessed by way of horizontal decks, elevated streets integrated in split-level sections.[Fig. 31, 32]

This idea of the elevated street was one of the main answers of the post-war modernists to the problem of how high-rise dwellings could become an integral part of the city and its network of public spaces. The 1952 Golden Lane competition in London became an early manifesto of this new way of thinking about collective urban housing. The famous competition design of Alison and Peter Smithson, Bakema's fellow members of Team 10, was an attempt to free the Corbusian concept of the Unité d'Habitation from its isolation and make it part of an (existing) urban fabric. The internal corridor of Le Corbusier was pushed towards the facade, opening it up to a view

54 The Ensemble

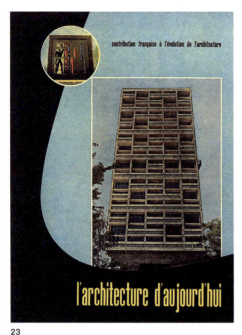
23

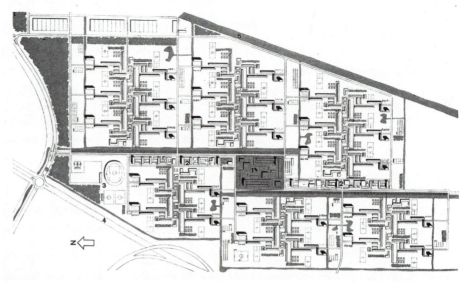
26

24

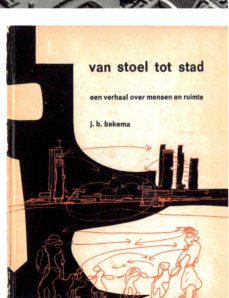
25

27

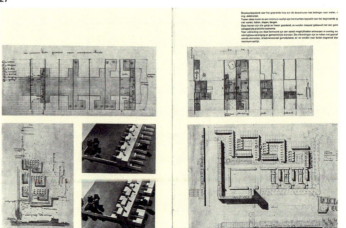
28

55   Palaces and Projects

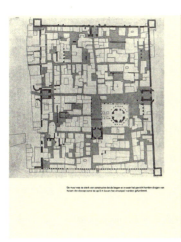

29a

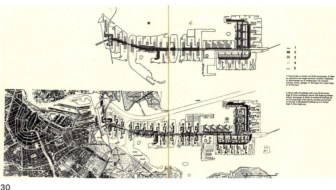

30

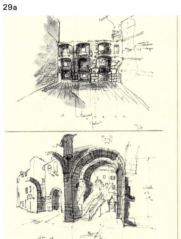

29b

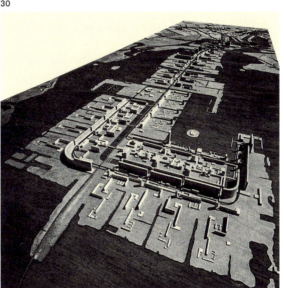

31

32

23   Issue of *L'Architecture d'Aujourd'hui*, dedicated to Le Corbusier's Unité d'Habitation in Marseille.
24   Le Corbusier's Plan Voisin for Paris.
25   *Van stoel tot stad*, the publication based on Bakema's lectures on public television in 1962 and 1963.
26   Urban design study for Noord Kennemerland, by Bakema.
27   Plan of Bakema's project for 't Hool in Eindhoven.
28   Early design sketches for 't Hool, published in the *Forum* issue devoted to Diocletian's Palace.
29   Spreads from Bakema's *Forum* publication on Diocletian's Palace.
30   Spread from the *Forum* issue dedicated to Bakema's Pampus plan for Amsterdam.
31   Model of the Pampus plan.
32   Pampus plan; sketch of one of the nodes of infrastructure, amenities, and services.

of the city, and connecting one building to the next, to make a network of streets 'in the air'.

The Golden Lane competition was eventually won by the architects Chamberlin, Powell and Bon, who proposed a mixed development of high-rise apartments and low-rise terraces, in a cheerful modernist aesthetic. The three architects received a further commission for a much larger development immediately south of the Golden Lane project, the Barbican area, which was almost completely destroyed during the Second World War.

When the City of London published the Barbican Report in 1959, with the final concept design for the massive regeneration of the Barbican area, the architects Chamberlin, Powell and Bon seemed to have the embodiment of Le Corbusier's ideals in mind. As a latter-day Plan Voisin, meandering housing blocks and tall towers were positioned in a continuous open space in the heart of the city.[Fig. 33] The report itself, however, reveals that entirely different sources of inspiration played a role, showing drawings and photos of the Adelphi and other references to London squares and streets. The reference to the Adam brothers' Adelphi project is obvious: the most prominent feature of the Barbican is its double surface level, with a system of decks and bridges for pedestrians about 6 to 10 metres above the original ground level, which primarily accommodates automobile traffic. The architects relate this not only to the project of the Adam brothers, but even further back in history, to Leonardo da Vinci's model of the ideal town, with a similar division of a lower level for transportation of goods and garbage, and an upper level for pedestrians.[Fig. 34]

When positioned next to the Adelphi, the Barbican has an almost identical layout: a substructure with space for (motorised) traffic and storage (car parks) and a superstructure with dwellings. The roof of the substructure forms a large, continuous pedestrian deck.[Fig. 35] The deck, called the podium, supports three high residential towers and several seven-storey residential blocks, whose meandering forms define a number of large, open green spaces at ground level, cut out of the substructure.[Fig. 36]

A total of 2,113 dwellings were built on the site. The three towers, comprising forty-three or forty-four floors, accommodate three spacious four- and five-room apartments per layer. The seven-storey blocks represent a catalogue of stacking options – from simple stair access configurations, internal corridors, some with Unité-like sections, to very complex scissor sections. A large number of amenities, such as schools and a library, were positioned in and around the podium. The Barbican Art Centre takes a central position under the podium and is the main cultural complex of the City of London, the central business district of London.[Fig. 37]

The design of the open space reveals a vital difference from the Plan Voisin: the latter's continuous but indeterminate green space between buildings has been redefined in the Barbican according to traditional urban planning models. The green spaces of London squares and parks were reinvented as collective and public gardens and squares between the residential slabs and towers. The juxtaposition of the green landscaping and the strong built masses of rough concrete resulted in a picturesque and sublime brutalist urban landscape.

'There is every hope that the Barbican area is going to be the showpiece of 20th century London', Pevsner wrote in the second edition of his volume *Buildings in England* dedicated to the City of London, published before the construction of the project started. The built result, however, led to many debates. In 1973 the *Architectural Review* was already describing the project, not even finished yet, as a 'model for a short-lived future'; Reyner Banham referred to it as a ghetto the middle class had erected for itself.[Fig. 38]

It is evident that the pedestrian system, due to its elevated position, is not properly connected to the city around it, turning the Barbican into an isolated enclave. This isolation was, however, intended by the designers; the residential project is a quiet place to live in the city, on top of a prestigious cultural complex. These qualities have been rediscovered, and the Barbican, well cared for by the Corporation of London, is now seen by many as an excellent place to live, proving wrong the pessimistic first reviews.

Just as the Barbican proved to be a model of urban living for the middle class, Thamesmead, a project in east London designed at the same time, was intended as a showpiece of council housing, a housing estate for the twenty-first century. In the mid 1960s, the Greater London Council (GLC) initiated a programme to design a new town for 60,000 people in east London called Thamesmead. The GLC had by then a long history of realising housing estates, many of them designed to replace the inner-city 'slums' consisting of Victorian working-class housing. This slum clearance process continued through the 1950s, 1960s, and 1970s. Thamesmead was intended, among other things, for the resettlement of families from the cleared neighbourhoods. A low-lying wetland area between the River Thames and the Abbey Wood hills had been deemed unfit for large-scale development for years due to poor soil conditions and the danger of flooding. However, lack of space and a high-pressured housing market encouraged a shift in perspective, and the location was developed despite the risks.

Unlike the first generation of English new towns, which were considered monotonous even then, Thamesmead was to become an example of the ideal new town, with a wider variety of building typologies and generous space for employment, services, and recreation.[Fig. 41] The original 1967 master plan, reminiscent of Bakema's Pampus plan of a few years earlier, shows a large number of meandering 'spine blocks' that form the backbone of the district along the main access roads to converge at a large central area around a marina by the River Thames.[Fig. 39] The spine blocks created a wind and noise buffer for the low-rise neighbourhoods positioned behind them. In accordance with the then-prevailing opinion that the separation of traffic modes by means of a raised pedestrian circuit would result in a safer living environment, an internal elevated system of routes through the spine blocks was developed. In the case of Thamesmead, this design also met the requirement that, because of the danger of flooding, there were to be no residential spaces on the ground floor and escape routes had to be present at a higher level. By connecting all first-floor pedestrian access decks, the built first phase of the project, called Thamesmead South, turned into one vast megastructure of interconnected townhouses, towerblocks, and amenities.[Fig. 40]

To deal with the conditions of the land and the flood danger as well, an intricate system of water courses was proposed for the purpose of water storage; the boggiest areas were transformed into small lakes. In advance of the construction on location, building firm Cubitts put a factory in place for the production of prefabricated elements to enable the quick construction of a large number of houses.

Only the first phase of this ambitious master plan, Thamesmead South, was completely realised. In accordance with the master plan, the spine blocks are situated along the north–south throughroute in the direction of the planned centre on the Thames. The complex composition, with a lot of height differences and staggered facades and balconies, provides the blocks with a varied and expressive exterior.[Fig. 43, 44] Located on the top of the parking garage is a raised pedestrian deck flanked alternately by stacked maisonettes and one-storey dwellings for seniors. Bridges also connect the deck to the community centre by the lake and to the two neighbourhoods immediately behind. Here, in a repetitive pattern of staggered short blocks, single-family dwellings are clustered around parking courts or, alternatively, green, car-free courtyards.[Fig. 43] In addition, a number of identical residential towers housing single or double households are situated along the fringes, some along the south shore of the lake and along the east–west access road.[Fig. 42]

Much more than the Barbican, Thamesmead can figure as a 'model for a short-lived future'. Already in the early 1970s, high construction costs and new insights led to drastic changes. As the original vision for the area was abandoned, Thamesmead quickly gained a bad reputation. Due to economic reasons the promises of a shopping area with international yacht haven, transport links to the City, and a

58 The Ensemble

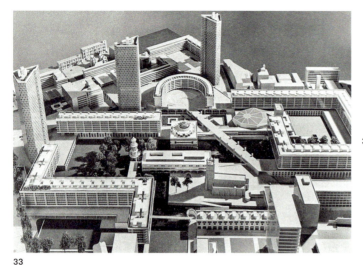

33

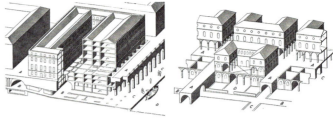

34

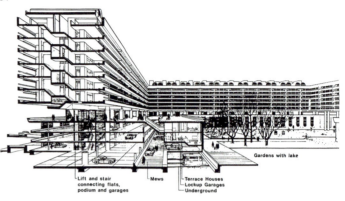

35

37

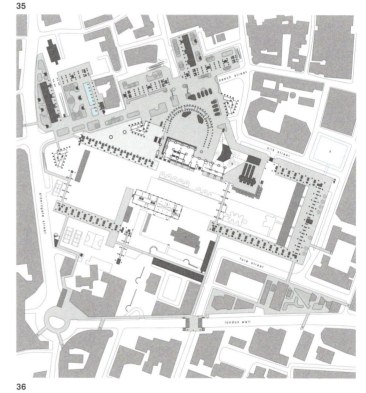

36

00

33 Preliminary design proposal for the Barbican development in London, design by Chamberlin, Powell, and Bon.
34 Schematic drawings of the Adelphi and of Leonardo da Vinci's proposal for an ideal town, as shown in the official presentation of the final Barbican master plan, taken from Bernoulli's 'Der Stadt und ihr Boden'.
35 Section of the Barbican, showing the relationship between the main components of the master plan.
36 'Nolli' plan of the Barbican deck level.
37 The Barbican as built.
38 1973 cover of the *Architectural Review*, with extensive documentation of the then-finished residential part of the Barbican master plan.

Palaces and Projects

39

42

40

43

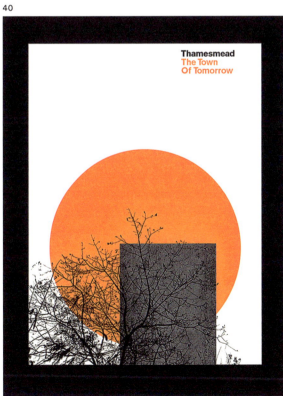

41

44

39 Model of the Thamesmead master plan, with Thamesmead South and Southmere Lake in the upper part.
40 Drawing of the first phase of the Thamesmead South megastructure as built.
41 Poster promoting the Thamesmead master plan by the Greater London Council.
42 Watching the construction of Thamesmead South, with the lake in the front.
43 The central raised deck with the spine blocks at the back, Thamesmead South.
44 One of the first residents of Thamesmead South, sitting near his front door on the raised pedestrian deck.

bridge across the Thames were unfulfilled, leaving the place in an isolated position. The experimental concrete housing construction developed technical problems such as leakages and draughts. Thamesmead's interconnected walkways and elevated living resulted in a neglected space without surveillance on the ground floor. Soon this led to a spiral of decline and the district became known as a 'sink estate' and served as a rough urban setting in various movies, such as Stanley Kubrick's *A Clockwork Orange*.

In spite of the criticism it received and its many failed examples, the ideal of urban life in an open green space hasn't disappeared. The recent Funenpark project in Amsterdam (1998–2010) shows a gentle reinterpretation of these ideas. It does not have the sublime shapes and contrasts of the Barbican nor the endless labyrinths of the Thamesmead megastructure, but instead has a small-scale domestic atmosphere. This is illustrated by the architect and master planner Frits van Dongen calling the plan a reinterpretation of the Garden City model, something the designers of the Barbican made a clear point of rejecting.[Fig. 45]

The Funenpark project brings together many previous concepts for collective housing in the city. While it distinguishes itself clearly from the surrounding city, it connects itself to these surroundings at the same time. It combines the idea of the closed building block or superblock with the idea of individual buildings in a continuous open green space, the idea of a protective wall of housing with that of an inviting open landscape.

This combination of distancing and connecting is obviously related to its context, situated between busy main railway lines on one side, and a typical nineteenth-century, densely built, working-class neighbourhood on the other side.[Fig. 46] The railway tracks are bordered by a *woonwand*, an uninterrupted structure acting as a sound screen or protective wall. Behind the housing wall, there is a car-free green space filled with a series of small apartment buildings or clusters of terraced and patio houses, all standing freely in the open green space, as collective villas or, as the Italians say, *palazzinas* (little palaces).

The park is designed as one continuous open space with a carefully designed web of paths. The paths continue in an open area between the Funenpark project and the bordering nineteenth-century neighbourhood. The careful way of connecting the new and the existing has stimulated regeneration of the adjacent neighbourhood. Thus, the project not only has created an idyllic landscape in the city but also functions as a catalyst for urban renewal.

The wall structure contains 305 dwellings in a large variety of dwelling types, from one-room studios to large penthouse flats and ground-floor atelier apartments. Also on the ground floor are offices, shops, and a women's refuge. An underground parking garage provides parking places for all inhabitants living in the wall housing and in the *palazzinas*. The sixteen *palazzinas* have been designed by a number of architects and show an even larger variety in dwelling types. Each design aims at a certain group of dwellers, from large families to singles.

D03   One of the *palazzinas*, designed for a housing corporation as part of the 30 per cent share of social housing in the project, manages to include a radical mix of housing types within its own small envelope.[Fig. 47]

All the designers had to deal with the question of how to make the connection between the dwellings and the park. Some apartments are raised above the ground level to create distance; others have their own outside deck as an in-between element. In most of the *palazzinas*, the front doors of the ground-floor dwellings are positioned on an internal street, open or closed, bisecting the building volume. These spaces and elements of transition, as Bakema would call them, play an important role in giving privacy to the dwelling while at the same time preserving the public character of the green in-between spaces.

The hybrid character of both the urban layout and the architectural expression of the individual buildings, and the mix of very different types of dwellings have managed to create an ensemble of collective housing that seems to have grown in time. It is possibly this aspect

Palaces and Projects

that anchors the project so convincingly in the city, and is a major reason for its appreciation by the inhabitants.

The desire to live in an urban environment close to work and services is still attracting many newcomers to cities such as Amsterdam and London. Increasing demand for housing in London evolved into a crisis in the 2010s as housing prices soared and the need for affordable houses became immediate, leading to the decision to start a radical regeneration project of Thamesmead, the failed housing ideal of 1970. The arrival of Crossrail at Abbey Wood, which will reduce journey times from Thamesmead South into central London dramatically, represents a mayor opportunity to regenerate the area, rehousing local residents as well as building new housing units to triple the original density.

The regeneration, commissioned by the Peabody Trust, will start with a complete rebuilding of the central part of Thamesmead South, its commercial and public facilities, and the north–south spine block. The original commercial and public facilities were already demolished and were partly replaced by some very low-quality new structures. The iconic spine blocks were in such a bad state that renovation proved both technically and economically infeasible.

D24   Its central position gives the first phase of the project a strategic significance in that it starts the larger process of regeneration of Thamesmead South and of Thamesmead as a whole. The project will provide a new urban structure for the area, characterised by a range of connected public squares, streets, and courtyards articulated by a cohesive composition of clusters of buildings, a clearly articulated mix of functions, and a variety of dwelling types.Fig. 48
Instead of the former spine blocks with a raised pedestrian deck, a ground-level street will make a meandering central connection within Thamesmead South and towards the surrounding neighbourhoods and landscapes, eliminating the disconnection of the old, abruptly ending deck system. The new road will be lined on both sides by buildings that vary in scale and together form a series of clusters or, in Bakema's terminology, *wooneenheden* (visual units) around collective courtyards. Fig. 49

The varied sizes and scales of the building clusters are tied together by the new pattern of streets, squares, and the courtyards that are in the centre of each building cluster. Entrance patios and large transparent entrance halls create clearly defined in-between spaces or thresholds between the public and the private and will make the green collective courts visible from the public space.Fig. 50

The structure of ensembles around the courtyards allows for the integration of existing housing that will be saved from demolition. In the first phase the first new cluster will connect two existing tower blocks with a new tower and several groups of terraced houses.Fig. 51

The larger regeneration project will not create another disconnected enclave or a new autonomous megastructure, but instead a new layer will be inserted over the existing, historic layers of landscape and previous patterns of housing. The result will be a palimpsest, a new urban fabric in which parts of the old patterns remain visible, creating a layered and anchored sense of place, as happened over many centuries in Diocletian's Palace.

> I turned my face to the Adelphi, pondering on the old days when I used to roam about its subterranean arches, and on the happy changes which had brought me to the surface.

The Adelphi, first the bleak scene of David Copperfield's lonely wanderings as a poor young man in London, later becomes the scene of a better future as Dickens's alter ego hires rooms in one of its large middle-class terraced houses on the podium level. The Adelphi thus becomes a symbol for the city as a whole, its diversity, its misery, and its hopes and aspirations. The unique character of the Adelphi

62 The Ensemble

45

46

47

↑ D03

63   Palaces and Projects

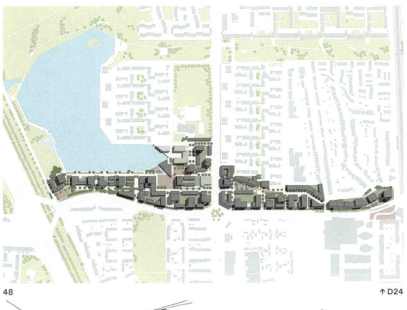

48 ↑ D24

50 ↑ D24

49 ↑ D24

51 ↑ D24

45 'Nolli' plan of the Funenpark, Amsterdam.
46 Aerial view of the Funenpark.
47 Funenpark, view of the car-free space between the *palazzinas* (D03).
48 Master plan for the restructuring of the spine blocks and the central area of Thamesmead South (D24).
49 Bird's-eye sketch of the Thamesmead South master plan (D24).
50 The first built cluster of the new Thamesmead South master plan, with view of the raised deck with the new apartments and townhouses to the right, and the integrated existing tower block to the left (D24).
51 The first built cluster seen from the south, Thamesmead South (D24).
52 The Funenpark *palazzinas* (D03).

fascinated not only Dickens, but many other writers as well, some even living in the Adelphi. One of them, H. G. Wells, seems to have been directly inspired by the Adelphi's two worlds – the dark subterranean one and the one on the surface, full of daylight – when writing some of his more dystopian science fiction works.

This brief and fragmented history of collective housing as urban projects shows remarkable continuities. The recurring inspiration found in the idea of the palace is perhaps the most striking one. The palace is a structure in which people can be part of a larger community, but at the same time find their own privacy and security. This ideal, already brought forward by Leon Battista Alberti in his *De Re Aedificatori*, is the essence of the collective housing project. The private house only takes space away from the city; collective housing gives space back to the city. Collective housing, by its nature and scale, needs to add space to the city, to create places of transition, to allow the residents simultaneously to connect to the city and find private space within the city.

Each project defines its own utopia, its own form of collectivity. The city made up of these palaces, of miniature utopias, is a diverse city. It is now clear that the homogeneous society of fifty years ago has changed for good. Highly divergent modes of life and culture are all seeking a place within our cities. This calls for a city with differences of its own, distinctive parts in which like-minded people can find one another, connected to the greater whole, but without imposing anything on others. The strength of the model lies in the proximity and the accessibility of 'the other'. Contrasts – and sometimes even confrontations – between differing visions propel the city's continual process of adaptation, change, and expansion forward. Assembling a variety of collective housing concepts is the key to give the city the layers and multifaceted identity befitting for our present-day society.

65 Palaces and Projects

3 The Plan

Patterns and Models

The architect [...] has to find somehow a realm of spaces where it is good to live. It is a realm of spaces really which you call 'house'. [...] Then there is one thing that the architect can do nothing about, and that is 'home'. A 'home' has to do with the people in it, and it is not his business, except that he must prepare this realm to make it suitable for 'home'.

Louis Kahn, in a talk at the conclusion of the
1959 CIAM congress in the Dutch village of Otterlo

Patterns and Models

Drawing parallels with the first chapter, in which the relationship between the public and private spaces in housing design was investigated, this chapter explores in detail the development of the plan of the individual dwelling, or in Kahn's words, 'the realm of spaces' that defines 'house'.

Looking to the design of a house – either terraced, free-standing, or an apartment – the plan appears to be the part that is most resistant to change. Whether it is a modest experiment in the functional set-up or a radical proposal to rethink the way housing should be planned and built, most efforts to introduce new ideas on the spatial layout of the individual dwelling have gained little or no foothold. Changes have most of the time been the result of efforts to rationalise building construction and to economise on construction costs rather than the product of architectural intentions. Following the slow process of adaptation and transformation over time, one can see how the standard housing plan has evolved while at the same time remaining firmly connected to conventions that go back centuries.

I The terraced house

The Dutch townhouse (*het stadshuis*) finds its origins in the first urban developments in medieval times. As discussed in the first chapter, the basic shape and structure of this type is still very much present in today's housing production in the Netherlands, not only in terraced housing, or *rijtjeswoningen*, where its impact is obvious, but also in apartment typologies.

The townhouse is characterised by a narrow width determined by the span between the load-bearing side walls, a large depth, and open, non-load-bearing street-facing and rear facades. The outward appearance of the Dutch house has shown a great variety over time, making it possible to date a house almost to a decade; however, the interior layout has changed at a much slower speed, seeing hardly any substantial change since the eighteenth century.[Fig. 2]

In the medieval and Renaissance periods, the townhouse layout was centred around one main space, facing the street, spanning the whole width of the house; at the rear, there was a split-level section with a higher-positioned back room and a partly sunken lower space, often used as kitchen and storage. The first townhouses had only an attic space crowning these main spaces, but gradually extra floors were inserted between the ground floor and the pitched roof, to provide more spaces for living and storage. The main front room on the ground level was a mediator between the public outside space and the private spaces behind and above. It was a space in which to receive guests, work, and do business.

In the second half of the seventeenth century, a major change happened with the introduction of a corridor, giving separate access to the back part of the house and reducing the width of the front room. The split level was abandoned, and the front room was elevated to the same position as the back room, thus creating a main floor raised above street level. The *stoep*, the narrow, paved threshold between the house and the street, was now used to position stairs up to the main front door at the so-called *bel-etage* level and down to the half-sunken lower level, the *souterrain*, which now extended to the street. This layout, with a division into a narrow bay for the entrance and corridor, and a wider bay for the main living spaces, proved to be very versatile and adaptable, and was, as we will see later, the starting point for the construction of the speculative multistorey apartment housing in the larger cities of the second half of the nineteenth century.[Fig. 6]

In this period, when the cities started once more to expand, the townhouse was brought back to its original modest size as a figure for suburban developments of working-class housing. In Agneta Park in Delft – one of the country's first garden cities, initiated by industrialist Jacques van Marken and built around 1884 – the architects Eugen Gugel and F. M. L. Kerkhoff introduced an interesting collection of low-rise housing types for the workers at Van Marken's factories. The standard type was a small cluster of four houses, with a plan going back to the centuries-old layout of a front room and a kitchen at the back, with an attic space under a pitched roof.

The Plan

Next to these small clusters of terraced houses in a linear repetition, groupings of four or eight units were laid out in a square plan; in the four-unit construction, each quadrant contained one house with a ground floor and attic, while the eight-unit cluster had a ground-floor unit and a separate first-floor unit, each with its own front door. These groupings looked like single farmhouses or villas in a rather romantic rural style, the favourite inspiration for suburban housing for many decades to come.[Fig. 3–5]

Agneta Park, however, was an unusual project. Most of the nineteenth- and early-twentieth-century low-rise, working-class housing was built by speculative builders with no ambitions for either the architecture or the urban layout, resulting in long, rather dreary rows of identical narrow terraced houses. This image became the spectre of those who argued against the pleas by architects and municipal housing agencies for both standardisation and the introduction of a limited catalogue of housing types to achieve higher-quality housing for the working class. In 1918 Berlage wrote a pamphlet, 'Normalisatie in Woningbouw' (Normalisation in housing construction), that made a strong plea for repetition as a way to build economically while creating a clear and coherent urban structure for the expanding cities. He rejected the desire to achieve individual expression and distinction in housing design, and emphasised the importance of making the individual house or unit a subordinate part of a larger architectural and urban composition. As examples he showed, among others, a street in Haarlem with a repetition of modest seventeenth-century step-gabled houses, and a number of contemporary garden villages.[Fig. 7, 8]

In the 1920s, Agneta Park in Delft was extended with a second housing ensemble for the factory employees. The main type was once more the terraced house. The new project was designed by the architect Jan Gratama, who had worked closely together with Berlage on several housing schemes in Amsterdam. The floor plans of the terraced houses were considerably larger than the first Agneta Park houses, each house now having a small bay with an entrance and stair in the front, and kitchen in the back, and, in a wider bay, a front and back room, divided by sliding doors.[Fig. 9, 10] The plan is almost identical to the plan of the ideal terraced house as published by the architect Gerrit Feenstra in 1920 in his book *Tuinsteden* ('Garden cities'), a handbook for architects, which advocated for the garden city as the ideal model for housing the working class. The preferred dwelling type was that of a single-family terraced house, without extensions at the back and based on the wide/narrow bay layout. The front and back rooms in the wide bay were divided by sliding doors, allowing the living spaces to be used together or separately. The bedrooms were all on the first floor, with a stair leading from the ground-floor corridor to a first-floor landing to give access to the bedrooms that was independent from the living spaces on the ground floor. The kitchen was positioned at the back of the narrow bay with a door leading to the back garden that could be accessed from a back alley. This became the dominant type of housing for at least another fifty years, with many new neighbourhoods of houses with this standard layout built in villages, towns, and small and large cities all over the Netherlands.[Fig. 11]

The long linear rows of identical terraced houses were becoming a familiar figure not only in the Netherlands but also in neighbouring countries such as England, Germany, and Denmark, where the similar *Raekkehus* has a pedigree that goes back centuries. Around 1900 there were many attempts to come up with more compact and varied configurations for terraced houses. The motivations varied from economic, seeking to save on the costs of roads and underground services, to aesthetic and social, aiming to create a stronger sense of community or to forge better connections with open spaces. An interesting attempt was published in a 1918 study by German architects Peter Behrens and Herman De Fries, titled *Vom Sparsamen Bauen, ein Beitrage zur Siedlungsfrage* ('About frugal building, a contribution to the problem of the housing estate'). They proposed in a series of plans and sketches a parcellation where the houses are clustered in two tiers behind one another, creating more diversity but also, more importantly, reducing the necessary length of access roads and services. The study was noted by Dutch architects and taken up in Dutch period publications on housing design.[Fig. 12]

Better known are the variations for clustering developed by Raymond Parker and Barry Unwin, the famous designers and advocates of the garden city in England. They proposed the 'close', a U-shaped grouping of terraced houses around a central collective open space that opens towards a larger public open space. They published these ideas in their book *Town Planning in Practice*, a study that today has lost nothing in importance and relevance. They realised their ideas in several English garden cities, with the closes in the Hampstead Heath Garden Suburb as possibly the best examples. The drawings of Parker and Unwin found their way into Dutch studies as well. Berlage copied the diagrams of the close in the above-mentioned pamphlet 'Normalisatie in Woningbouw'.[Fig. 13, 14]

Despite these publications on the ideas of the close and of a denser, double-tier clustering, actual realisations of these ideas in the period between 1918 and 1940 were very rare in the Netherlands. The best example, and a very original interpretation, is the Papaverhof, designed by architect Jan Wils, one of the most inventive and important housing designers of the Dutch interbellum period. Wils was a member of the avant-garde group De Stijl and published with Berlage and others one of the first surveys of designs for working-class housing in the Netherlands. The Papaverhof in The Hague was built in 1921. A ring of semi-detached houses is connected back-to-back to a second outer ring of the same type of houses.[Fig. 15] The semi-detached typology and the shift in position of the houses between the inner and outer rings enables each unit to have openings to the rear as well. The space made available by the elimination of the usual back garden was used to create a central collective green space in the heart of the two rings of houses. Two changes to house layouts that the plan afforded were taking advantage of the semi-detached structure to position the front door in the side facade and relocating the kitchen at the back of the living room with a window opening to the small alley leading to the front doors of the opposite ring of houses. The result was that the ground floor of the narrow bay of the conventional two-bay structure only had to accommodate a now very generous entrance hall, instead of the narrow corridor and equally narrow stairs squeezed together in the narrow bay of the standard terraced house type.[Fig. 16, 17]

A few years later, the architects of the Amsterdam Municipal Housing Office used the same principle in an extremely condensed form for the design of small apartments for elderly people with very little means. This ring-shaped cluster forms the heart of Floradorp, part of the Buiksloterham Garden City in the north of Amsterdam.[Fig. 18-20] A ground-floor unit and a first-floor unit each with its own access at the ground level were designed in a repetition of individual houses with steeply pitched roofs, a characteristic house type of the region north of Amsterdam. The project sadly didn't survive the Second World War. The elderly inhabitants were forced to move in with family in the harsh winter of 1944 when famine and lack of heating caused a lot of suffering. The abandoned homes were then vandalised by those who were desperately seeking for firewood. Nevertheless, the apartment cluster, and the Buiksloterham Garden City as a whole, are still a remarkable example of the advocacy of the Amsterdam Municipality to build low-rise garden villages for the working-class population and to create non-institutional housing for the elderly that is integrated into a residential neighbourhood.

Attempts by architects to look for new and innovative construction methods were even scarcer. A radical proposal was made by the architects Jan Duiker and Bernard Bijvoet. They designed and received a patent in 1925 for a prefabricated concrete building kit, made out of columns, beams, and floor elements. They proposed a project for terraced houses using these kits that had alternating narrow and wider frontages. They argued that the living room facade needed more width than the kitchen facade. With an interlocking system they reduced the frontage of two adjacent units

72 The Plan

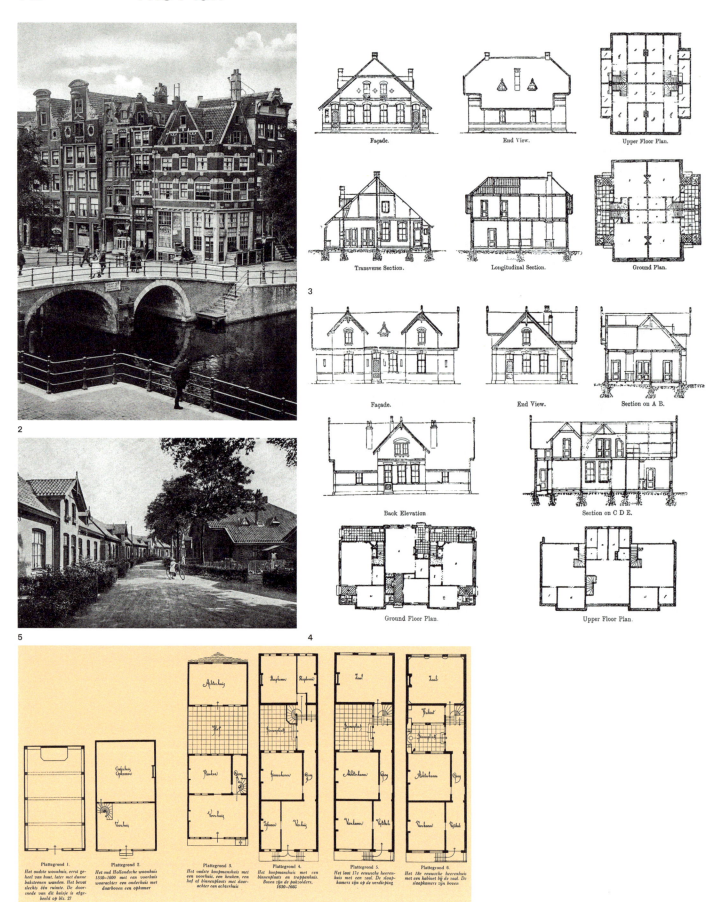

73 Patterns and Models

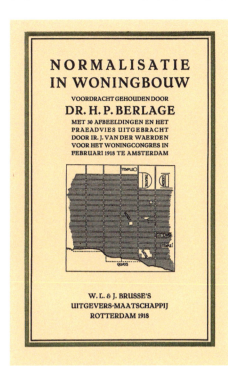
7

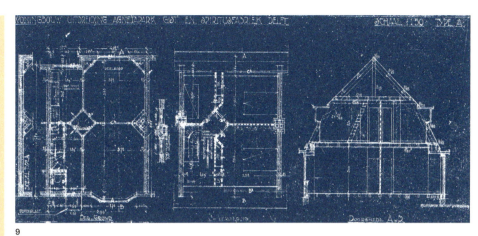
9

10

8

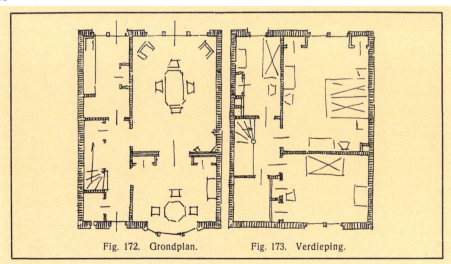
11

1   Slotermeer, part of the Amsterdam Western Garden Cities, 1962.
2   Corner of Prinsengracht and Brouwersgracht in Amsterdam showing the variety in size of the canal houses.
3   Four dwelling units clustered in a single 'farmhouse', Agneta Park, Delft.
4   Cluster of three terraced houses, Agneta Park, Delft.
5   Agneta Park, showing the two housing types on either side of the street.
6   Evolution of the Amsterdam townhouse plan: (left) the early medieval house with one undivided ground floor space, developing slowly towards the eighteenth-century plan (right) with a corridor and internal courtyard dividing the *voorhuis* from the *achterhuis*.
7   'Normalisatie in Woningbouw', Berlage's plea for standardisation and repetition in housing design.
8   Illustration from Berlage's pamphlet 'Normalisatie in Woningbouw', showing a row of identical seventeenth-century townhouses in Haarlem.
9   Plans and section of the standard type of Gratama's project for the extension of the Delft Agneta Park.
10 The extension of the Agneta Park in Delft.
11 Drawing of the ideal standard plan of a terraced house, as published by Feenstra in his study on garden cities.

The Plan

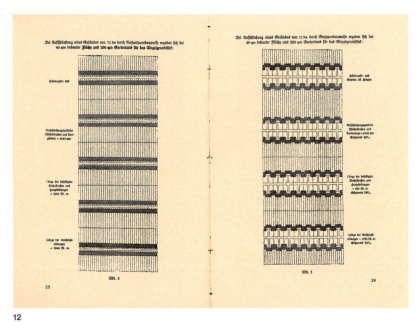
12

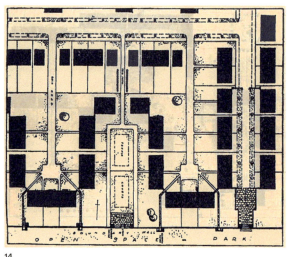
14

13

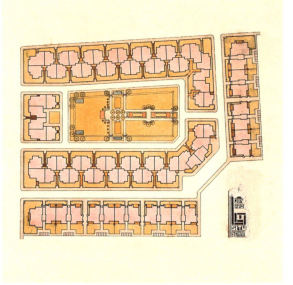
15

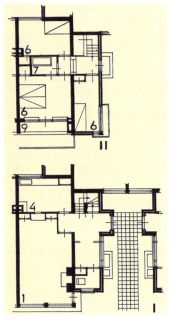
16

17

75 Patterns and Models

18

19

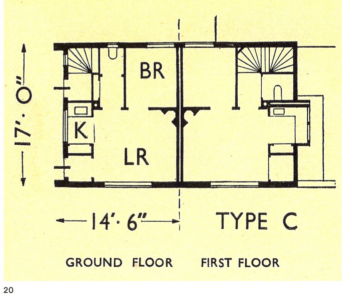

20

12 The proposal for a more varied, and more economic, way of clustering terraced housing (right), compared to a drawing of the usual clustering (left). Drawings from the study of Behrens and De Fries.
13 Drawing of a close in Hampstead Heath Garden Suburb, London.
14 Diagrammatic drawing of a close and a street oriented towards an open green space.
    From Unwin's *Town Planning in Practice*, reproduced by Berlage in his pamphlet on standardisation.
15 Plan of the Papaverhof project, The Hague, design by Wils.
16 Ground-floor and first-floor plan of the standard house type of the Papaverhof.
17 Papaverhof.
18 Several stages of the construction of the Buiksloterham elderly housing. Following centuries-old methods, construction starts with the erection of the wooden structure and window frames, followed by the load-bearing brick walls.
19 Plan of Tuindorp (garden village) Buiksloterham in Amsterdam North, design by the municipality. In the hexagonal centre, the Papaverhof parcellation of elderly housing.
20 The plan of the elderly housing in Tuindorp Buiksloterham, as published in a 1936 English survey of housing in Europe. There are two minimal units on top of one another, with individual front doors.

from 11 metres to 7.80 metres to save land and infrastructure. Their design was published in the official publication of the third CIAM congress in 1931, titled *Rationelle Bebauungsweisen* ('Rational land development'). The project was perhaps less rational, however, than promised. The structural system was quite complicated, and the proposed plan could just as easily be built with traditional brick walls. Also, the interlocking plans, with the living rooms changing position from front to back, didn't result in an alternative urban structure. It was never built.[Fig. 21, 22]

The project proved how difficult it was for the modernists, the brilliant Duiker and Bijvoet among them, to come up with new alternatives for the traditional terraced house. Its efficiency and rationality were almost impossible to match. As was shown in Wils's Papaverhof, and, for example, in architect J. J. P. Oud's project for the Kiefhoek in Rotterdam, the aesthetics and even the clustering could be changed, but the basic layout of the plan and the applied construction methods and materials remained essentially the same.

The post-war period was characterised by an enormous need for new and affordable housing amid a time of scarcity of both financing and material. The well-known standard terraced house remained as popular as before. An interesting case of the period is the housing in the village of Nagele, a modernist showcase in the new land of the Noordoostpolder that was created before the war, but finally populated with a series of villages and one central town in the 1950s. While most villages were designed in line with traditional concepts, Nagele was selected to be designed by the two leading groups of modernist architects, Opbouw and De Acht. They intended to design the village as a collective of architects. The members proposed many solutions and variations for a village layout that would introduce a radical new way of planning and building a village from scratch.

One of the most extreme proposals was drawn by Gerrit Rietveld, who before the war was a protagonist of the De Stijl movement. He designed a cluster of free-standing, single-family houses, giving them each a view of the open, green heart of the village. Although a need for economy dictated a return to the familiar patterns of terraced housing in linear clusters, the abundance of space on the new land still permitted experimentation in the positioning of the linear terraces. In the final plan for Nagele, drawn by Aldo van Eyck but with the clear influence of Bakema's earlier urban studies, groupings of terraced houses around central collective green spaces, obviously inspired by the concept of the *wooneenheid* (visual unit), were repeated to form a ring around the very generous central village green, where four churches and three schools were located.[Fig. 23] Gerrit Rietveld and his son Jan designed two of these *wooneenheden*. The terraced house plans were conventional, reaching to even older traditions – of the rural house – with a living room facing the front and a kitchen with a large storage space at the back. To make a statement as innovative modernists, as compared to the traditional, so-called Delft School architecture of the other villages, all the architects, including Rietveld, designed the housing without pitched roofs, depriving the residents of the customary attic space. The overall absence of pitched roofs was considered so exceptional that Nagele received national fame as the village with the flat roofs.[Fig. 24, 25]

A typical dilemma of implementing the modernist ideals of free-standing housing in a continuous public or collective green space was how to position the traditional terraced house type. The type has a public front, and a private back with a kitchen, storage, and garden that the Dutch will inevitably close off with high fencing for privacy. The problem became quite visible in Nagele, where the terraces of houses were positioned one after the other, without mirroring, thus confronting fronts with backs.

In a slightly later design for terraced houses in the village of Reeuwijk, Gerrit Rietveld tried to address this issue by turning around each house in relation to the neighbouring house. A linear cluster would then result in two equal frontages, with alternating back and front yards. The project was named the *om en om woningen*, or the alternating houses. In this manner, there would be no continuous rear to a terrace, and the row of houses was surrounded by public space on all sides. The plans of the units demonstrate an attempt to improve the familiar layout of what was now called the *doorzonwoning* (sun-pierced dwelling, or a house with a living space that continues undivided from front to back). Gradually, the typical interbellum solution with sliding doors dividing the living space had been replaced by a completely open layout. By omitting the corridor connection between the entrance and staircase hall at the front, and the kitchen at the back, Rietveld created an internal niche, or inglenook, to make the main living space more interesting. It also resulted in a stronger connection between the kitchen and the living room by the design of an 'open' corner, a typical Rietveld detail. The kitchen extends partly into the backyard, with an additional storage room. This protruding volume divides the front yard of one house from the backyard of the next house. However, tenants inevitably closed off the backyard with a high fence, thereby spoiling the intended open character of the cluster of houses.[Fig. 26, 27]

The alternating repetition of terraced houses was not a new discovery. In Scandinavia one can find earlier and more successful projects. The Friluftstaden project (1944) in Malmo is a remarkable example that remains unspoiled today. Scandinavian, and especially Swedish, housing became an important inspiration for the post-war Dutch housing architects. While housing production in the Netherlands came to a complete standstill in the 1940s, architects in neutral Sweden continued to build and develop a rich catalogue of new standards that, with their gentle and simple brick architecture, found great appeal among the Dutch. The Swedish habit of building housing amid a collective open space rather than having fenced-off private gardens, however, was almost impossible to reproduce in the Dutch context.[Fig. 28, 29]

Another innovation in the traditional layout, explored in the 1960s, proved more successful. The change was certainly triggered by Scandinavian examples, but precedents can also be found in the Netherlands. As a first experiment in drastically changing the internal layout of the terraced house type, the beautiful Tuinwijk Zuid project in Haarlem, designed by Johannes Bernardus van Loghem and built between 1920 and 1922, deserves mention. Continuous terraces of two- and three-storey, middle-class houses give at the back onto a generous collective green garden. To create a strong connection between the living spaces and this garden, Van Loghem reversed the order of the usual plan, moving the kitchen and storage to the street front, and using the entire width of the house at the back for the *doorzon* living room and a dining room that was open to the living room. A 4-metre-long back garden was bordered by a privet hedge that was required to be clipped to below eye-level by the homeowners' society, forming a private outside space between the interior of the house and the collective garden.[Fig. 30, 31]

The close as a connection between the individual house and the larger public space came once again to the fore in Scandinavian examples, like Kay Fisker's Egeparken project designed in 1942 and built in the years after 1949 near Copenhagen, where public and collective spaces are combined in a network of small paths and wider access courts. Another is the much-better-known Kingo and Fredensborg housing projects of Jorn Utzon from 1956, which can be read as a combination and reversal of the principles of the English close and of Van Loghem's Garden City.[Fig. 32, 33]

Van Loghem's early ideas and the Scandinavian examples came back with a vengeance in Dutch housing in the 1960s. The 1960s and the 1970s can in retrospect be seen as the most experimental and innovative period in the history of housing design. Between 1968 and 1980 projects with experimental ambitions could get an official Experimentele Woningbouw (Experimental Housing) government seal. Most of the experiments of this period remained one-offs, and many of the ideas introduced then can be seen coming back again today, once more labelled as experimental and innovative.

Architects and urban planners who were part of the Experimentele Woningbouw programme were looking for alternatives to the industrial mass production of housing that

The Plan

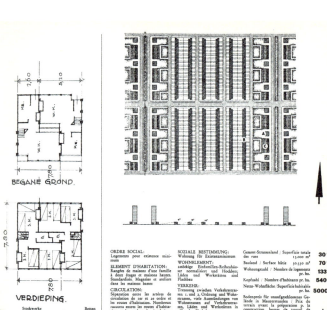

21

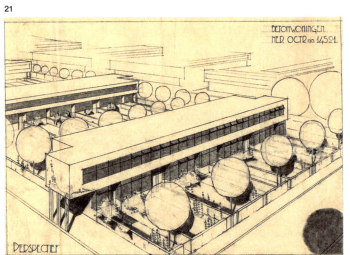

22

24

25

79 Patterns and Models

26

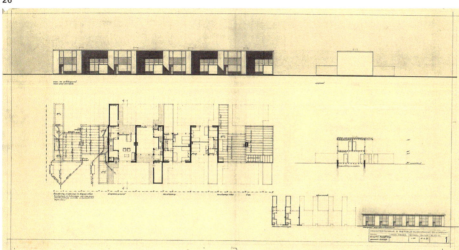
27

28

29

21 Proposal for terraced housing with a prefabricated concrete structural system, design by Duiker and Bijvoet, as published in the 1931 CIAM study *Rationelle Bebauungsweisen*.
22 Bird's-eye view of Duiker and Bijvoet's proposal.
23 Plan of the definitive design for the village of Nagele by De 8 en Opbouw.
24 Cluster of terraced houses in Nagele, design by Gerrit and Jan Rietveld.
25 Plan and facade drawing of the Rietveld design for Nagele.
26 Model of Rietveld's design for terraced housing in Reeuwijk.
27 Plans, facade, and section of Rietveld's Reeuwijk project.
28 Aerial view of Friluftstaden in Malmö, design by Persson.
29 Photo collage promoting Friluftstaden: 'borders without fences, freedom of movement for children, better space, easier work'.

had become dominant in the 1960s while also trying to avoid the lack of identity and collectivity of the ubiquitous suburban terraced housing neighbourhoods. The sixty-four realised projects introduced concepts such as shared outside spaces, participation, incremental growth, and adaptability of individual dwellings.

The period saw the introduction of *het woonerf*, a concept inspired by traditional collective farmyards in the east of the Netherlands and a term coined by the urban planner Niek de Boer. Even more than the words *doorzonwoning* and *rijtjeshuis*, the word *woonerf* is difficult to translate and was introduced as a term all over the world without translation. The idea of the *woonerf* was to create a sense of community and of individuality at the same time by making fractal-like clusters of terraced houses in which each house was individually recognisable, while being connected to a common, an informal yard where pedestrians, children, and cars could co-exist.

The idea of the *woonerf* required a rethinking of the plan of the terraced house, in line with Van Loghem's Tuinwijk Zuid. The designers who developed the first *woonerven* in the 1960s envisioned the street – or as they preferred to call it, the yard (*erf*) – as the catalyst for achieving a sense of community. The yard was above all an informal collective meeting place for the residents. To emphasise its informality and the importance of everyday encounters, the designers moved the informal work space – the kitchen – to the front of the house. The living room was relocated to the back of the house, connecting to a private terrace or garden, which in turn led to a collective green space at the rear of the houses.[Fig. 34]

One of the first *woonerf* projects, Emmerhout in Emmen, has all the characteristics that would become typical of the housing form as it became dominant in the 1970s and 1980s. The kitchen was placed in the front while the living room adjoins the back garden. To increase the privacy of the living room and to emphasise how daily activities connect to the communal *woonerf*, the storage and bicycle shed were also moved to the front of the house. Cars could be parked in front of the house, making the banal everyday activities of arriving and leaving part of the shared space.[Fig. 34, 35] The first designs show a complex configuration of the terraced houses. The standard simple rectilinear plan between the parallel partition walls was changed into meandering L- or Z-shaped spaces. This resulted in many options for clustering, articulating the individual unit.[Fig. 36]

The figure of the *woonerf* certainly had precedents in the aforementioned examples from the Netherlands and Scandinavia. A sketch showing the quintessential shape and idea of a *woonerf*, which has often been attributed to Niek de Boer, proved to be a proposal of the German architect Walter Schwagenscheidt published in his 1957 book *Ein Mensch wandert durch die Stadt* ('A wanderer in the city'),[Fig. 37, 38] showing how architectural ideas circulate over time and place. It is interesting to note that Schwagenscheidt's book advocates the positioning of kitchen and storage at the entrance side of the house, not to stimulate informal community life, but instead to create a barrier between car traffic and the living spaces that were located at the back of the house, connected to small private gardens and continuous collective green spaces. The noise, pollution, and danger of the car were thus addressed, as in that other better-known study on the design of the private house in the car-dominated suburbs of the post-war period, Serge Chermayeff and Christopher Alexander's 1965 book *Community and Privacy*.[Fig. 39, 40]

Whether the *woonerf* has managed to solve the conflict between motorised traffic and the home environment remains to be seen, but it did result in the demise of the *doorzonwoning*, a process that continued in the later period of large-scale suburban housing development, the so-called Vinex project of the 1990s and early 2000s. Shifting kitchen and shed to the front of the house played a decisive role in the development of a standard terraced house layout for the *Vinex wijken*, the next generation of Dutch suburban planning after the *woonerven*. The traditional *doorzonwoning* from the period before the *woonerf* had required a wider floor plan, but the *woonerf* typology made it possible to narrow the individual unit, which then allowed for an increase in density. However, the Vinex developments saw the disappearance of the shared yard as a communal intermediate space, something undesired in the individualistic neoliberal atmosphere of the 1990s, which resulted in the emergence of very introverted living in which the collective ideals were replaced by an overpowering emphasis on privacy.

D31
D30 In the project for a new neighbourhood of social housing, Grootstal in Nijmegen,[Fig. 42] collective car-free spaces were introduced as a new interpretation of the *woonerf*. The plans of the different types of narrow, 4.8-metre-wide terraced houses were all designed with a central core containing stairs and the kitchen, thus allowing each house to have glazed doors open to the collective spaces in front of the house, making the kitchen area part of an hourglass-shaped, *doorzon* living room.[Fig. 43] In a later project in Nijmegen, Woonpark Oosterhout, the inverted close, as shown in the projects of Van Loghem and Scandinavian architects, was revived. The brief for social terraced housing asked for the lowest possible building costs. This resulted in a design for one-storey linear clustered patio houses with a minimal width of 4 metres and a depth of 24 metres, as a modest version of Chermayeff and Alexander's ideal plan in their study *Community and Privacy*.[Fig. 41] The narrow one-storey volume minimised the facade surface, thus reducing the costs of the most expensive building component in housing. A small patio brought daylight to the bedrooms; and the living room at the end opened to a small private outside space with a low brick wall separating it from a large, central collective green space.[Fig. 44]

D29 The close was also used in the projects for 650 houses in the Vinex area of Ypenburg near The Hague. The closes are connected to the green park that borders the area, almost like green fingers working their way into the high-density, low-rise project. There were various different house types designed to line the green fingers, intended to create a catalogue of alternatives of the well-established single-family terraced house.[Fig. 49]

A crucial element in designing new housing neighbourhoods is the issue of providing parking spaces for all of the cars. An often-adopted solution in *woonerf* and Vinex areas is a carport or open parking place in front of the house. This is obviously detrimental to the connection of the house with the street. Another solution to create a direct connection between the parked car and the house is the drive-in *woning*, first introduced by Mart Stam en Van Tijen in Berlage's Amsterdam South in their 1935 project for five terraced houses,[Fig. 50] creating an almost-displaced appearance with their large steel windows among the brown bricks and heavy timber window frames typical of the area. The drive-in house had a short-lived popularity in the 1970s but suffered from the lack of direct connection between the living spaces and the street.

D28
D26
D05 For Ypenburg and other projects such as the Talmalaan urban regeneration project in Utrecht and the IJburg Blok 51C,[Fig. 46] a reversed drive-in house was developed. The reversed type makes it possible to place a workspace or dine-in kitchen on the ground-floor facing the street that is connected by a void to the main living space on the first floor. A first-floor terrace at the back of the living space covers the collective access road to the individual parking garages, hiding cars from view. A more condensed version of this solution was made for the project on Borneo Eiland in the Amsterdam Eastern Docklands district.[Fig. 47]

The architects of the housing projects on Borneo and Sporenburg had to design car parking inside the envelope of the house, resulting in a reworking of the traditional townhouse typology. Many designers chose to make a ground-floor carport on the street as an open variation of the drive-in type. This, however, greatly affected the intended direct connection of the private

HET STADSWOONHUIS IN NEDERLAND

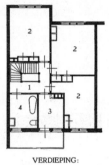

BEGANE GROND:
1. Ingang.
2. Hal.
3. Woonkamer.
4. Eetkamer.
5. Keuken.
6. Bergplaats.
7. W. C.

VERDIEPING:
1. Portaal.
2. Slaapkamer.
3. Kamertje.
4. Badkamer.

HEEMSTEDE. WONINGCOMPLEX „TUINWIJK."   ARCHITECT: J. B. VAN LOGHEM. Bouwk. Ing.

30

31

19

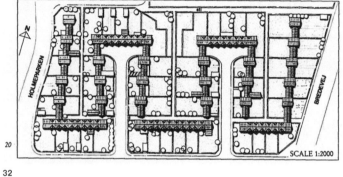

20

32

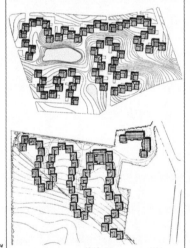

34

33

83 Patterns and Models

34

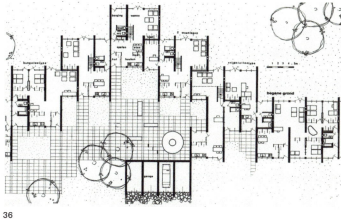
36

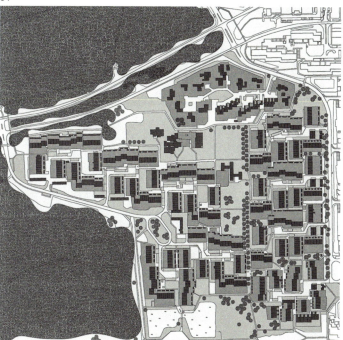
35

37

38

30 Street view and plans of standard terraced house type of Tuinwijk Zuid, Haarlem, design by Van Loghem.
31 View of the collective central garden, Tuinwijk Zuid.
32 Project for a clustering of terraced houses around closes and alleys in Copenhagen, Fisker.
33 Utzon's Fredensborg and Klingo housing projects.
34 Emmerhout today.
35 Plan of Emmerhout, introducing the idea of the *woonerf*.
36 Study for a clustering of houses around a *woonerf*, by A. de Jong.
37 Sketch showing an alternative clustering of patio houses, by Walter Schwagenscheidt.
38 Schwagenscheidt's study *Ein Mensch wandert durch die Stadt*.

84 The Plan

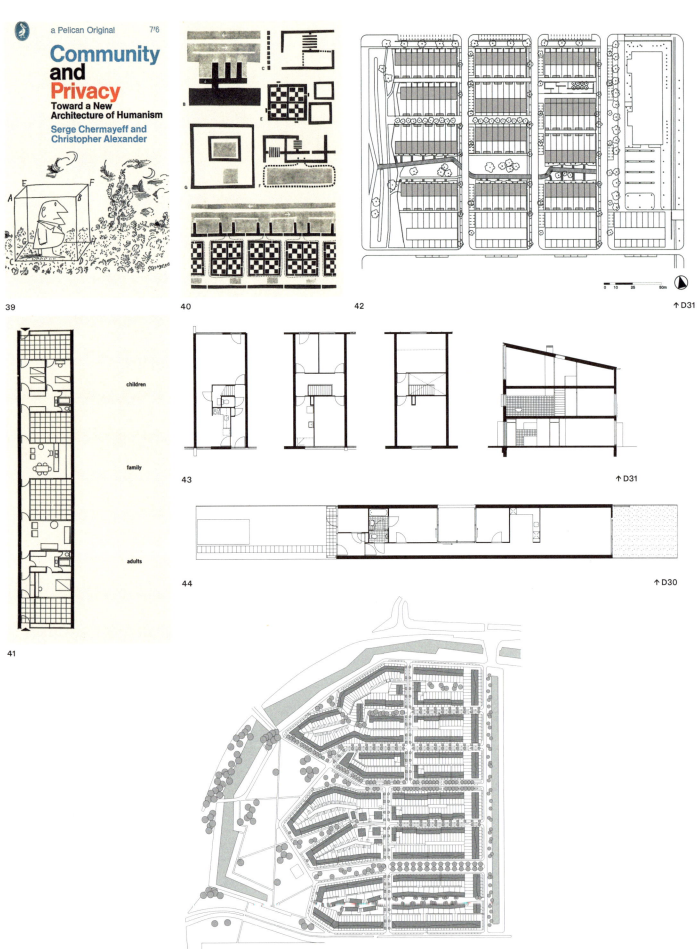

85 Patterns and Models

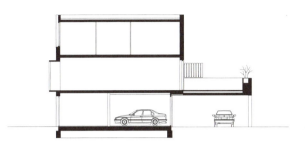

46 ↑D28

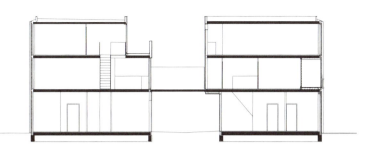

47 ↑D05

48 ↑D05

49 ↑D05

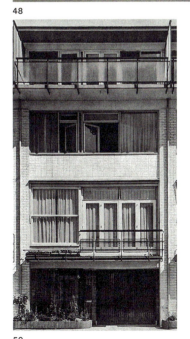

50

39 Chermayeff and Alexander's *Community and Privacy*, on the ideal suburban house.
40 Diagrams from *Community and Privacy*, searching for ways to disconnect car circulation and parking from the home environment.
41 Plan of an ideal suburban home, according to Chermayeff and Alexander.
42 Plan of Grootstal garden village (D31).
43 Basic type of terraced house for Grootstal (D31).
44 Plan of one dwelling unit in Park Oosterhout (D30).
45 Urban plan for the most western part of the Vinex neighbourhood Ypenburg between Delft and The Hague (D29).
46 Section of 'reversed' drive-in townhouse, Talmalaan, Utrecht (D28).
47 Section of block on Borneo Eiland, Amsterdam, with internal parking street (D05).
48 View of the parking street inside the Borneo Eiland project (D05).
49 Street view of the Borneo Eiland project with ground-floor workspaces opening to the street (D05).
50 Drive-in townhouse, Amsterdam, design by Mart Stam and Lotte Stam-Beese.

interior with the public street, a main characteristic of the Dutch townhouse on which the urban project for Borneo Sporenburg was based. The streets ended up lined with carports instead of front doors and living and working spaces.

D05 To avoid this conflict, in the project for fifty-six houses at the end of the Borneo Eiland pier, the section of the houses was reversed, placing the carports on the inside of the building block accessible via a closed-off and partly covered interior street. This allowed the public frontages to be used for the entrances to the houses, and the work or living spaces could face the street at ground level.[Fig. 48, 49]

II The free-standing house

The free-standing individual house has always been an exception in Dutch housing production. It was the arrival of railways and trams at the end of the nineteenth century, and a growing middle class that sought to escape the overcrowded and polluted city centres that triggered the first move to the countryside, in particular to the areas with sandy soil, which were considered a healthier environment than the Dutch peat and clay polder lands. The houses built for the commuters were very much inspired by the local vernacular architecture of farmhouses in these originally poor rural areas. The houses' main characteristic was a low-lying, steeply pitched thatched roof. The plans were conventional and quite similar to the plans developed for townhouses, but now in a rural and picturesque disguise, blending in with the existing environment.

A project that brought this dominant way of building private houses in the countryside to the next level of development was Park Meerwijk in Bergen, built on sand behind the dunes of the North Sea. Initiated by an Amsterdam tile manufacturer, the project involved five architects belonging to the Amsterdam School designing seventeen houses.[Fig. 51] The houses designed by architects such as Margaret Kropholler, Arthur Staal, and Piet Kramer are modest in size, but have remarkable exteriors and interiors, where references to vernacular farmhouses, maritime architecture, and details inspired by vernacular buildings from the Dutch East Indies converge in an imaginative way.[Fig. 52] The floor plans reveal a different inspiration: the English country house with a central living hall opening towards inglenooks and smaller annex spaces with specific functions. The houses and their interiors were built more on the scale of a cottage than a country house and are maybe best represented by the examples published in the British architect Hugh Mackay Baillie Scott's book *Houses and Gardens* from 1906.[Fig. 53] Influenced by his work and other contemporary British architects, the interiors of the modest Park Meerwijk villas start to open up internally, but remain rather disconnected from the outside world, with small-paned windows and protective overhanging thatched roofs. The project opened initially as a housing exhibition, showcasing the expressive architecture and the beautifully coloured and shaped tiles of tilemaker Heystee in the halls and other living spaces.[Fig. 54]

The project was extensively published in *Wendingen*. This magazine, published between 1919 and 1932, promoted the expressionist Amsterdam School's architecture, and, in its first year, dedicated an entire issue to Park Meerwijk. Two years later another issue was devoted to one single project: the villa 't Reigersnest in Oostvoorne, designed by architects Pieter Vorkink and Jacobus Wormser, and built on sand, in the dunes south-west of Rotterdam. The villa grows out of the landscape, with a roof that raises up and comes down in one large, organic gesture, like the surrounding terrain.[Fig. 55, 56] The final page of this issue of *Wendingen* was dedicated to another intriguing design for a house on the sands of the Veluwe, the wild natural area in the centre of the Netherlands. There is an image of a model made of clay, emphasising the house's earthbound character. The plan seems to be that of a modest English country house gone wild. The central hall is the heart of the building, like the dining hall in Het Reigersnest, with two wings spreading out, one with the service spaces and another with the family rooms.[Fig. 58] The design of the free-standing house took a new turn when the work of Frank Lloyd Wright became known in Dutch architectural circles. The famous German *Wasmuth Portfolio* had a major impact, as did the later publications in *Wendingen*, which devoted a total of eight issues to his work. The brick facades and low, overhanging roofs of Wright's Prairie Houses likely resonated with Dutch country house architecture and the flat landscapes, though he clearly introduced a new formal, modern language, different from Dutch vernacular inspirations. In 1921, the architects Jan Duiker and Bernard Bijvoet designed a cluster of *landhuizen* (houses in the countryside) in the sand dunes near The Hague, called Villapark Meer en Bosch.[Fig. 57] They combined two or three houses under one roof, creating large horizontal volumes in a clearly Wright-inspired vocabulary. The plans, however, remained rather traditional, showing little influence of Wright's open plans with a central core of fireplace, chimney, and stairs. In 1922, architect Jan Wils, known for the Papaverhof project, published two volumes on how to design and build a private free-standing house, titled *Het Woonhuis*. In this publication he explains how the design and actual construction of a villa should take place. The proposed design could have been one by the American master himself. Next to the obvious exterior characteristics, Wils's plan reproduces the typical Prairie House layout very clearly. Even the perspective images of the design show clear parallels to the famous line drawings of the *Wasmuth Portfolio*, with the low viewpoints and the merging of house and nature.[Fig. 59]

The traditional, vernacular-inspired architecture of Dutch *landhuizen* became a laughing stock for progressive architects when the Modern Movement started to gain momentum in the late 1920s and 1930s. In 1935, architect Ben Merkelbach designed a small holiday house, quite close to Park Meerwijk, that is in plan and appearance the complete opposite of the Meerwijk houses. Strikingly, it was built just outside the dunes, where the polder landscape starts, and seems entirely disconnected from its surroundings: a white cube with a flat roof set off against the typical pyramidal and thatched farmhouses of the region. The plan is simple, and the emphasis is not so much on the spatial connections inside the house, but on the relation between inside and outside space. In the corner of the square living room, two very large, glazed, and segmented sliding doors can open fully to the outside, creating in the open position two wind screens. In a publication in *De 8 en Opbouw*, the magazine that was in its design and content the very opposite of (the by-then no longer in publication) *Wendingen*, Merkelbach describes how designs for countryside houses are 'forced' to imitate farmhouses, although they are intended for occupants with completely different demands: 'Rurality reigns, and leads to the jaded architecture that in its duplicity destroys nature and in its untruthfulness creates a permanent dissonance.'[Fig. 60]

Therefore, while modernists were unable to find a clear alternative to the terraced house, here, with the free-standing house, they could. This aligns with the evolution of the house in twentieth-century architecture from a space confined within walls to an infinite space, only delineated by glass, roofs, and free-standing walls or columns; in other words, with the opening of the 'box'. In Dutch architecture, this shift is epitomised by the work of Gerrit Rietveld, most of all in the Rietveld-Schröder house in Utrecht, and later, by the refined post-war designs of Herman Haan.

The dominance of the farmhouse style was so persistent, however, that the Swiss architect Paul Artaria in his 1947 survey, titled 'Weekend- and Country-houses', showed only two very traditional projects from the Netherlands, stating that 'for apparent reasons – the similarity of the form of society and of national character – this influence (of the English country house) was stronger in Holland than in other countries'. The Dutch examples make a rather regressive appearance in his book among the more progressive designs of Richard Neutra, Marcel Breuer, Le Corbusier, and others.[Fig. 61, 62]

Architect Bernard Bijvoet, who worked with Duiker on the Wright-inspired houses of Villapark Meer en Bosch in the dunes of The Hague and later collaborated with Pierre Chareau on the legendary Maison de Verre in Paris, designed together with his new partner

51

52

53

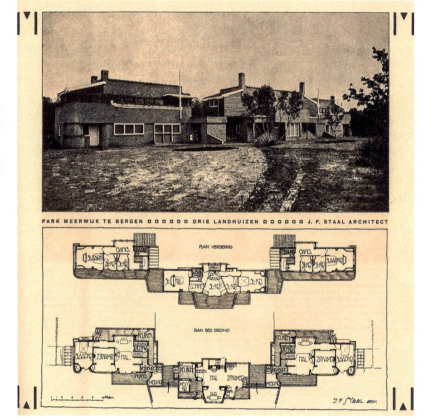

54

51   Plan of Park Meerwijk in Bergen, as published in *Wendingen*.
52   View of the entrance to Park Meerwijk, with garden pavilion and house designed by Staal, as published in *Wendingen*.
53   Design for a living hall by Baillie Scott.
54   Three connected *landhuizen*, with central living hall, design by Staal, as published in *Wendingen*.
55   Plans of 't Reigersnest, Oostvoorne, near Rotterdam. Design by Vorkink and Wormser, published in *Wendingen*.
56   Garden view of 't Reigersnest, from *Wendingen*.
57   Plan and perspective of Driedubbel *landhuis*, triple villa, Villapark Meer en Bosch, The Hague, design by Duiker and Bijvoet.
58   Unbuilt project for a landhuis, design by Vorkink and Wormser, from Wendingen.
59   Plan and perspective of Eenvoudig *landhuis*, from Jan Wils's publication *Het Woonhuis*.

Patterns and Models

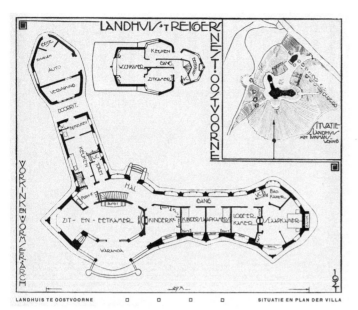

55
LANDHUIS TE OOSTVOORNE — SITUATIE EN PLAN DER VILLA

56
LANDHUIS TE OOSTVOORNE — ACHTERGEVEL EN ZIJGEVEL

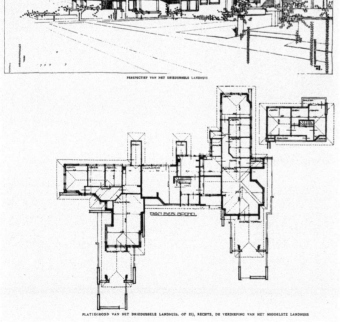

57
PLATTEGROND VAN HET DRIEDUBBELE LANDHUIS, OP ZIJ, RECHTS, DE VERDIEPING VAN HET MIDDELSTE LANDHUIS

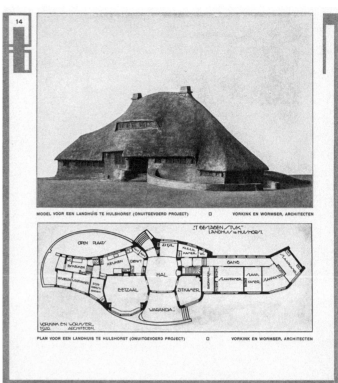

58
MODEL VOOR EEN LANDHUIS TE HULSHORST (ONUITGEVOERD PROJECT) — VORKINK EN WORMSER, ARCHITECTEN
PLAN VOOR EEN LANDHUIS TE HULSHORST (ONUITGEVOERD PROJECT) — VORKINK EN WORMSER, ARCHITECTEN

59a

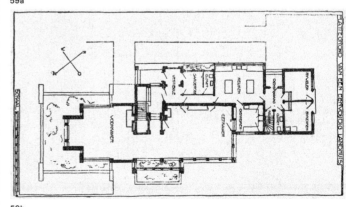

59b

90   The Plan

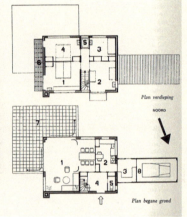

60

61

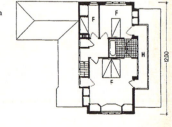

62

91 Patterns and Models

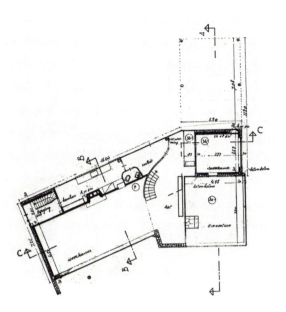

64

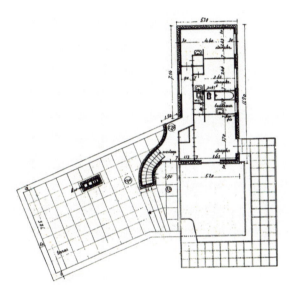

63

65

60 Weekend house in Groet near Bergen, design by Merkelbach, spread from *De 8 en Opbouw*.
61 Dutch small countryside house, as published in Artaria's 1946 survey 'Weekend- and Country-houses'. Design by Smits and Van de Linde.
62 Plans of the Dutch house in Artaria's 'Weekend- and Country-houses'.
63 Plans of Villa Looyens in Aerdenhout, design by Bijvoet and Holt.
64 View from the south, Villa Looyens.
65 View into the protected patio garden, Villa Looyens.

The Plan

66   ↑D37   67   ↑D37

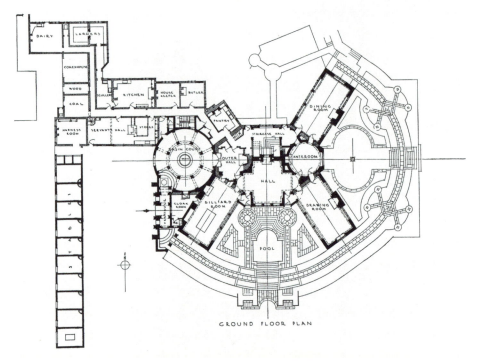

68

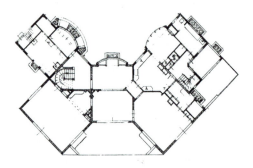

69

66 Villa with butterfly plan and patio (D37).
67 View of the villa towards the entrance (D37).
68 Butterfly plan of Papillon Hall, design by Sir Edwin Lutyens.
69 Butterfly plan of Hotterhof near Lonneker, design by De Clerq.
70 The House on the Lake (D39).
71 View from bedroom to the lake (D39).
72 Ground-floor plan of the House on the Lake (D39).
73 Master plan for the Netherlands Embassy compound in Addis Ababa with section through the staff houses (D40).

93 Patterns and Models

70 ↑D39

71 ↑D39

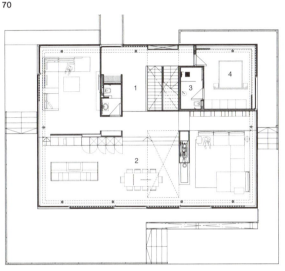
72 ↑D39

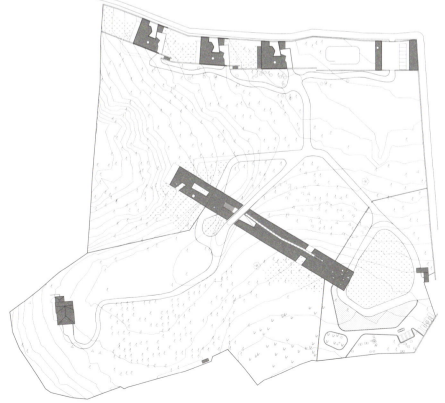
73 ↑D40

Gerard Holt a remarkable villa in the sandy dunes west of Amsterdam. Villa Looijen (1948–1950), located in Aerdenhout, can be seen as an attempt to blend the sensitivity of an expressionist, earthbound architecture with the abstract detailing and straight lines of modernist houses. The house carefully reacts to the conditions of the site: the entrance side is relatively closed, oriented towards the north and the rising landscape, and the south side is almost completely open, connected to the garden.[Fig. 63] The central space in the house is a generous hall, open to the living room, with an elegantly curved stair leading to the first-floor bedrooms. Between the hall and the garden lies a protected patio, forging an extraordinary link between exterior and interior. The steel and glass screen of the patio is crowned by a narrow walkway that can be accessed from the large first-floor roof terrace. The sculptural volume of the house is covered in an irregular stone pattern, making yet another connection between the house and its natural surroundings.[Fig. 64, 65] The house remains a unique project and is arguably one of the most interesting contributions to the development of free-standing house design in the last 100 years in the Netherlands.

D37 Villa Looijen was one of the main inspirations for the rebuilding of an existing villa near Naarden. The original house, a poorly built, hexagonal Frank Lloyd Wright-inspired bungalow of the 1960s, was enlarged several times, turning the house into a labyrinthine and dark place. The redesign imposed a series of drastic interventions and added another wing to create a butterfly plan. The four wings open onto the beautiful surrounding gardens and landscape. Each wing has its own programme and views, relating to the more densely planted parts of the garden or to wide perspectives on the surrounding streams and meadows. The wings are all connected to the central living hall, a space that is both inward- and outward-looking. This spatial organisation is reminiscent of the aptly named Papillon Hall, an equally drastic rebuild of an existing house by the great English country house designer Sir Edwin Lutyens, and, closer to home, the countryside house 't Holterhof, designed by architect Samuel de Clerq in the eastern part of the Netherlands, near the village of Lonneker.[Fig. 66, 68, 69]

As in Villa Looijen, the house in Naarden has a patio that creates a strongly layered connection between the outside and the interior, while the overall sculptural shape of the house stretches out to the surroundings. In order to preserve privacy, the existing landscape and the new landscaping immediately around the house are used to protect the house from view, acting as a protective screen for the open, transparent facades.[Fig. 67]

D39 The design for the House on the Lake, a project in the English Cotswolds, takes this idea even a step further. The fully glazed house is visually hidden from the access road and the neighbouring plots by a series of interventions in the landscaping. By making open, glazed corners in the living room, kitchen area, and other spaces, a feeling is evoked of literally living on the lake. Solid elements, such as the fireplace and storage cupboards, divide the interior of the house, creating more intimate and private spaces within the large transparent volume.[Fig. 70-72]

D40 In a different way, the residence and the three staff houses for the Netherlands Embassy in Addis Ababa, a Dutch enclave in the sprawling capital of Ethiopia, are anchored in the surrounding landscape as well. Here the topography of the sloping terrain and the abundant vegetation of shrubs and trees were used to create optimal privacy between the houses, while still taking maximum advantage of the views to the hills that surround the city.[Fig. 73]

The embedding of a house in its surroundings links these projects to one another, and to the earlier examples of Dutch houses that didn't want to stand out, but rather preferred to blend in with nature.

III The apartment

The apartment has a long history of being considered a necessary evil. In his book on the design of garden cities, Feenstra showed in a range of plans the development of the principal Dutch apartment and its gradual improvement, from the abominable alcove back-to-back units on one floor to the much-improved design of Berlage for the pioneering Javastraat housing. Regardless of the changes over time, however, all of Feenstra's examples fit in the basic structure of a narrow bay and a wide bay.^{Fig. 74}

His general conclusion was that the terraced house was very much preferred over the common apartment, explained with the help of the plan as discussed in the beginning of this chapter. It is remarkable that this plan of the ideal terraced house is in essence not very different from the plan of the units in the early Dutch apartment buildings. The combination of a narrow and a wide bay makes for a clearly organised floor plan, whether for a low-rise terraced house or a high-rise apartment.^{Fig. 76}

Arie Keppler, the highly influential head of the municipal housing department of Amsterdam, expressed in 1938 in the publication *Beter Wonen*,^{Fig. 75} celebrating the twenty-fifth anniversary of the National Confederation of Housing Corporations, his aversion to the ubiquitous four-storey apartment blocks in Amsterdam and elsewhere. Keppler was a strong advocate of *het tuindorp*, the garden village, as the optimal model for affordable housing. The municipality itself set the example by building in the interbellum period a series of garden villages on the northern and eastern borders of Amsterdam, such as the Tuindorp Buiksloterham. However, even with this disapproval, the housing corporations continued to build the four-storey apartment block as its brick-and-wood structure remained the most economic model for urban housing production.^{Fig. 77}

Keppler was not alone in his aversion to the four-storey blocks that had evolved out of the structure of the traditional Dutch house. Many Dutch studies on housing design in the period before the Second World War echoed the promotion of the low-rise terraced house.

Another influential figure, Herman van der Kaa, chief housing inspector of the national government in The Hague, expressed his scepticism about apartments in 1927 in a paper called 'Het Eengezinshuis en zijne mogelijkheden' (The one-family house and its potentials), stating 'There is no doubt that the apartment buildings as seen in Amsterdam and Rotterdam with six or eight families sharing a stair, can only be accepted out of necessity'. He added, 'The single-family house has to be mentioned as the designated housing for a happy family life of the Dutch population'.

The main issue of the apartment building was clearly the loss of the direct connection between the private house and the public street. A compromise that became quite popular was the *boven-benedenhuis* (upstairs-downstairs) typology. Two units of two floors each were stacked on top of one another, with two front doors on street level beside each other. The narrow bay was just wide enough to accommodate the two front doors, one to the *benedenwoning*, and the other door giving access to a steep, 6-metre-long stair climbing up to the floors of the *bovenwoning*. The double-floor units themselves were quite generous and became a new standard for urban middle-class housing in Amsterdam. With the addition of a half-sunken basement, a *souterrain*, to the lower unit as storage, and an attic floor to the upper unit, these were spacious apartments that inside had a plan almost identical to that of a terraced house.^{Fig. 78}

The search for a higher standard of urban working-class housing was a much more complicated one. The earlier, much-criticised, back-to-back division of two units on one floor disappeared soon after the introduction of the Woningwet (Housing Law). Combining the two units into one was relatively simple and required only the addition of doors in the central partition wall. Some hybrid solutions appeared in the early housing corporation projects, such as the housing on the Roggeveenstraat in the first, pre-1914 phase of the Spaarndammerbuurt in Amsterdam. The project designed in 1911 by architect Herman Walenkamp, who later contributed to the design of the Zaanhof in the second phase of this working-class quarter,

The Plan

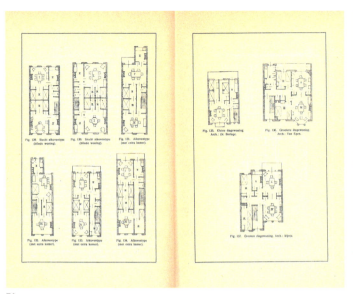
74

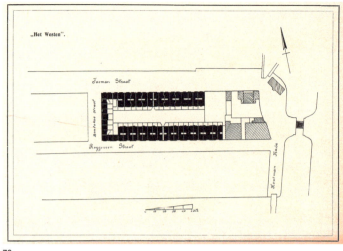
79

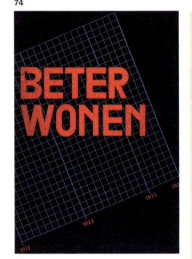
75

77

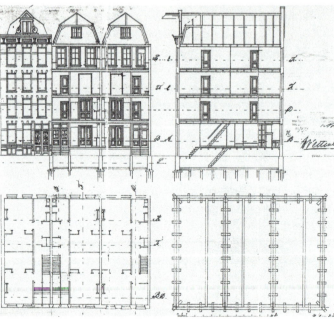
76

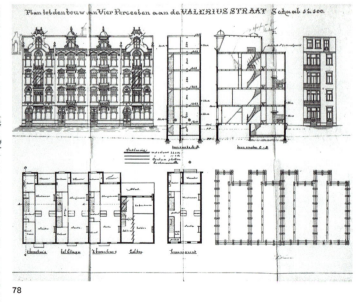
78

Patterns and Models

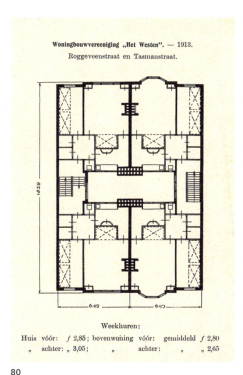

80

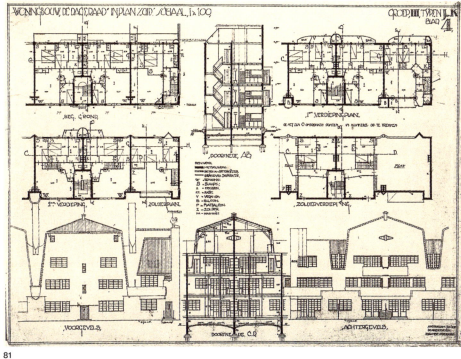

81

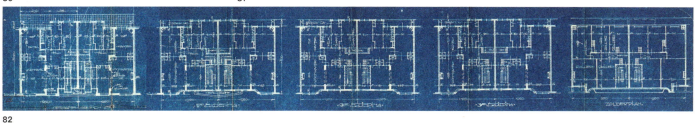

82

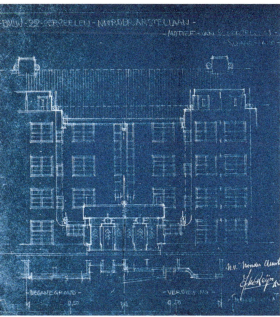

83

84

74 Development of the Dutch 'standard' apartment, as drawn by Feenstra in his study on garden cities.
75 *Beter Wonen*, celebrating the twenty-fifth anniversary of the National Confederation of Housing Corporations, design by Lotte Stam-Beese.
76 Contractor's drawing of typical late-nineteenth-century speculative working-class housing. The plans show two single orientation units on each floor.
77 Photo collage in brochure on the achievements of housing corporations in Amsterdam, with the statement: 'The dwelling is a gauge of the level of civilisation of a people.' Image by Emmy Andriesse.
78 Contractor's drawing of a block of middle-class *boven-benedenwoningen*, Valeriusstraat in Amsterdam.
79 Plan of a project for an Amsterdam housing corporation on the Roggeveenstraat, part of the first phase of the Spaarndammerbuurt extension in the western part of the city, design by Walenkamp.
80 Plan of typical cluster of four units of the Roggeveenstraat project, design by Walenkamp.
81 Plans, sections, and facades of De Klerk's design for De Dageraad, Amsterdam South.
82 Building permit plans of the housing block on the Churchilllaan (named Noorder Amstellaan before the Second World War) in Amsterdam South, design by Gulden and Geldmaker (plans) and Van der Mey (facade).
83 Facade drawing of the design by Van der Mey for the Churchilllaan, with a cluster of six front doors.
84 The front doors of the Churchilllaan project.

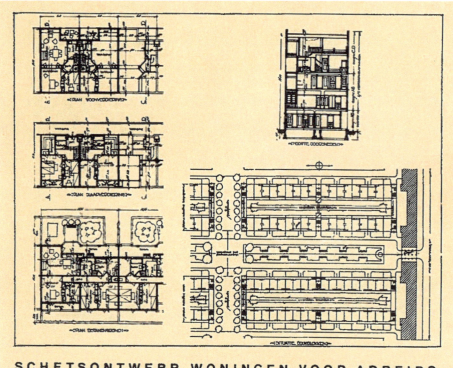

85 Entry for a competition for labour-saving housing, design by Boterenbrood.
86 Perspective of Boterenbrood's proposal for labour-saving housing.

improved the back-to-back typology by introducing small internal courtyards that provided light and ventilation to the units that looked either to the street or to a collective courtyard. The solution fit well in the narrow bay–wide bay structure, proving once more its versatility.[Fig. 79, 80]

Gradually, one sees that the two staircases of neighbouring segments were combined into one central staircase, now serving two units on each landing. This became a standard plan in the Amsterdam School housing, as demonstrated by the housing designed by Amsterdam School protagonist Michiel de Klerk for the housing corporation De Dageraad in Berlage's Amsterdam South urban plan and his project Het Schip in the Spaarndammerbuurt.[Fig. 81] This, however, didn't solve the front door issue; on the contrary, it made it worse as now the staircase had to be shared not by four apartments, as in Berlage's early Javastraat housing, but by six units. To mitigate this undesired presence of collective access space and the loss of the direct connection of one's front door to the street, architects introduced individual front doors for the ground- and first-floor units, next to an entrance for the second- and third-floor units, as explained in chapter 1 (see p. 26). This led to a slightly more complex plan, but still adhered to the two-bay structure. The plans of a large housing block along the Churchilllaan, one of the main thoroughfares of the Amsterdam South project, show the adopted solution. Accommodating several front doors was more costly than the shared staircase for six units and, therefore, was mainly used for middle-class apartment buildings. The resulting six front doors immediately next to one another repeated many times led to a succession of quite spectacular pieces of woodwork along the Churchilllaan. Typically, the street facades and front doors were designed by a leading Amsterdam School architect, in this case Joan van der Mey, whereas the plans and other elements were drawn by another firm. Here Van der Mey, as in many other of his housing projects in Amsterdam, worked together with Zeeger Gulden and Melle Geldmaker. These architects were probably the most prolific housing designers in the interbellum period in Amsterdam, responsible for thousands of dwellings in the new extensions of the city.[Fig. 82–84]

A few architects looked for alternative and more efficient solutions. In 1920, a lesser-known Amsterdam School architect and co-editor of *Wendingen*, Jan Boterenbrood, made an intriguing but unbuilt proposal for *woningen voor arbeidsbesparing* (housing for the reduction of labour). On top of single-storey, ground-floor units, there were four floors with maisonettes, accessed by means of internal corridors or interior streets that could be reached via a central staircase. Next to a more rational access system, the proposed typology allowed for a less repetitive facade design, and it was one of the first proposals in which the private outside space, here a loggia connected to the kitchen and living room, was facing the street and was wide enough to allow for sitting outside.[Fig. 85, 86]

The persistence of the four-floor typologies in Amsterdam was the result of not only the continued use of the most economic building methods but also building regulations that didn't allow for collective staircases leading to more than six units. In the city of The Hague, the local building regulations led to a dominant, but quite different typology of housing. The regulations demanded a direct connection between each unit and the street, for the reasons discussed earlier, leading to an open staircase design, the *Haagse Portiek* solution. As the staircase occupied a considerable part of the floor plan, the apartments on each floor were extended at the back with a long and narrow volume containing several bedrooms one after another, occupying most of the courtyard space. The lack of light and fresh air caused by this solution led to revised building regulations, prohibiting the back extensions. This was then subsequently solved by adding an extra bay to the dwelling,[Fig. 88] creating a bay with a front and back living room, and a bay with bedrooms, thus juxtaposing the two floors of the standard terraced house into a one-floor unit. Comparable with the Roggeveenstraat housing in Amsterdam, attempts were made in The Hague to create a double-row typology, with units facing the street or the inner courtyard. The 1904 block on the Fahrenheitstraat –

built by the Society for the Improvement of Working-Class Dwellings (Vereeniging tot verbetering der woningen van de arbeidende klasse), later the Royal Housing Corporation of the Hague (de Koninklijke Haagse Woningvereniging) – is an interesting example, where an open ground-floor passage, lit from above by a roof light, connects the front doors of four ground-floor apartments and six first-floor maisonettes directly to the street.[Fig. 87, 89–91]

The regulations in Amsterdam and The Hague made housing with gallery access an impossibility. Experiments with this access system, which would become standard in the post-war period, happened only in Rotterdam, exemplified by the construction of two pioneering buildings (see pp. 20, 27): the Spangen block designed by architect Michiel Brinkman and the Bergpolderflat designed by Willem van Tijen, who specialised in housing design and collaborated with many other prominent architects such as Brinkman's son Johannes, Leen van der Vlugt, Ben Merkelbach, and Gerrit Rietveld. While the Spangen block used a typology for the individual unit clearly based on a minimal version of the well-known terraced house, the radical Bergpolder project introduced a new layout for the dwelling units. The units were designed within a single span of the likewise revolutionary steel-frame structure. The kitchen was positioned near the front door, the living room at the back of the unit facing the private outside balcony that was in size and structure the exact mirror of the access gallery on the other side of the unit. One bedroom faced the access gallery, the other bedroom was next to the living room, connected by glazed double doors. The repetition of identical units and the reduction of the vertical access system to one main staircase and lift, in other words, the *galerijflat*, introduced an efficiency that could not be beaten and would become a standard that is still used today. The reception of the project was, as could be expected, very mixed. Two professors of the Department of Architecture in Delft reacted in opposite ways. Marinus Jand Granpré Molière compared the Bergpolderflat with an American prison where the Rotterdam workman had to search on the access gallery for the number of his home.

Professor Janus Gerardus Wattjes considered the project as 'a healthy and honest piece of work' that exposed the banality and lack of character of the surrounding housing blocks (which were designed by his colleague Granpré Molière!).[Fig. 93–95]

The Bekkerstraat project (1935), also in Rotterdam and a contemporary design by Van Tijen, utilised an access system of a staircase shared by two units on each floor. But the structure was again radically different. Similar to the Bergpolderflat, Van Tijen used a steel-frame structure with a lightweight facade infill and continuous bands of wooden window frames.[Fig. 92] The internal layout introduced a central narrow bay with a shared staircase facing the street, and at the back of the access bay, called the *wisselbeuk*, or the switch bay, a bedroom was added to one of the two units. This allowed for a rational way of differentiating the apartments' sizes.[Fig. 96, 97] The addition of another narrow bay to some of the units increased the possibilities for differentiation further, allowing for apartments with another two extra bedrooms. Next to the gallery access building, the *galerijflat*, this layout, the *portiekflat*, became the other standard housing type in the post-war period.

Jan Duiker, together with Bernard Bijvoet, published in 1930 a booklet called *Hoogbouw* ('Highrise'), making a plea for high-rise towers in open green space, acknowledging Le Corbusier's advocacy for such developments. The units in the proposed design spread out around a central access core. The design included collective spaces, considered by Duiker as one of the main advantages of high-rise housing.[Fig. 98, 99] As in his proposal for terraced housing, the project was never realised but testifies to his reputation as one of the most experimental modernists in the Netherlands. One innovative housing project by Duiker that was built is the Nirwana Flat in The Hague, literally a white elephant with concrete legs in the brick universe of its surroundings. The plans of the flat introduced another new and meaningful idea: a flexible layout within a concrete column structure that could by adapted and changed over time by the residents.[Fig. 100]

Patterns and Models

After its introduction by Van Tijen in the Bekkerstraat project, the *portiekflat* was further developed in the study *Woonmogelijkheden in het nieuwe Rotterdam* (1941) by Van Tijen and the young architect Jaap Bakema. The study was intended to provide an answer to the task of rebuilding Rotterdam after the city's disastrous bombing in 1940 by the German Luftwaffe. In the first decades of the post-war reconstruction, lifts were considered too costly, and the three- to four-storey *portiekflat* became the standard for social housing all over the country. Gradually, traditional building methods were replaced with concrete floors and load-bearing walls, although still based on the bay structure with spans not exceeding 4 metres. The *portiekflat* was built in large numbers, with hardly any variation in the layout.[Fig. 101, 102]

Both Willem van Tijen and Jaap Bakema became leading figures in post-war housing design and production. Van Tijen continued to improve the gallery type, pioneered in the Bergpolderflat project, while Bakema, who joined forces with architect Jo van den Broek in 1948, started to develop new housing typologies.

Bakema's best-known contribution to housing design is probably the tower block in Berlin's Hansaviertel from 1957. The complex section of split-level units in a repeated sectional fragment of three floors with a central access corridor on every second floor resulted in a very economic access system. The split-level section divided the apartments into two or three different levels, one with living room and kitchen, and the other with bathroom and bedrooms. In this way living spaces and bedrooms were separated from one another as in a terraced house. The type was further developed over time in a series of built and unbuilt projects. It could be applied in tower blocks such as the Berlin example, longer slab blocks as in 't Hool, and eventually in long wall-like structures or spine blocks, as can be seen in the Pampus project.[Fig. 103–105]

The basic types of the *portiekflat* and the *galerijflat* were best suited to an industrialisation of the construction methods. The large honeycomb structures of the Amsterdam Bijlmermeer were designed with an open access gallery on all levels, sometimes more than 500 metres long. Most of the dwelling units were still held captive in a two- or three-bay structure of load-bearing side walls and relatively small spans, all to minimise the cost of materials. Both the inflexibility of the structural system and the minimal floor and wall thickness meant the buildings were not future-proof.[Fig. 106, 107] Another system introduced in the period of industrialisation, the so-called ERA flat, tried to address the flexibility of the internal layout. The units, also accessed from long galleries, were built in an unprecedented single span of 7.20 metres, thus allowing for many configurations, including, in the most extreme option, a single open loft space.[Fig. 108]

The most radical proposal to rethink housing design and housing construction was probably John Habraken's plea for 'open building', published in 1961 in his first book, *Supports: An Alternative to Mass Housing*. The Stichting Architecten Research (SAR, Foundation for Architects' Research) made Habraken its first director. The SAR, started by several Dutch architects active in post-war housing construction, had the ambition to change the design and production methods of housing. Habraken's ideas were based on a clear separation of the different elements of construction, thus achieving an optimal flexibility and adaptability over time. Participation of the people for whom the housing was made, both during and after the design phase, was a crucial part of the proposed new approach. Habraken's ideas, which over time have been further developed and enriched, resonated globally, and are a focus of interest again today.

A main point of study for the SAR was finding ways to escape from the straitjacket of the industrial building systems with load-bearing walls. The design for a pilot apartment project in Rotterdam Ommoord proposed to make the facades and an in-between interior wall the load-bearing system, rather than utilising the centuries-old method of load-bearing partition walls between the units and a completely open facade.[Fig. 109, 110]

A couple of projects based on the open-building concept were designed and built in

The Plan

87

88

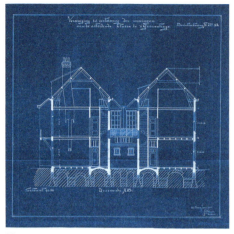

89

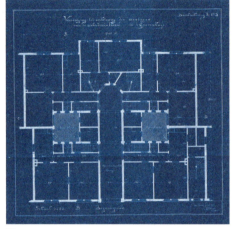

90

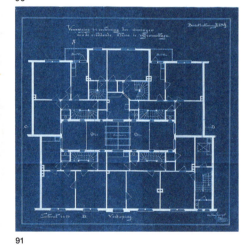

91

103 Patterns and Models

92

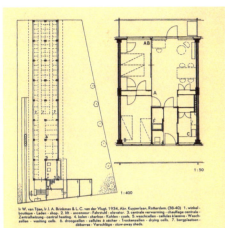
93

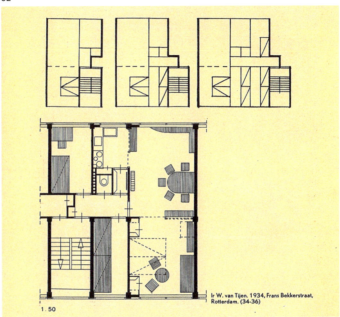
96

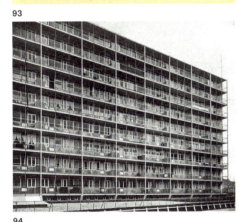
94

97

95

87 The Fahrenheitstraat block after completion.
88 Development of housing types in The Hague: 1866, courtyard houses, *boven-benedenwoningen* with front doors on both sides; 1908, early *Haagse Portiek* type; 1914, *Haagse Portiek* with extension at the back; 1923, improved *Haagse Portiek* with two wide bays and no back extension.
89–91 Section, ground-floor, and first-floor plan of the *boven-benedenwoningen* on the Fahrenheitstraat in The Hague: 10 of the 11 front doors are connected to the street via a partly covered passage.
92 View of the Frans Bekkerstraat housing block, *portiekflat* typology, design by Van Tijen.
93 Ground-floor plan and typical unit of the Bergpolderflat in Rotterdam, *galerijflat* typology as introduced by Van Tijen.
94 View of the private balconies, the Bergpolderflat.
95 Interior view of a Bergpolderflat unit.
96 Floor plan of typical unit of the Frans Bekkerstraat project, with diagrams showing the differentiation in unit size made possible by the *wisselbeuk* and/or the addition of extra narrow bays.
97 Interior view of unit of the Frans Bekkerstraat project.

104   The Plan

98

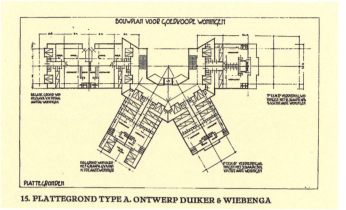

99

101

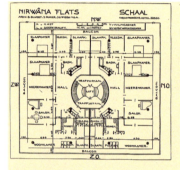 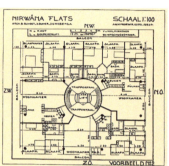

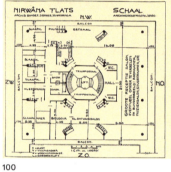 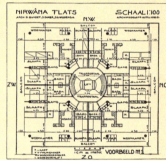

100

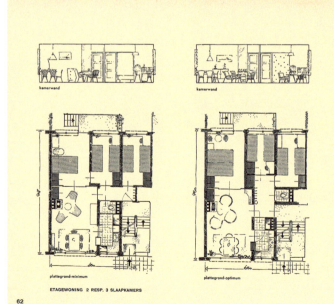

102

98 Duiker's *Hoogbouw* manifesto on high-rise residential buildings.
99 Floor plan for affordable housing in high-rise tower block with eight apartments varying in size around a spacious and day-lit central core, proposed in Duiker's manifesto.
100 Preliminary design for the Nirwana Flat with flexible layout and variation of unit sizes, design by Duiker, Bijvoet, and Wiebinga.
101 Cover of the study on new housing options for Rotterdam, with design proposals by Van Tijen, Brinkman, Van den Broek, and Maaskant.
102 Proposal for the floor plan of *portiekflats* with *wisselbeuk*, published in the study *Woonmogelijkheden in het nieuwe Rotterdam*.
103 Model of Bakema's design for a tower block at the Berlin Hansaviertel Interbau Exhibition.
104 Floor plans of Bakema's Hansaviertel project as built.
105 Sketch by Bakema, showing the access system and split-level typology of the Hansaviertel project, and explaining its advantages.
106 Design of the Bijlmermeer, in south-east Amsterdam. The ten-storey honeycomb structures can be reached via the parking garages (grey volumes) that connect to the elevated ring road.
107 Typical floor plan of a Bijlmermeer apartment with one wider bay (3.70 metres) and two narrow bays (2.70 metres).
108 Floor plan of an ERA flat, showing two options for the internal layout within the 7.20-metre-wide structural bay.

105 Patterns and Models

103

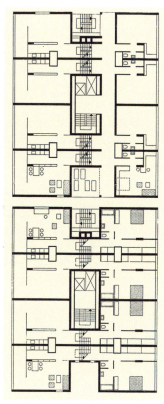

104

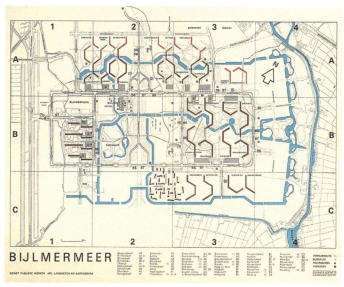

106

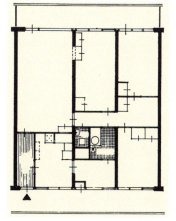

107

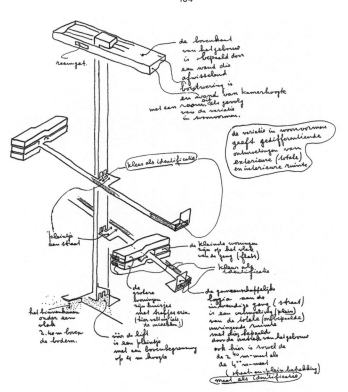

105

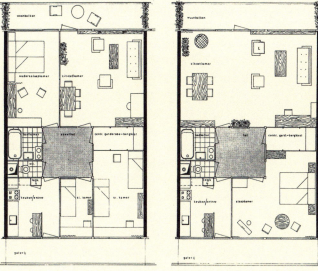

108

the 1970s. The plans of the units were designed with the participation of the future residents, but, or maybe because of this, hardly differed from the standard of the time. In the end, the studies and pilot projects had little impact, and the SAR came under fire for only propagating a system and stopped its activities in 1990.

The lack of typological variation in apartment buildings remained persistent despite some built experiments. In the 1980s the standard repertoire was slowly widened, especially with the introduction of what Dutch architects called the *stadsvilla*, or the urban villa, a type already known for decades in Italy as the *palazzina* or in Scandinavia as *tjockhus* (the thick building). The type avoided the open access gallery but was still more economic than the *portiekflat* as the access core now served four to six units per floor instead of two. The corner units that characterise the urban villa also allow for more variation in the floor plan, getting away from the tunnel vision of the previously standard types.

D03 D10 D21 The projects in Funenpark show two variations on the *palazzina* typology and demonstrate how within the envelope a large variation in plans and unit sizes can be combined. The *tjockhus* typology becomes especially efficient when a maximum number of units is grouped around a central access lobby on each floor.Fig. 111 This can be seen in the Nierkerkestraat project, part of the regeneration of the Amsterdam Western Garden Cities. Seven units are clustered on one floor with a variation of apartment layouts and sizes, all fitting, however, within the 5.4-metre span of the concrete tunnel construction system.Fig. 112

Although the open gallery-access building is probably the most despised housing type, considered 'cheap and anonymous', it is still a much-used solution. The early project in Nijmegen on the Gerard Noodtstraat has a gallery access typology, but by cutting the gallery in two with separate points of vertical access and positioning the access galleries on alternating sides of the building, a long and anonymous gallery has been avoided. The unit plans also try to escape from convention. Instead of a basic layout of a 'tunnel' between two side walls, two apartments interlock in a shared third bay, thus providing each unit with a wider two-bay part and a narrow single-bay part.Fig. 114

D11 The Berkenstede care home in Diemen avoids the ubiquitous tunnel system in the plans for the pavilions with small individual units. The Berkenstede project was designed to replace a twenty-five-year-old care home. The existing structure was built with load-bearing partition walls between the tiny single-room units. This made it impossible to adapt the building to today's standards. To avoid the same happening again in the future, the project was designed with a load-bearing core and load-bearing facades, allowing for an optimal flexibility over time as the size of the individual units can now be changed without structural interventions.Fig. 113

D04 The tower type was investigated in the project for the former sewage plants of the Amsterdam Western Garden Cities. Each floor has four units, but using a system of interlocking and maisonette units avoided any apartments having only a north-east orientation, which on this site would mean no sunlight or views towards the park and lake.Fig. 115

D15 D07 In a number of projects, more hybrid combinations of different types and access systems were explored. The three-storey *palazzinas* in Huizen are a combination of terraced houses with apartments, all centred around a covered and hidden ground-floor parking garage.Fig. 116 The social housing project near Delflandplein, another project for the regeneration of the Western Garden Cities of Amsterdam, contains an almost extreme differentiation of types and sizes in one building. Gallery-accessed one- and two-room studios with collective spaces, apartments around compact interior lobbies, and large

Patterns and Models

maisonettes with ground-floor access via individual front doors are just three of the many types clustered in the U-shaped building. These hybrid solutions make it possible to better anchor new projects in existing urban sites, as they can adapt more easily to a context with different kinds of adjacent open spaces and buildings.[Fig. 117]

New housing now has to find ways to fit within existing urban and suburban fabrics. Densification and renewal of older and more recent housing neighbourhoods will make these more attractive and more diverse and will increase the viability of amenities, schools, and other vital services. The mass production of single typologies with fixed plans has proven to be a short-lived solution. The adaptability of housing of the first decades of the twentieth century stands in sharp contrast with the concrete inflexibility of the later years. A varied range of housing types that can be adapted over time is necessary to create neighbourhoods that withstand time and result in strong communities. Variety and adaptability give residents the possibility to remain in their neighbourhood and community if their housing needs change. The design of housing shapes the conditions for this to happen.

108 The Plan

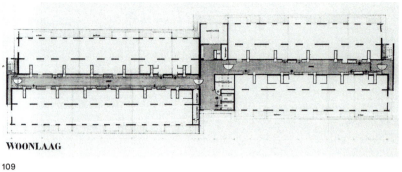

WOONLAAG

109

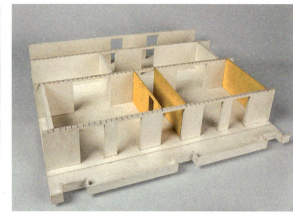

110

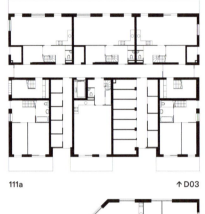

111a ↑D03

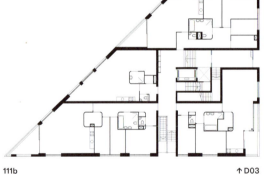

111b ↑D03

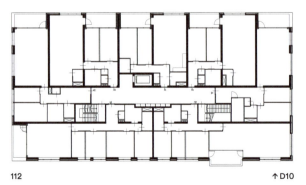

112 ↑D10

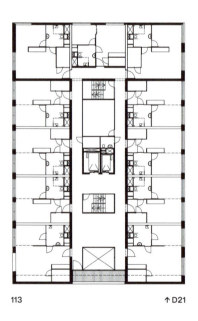

113 ↑D21

114 ↑D11

Patterns and Models

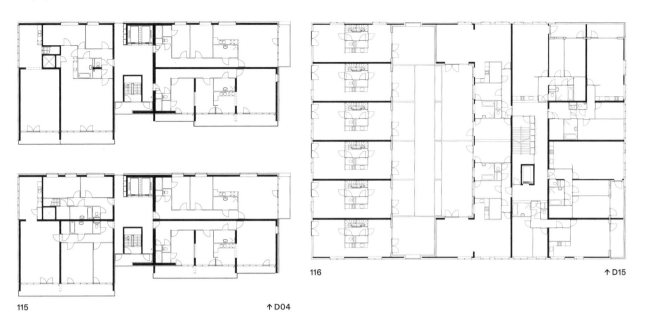

115   ↑ D04

116   ↑ D15

117   ↑ D07

109 SAR proposal for an experimental apartment building with a load-bearing facade and corridor walls, not realised.
110 Model of the experimental SAR proposal.
111 Ground-floor plans of two urban villas, or *palazzinas*, in Funenpark (D03).
112 Compact apartment block with internal corridor (D10).
113 Apartment building with *galerijflat* access system. The access gallery moves from front to back (D21).
114 Care-home apartments with load-bearing facade and corridor walls, allowing for internal flexibility in unit size over time (D11).
115 Tower block plan, with maisonette type to avoid unit with only north-east aspect (D04).
116 Combination of townhouses and apartments in one building (D15).
117 First-floor plan of building block, combining different unit types within framework of 5.40-metre-wide bays (D07).

4 The People

Cooperation and Customisation

The People

The intimate and unceasing interaction between people and the forms they inhabit is a fundamental and fascinating aspect of built environment. We are all players; agents who inhabit the environment, transforming it to our liking and making sure things stay as we choose.

John Habraken, *The Structure of the Ordinary*

Cooperation and Customisation

Dutch housing has been dominated since the end of the nineteenth century by projects initiated by housing corporations or commercial developers, rarely by individual clients. This has led on the one hand to a clear and consistent connection between housing production and urban development, but on the other hand to a focus on large numbers and an almost complete lack of direct participation of residents in the design of their own domestic spaces.

This chapter looks at projects of the last hundred years that started from the viewpoint of the residents, who either took up the role of developers themselves or were involved in the design and building process in other ways. Projects initiated or directly guided by the future residents show a diversity of approaches, and sometimes an innovative power that the projects led by architects, builders, and developers cannot achieve. These projects can play a vital role in creating housing and neighbourhoods that acknowledge the diversity of today's society and establish the right conditions for a community of people from different backgrounds and cultures.

In the recent Dutch housing market crisis, resulting from the 2008 credit and banking crash, local governments started to promote the practice of private commissioning. Housing production had fallen dramatically; sites that had been purchased by commercial developers for large sums of money and were ready for building, were left undeveloped. Next to the developers, housing corporations were dropping out as well. They were affected not only by the stagnant housing market, impacting their mixed development projects in which the housing market financed the social housing, but also by a political decision to tax the corporations in an unprecedented way. This all seemed to clear the way for private initiatives, whether individual or collective.

In the last five years, the market has opened again. The drop in production caused by the crisis has resulted in a significant shortage, leading to a steep rise in house prices, and inevitably to a parallel surge in the demand for affordable housing. Collective projects continue to be initiated to address the shortage of affordable housing, but whether the promotion of private initiatives indicates a definitive shift in the Dutch housing market is impossible to say at this time. But one can try to assess whether the increase in private initiatives is resulting in the construction of more varied types of dwellings. Of special interest is the practice of collective commissioning, in which the balance between individual requirements and collective interests seems to offer a new principle for housing design.

I Self-build

The stimulation of private commissions has been a factor in the debate on housing policy for much longer. It reflects the political developments of recent decades in the Netherlands, where both the left and the right were gradually abandoning the welfare state. Citizens are expected to take on more responsibilities, while they should at the same time be given more freedom in how and what to build for themselves. In 1997 Carel Weeber, the architect of several large-scale and often controversial social housing projects, took a polemical stand against 'state architecture' in the housing sector, embodied by the endless rows of terraced houses in the so-called Vinex neighbourhoods. Through his concept of *het wilde wonen* (wild or unregulated housing),[Fig. 2] he put forward the idea that everyone should be given the opportunity to build their own home, unhindered by (aesthetic) rules and regulations. In response, Dutch member of parliament Adri Duivesteijn (social-democrat) successfully tabled a motion in 1998 proposing that a third of all housing production should be in private hands. In the policy document *Mensen Wensen Wonen. Wonen in de 21ste eeuw* ('What people want, where people live. Housing in the twenty-first century', 2000), Deputy Minister Remkes (VVD) argued for more room for individual 'housing preferences', and reiterated Duivesteijn's target that by 2005 at least 30 per cent of Dutch housing production ought to be in the hands of private owner-occupiers. Reality refuses to be pinned down, however, and these targets were never met.

Housing in the Netherlands has long been geared towards repetition, standardisation, and the resulting cost savings. It was this strategy that made it possible to build over a period of almost a hundred years, since the introduction of the Woningwet, so many social housing projects at an average construction standard that is, compared to many other countries, quite high. Berlage's plea for standardisation, as mentioned in the previous chapter, to achieve quality and a coherent urban structure in Dutch cities can thus be considered successful. It was, however, exactly this Berlagian paradigm, as Weeber called it, that the *wilde wonen* followers opposed, in line with the neoliberal turn in Dutch politics in the 1990s. 'Het Wilde Wonen' postulated that the contrast between city and countryside was an outdated planning misconception, and that total liberty to build one's own house would bring freedom, leisure, and fun(!).

The idea to promote self-built houses was, however, not a new one. One interesting example is the 1960s campaign by the Dutch government to stimulate individual commissioning and building of houses. If the house were designed by a local architect, built by a local builder, and cost less than 16,000 Dutch guilders, the government would give a subsidy of around 5 to 10 per cent of the costs and a bank guarantee for the remaining loan.[Fig. 3] The government issued a book with seventy designs for housing costing less than the maximum indicated. Not surprisingly, the designs are almost identical and can be found all over the country, mostly in rural areas.

Despite all this, the average person looking for accommodation has not had the option of commissioning his or her own home for centuries, especially in an urban context. And while there have been since the 1990s several attempts at facilitating individual commissioning in the Vinex neighbourhoods, these seldom went beyond a small area with plots for detached houses, with or without aesthetic supervision.

→D36 The individually designed and built townhouses on the Scheepstimmermanstraat in Amsterdam are a clear example. Aesthetic supervision was focussed on a prescribed building envelope but left the design of the facade and interior layout open.[Fig. 4]

In Almere, where the housing sector was under the control of Adri Duivesteijn in his role as city councillor from 2006 to 2013, efforts to stimulate private commissioning are continuing apace. They are mainly centred on the Homeruskwartier, the largest new development based on private commissioning in the Netherlands to date.[Fig. 5]

Needless to say, project developers have embraced the appeal of the self-built house. Projects with names like Wonen à la carte and Wenswonen (Wishful Living) offer a set of often purely cosmetic options for making a standard dwelling 'individual and unique'. But the options fail to shrug off the straitjacket of the construction methods; the industrialised construction process, a lasting heritage from the 1960s, is literally masked by different facades. Excepting a few projects, such as the Homeruskwartier, private commissioning on a large scale without the intervention of a developer has not really taken off.

After decades of large-scale housing, there is undeniable demand for more individual participation in the design of both the house and the living environment, but it is not necessarily coupled to private commissions. Likewise, there are signs of a resurgence of the appreciation of shared, collective space in the living environment. Individual commissioning appears to be of limited benefit to these developments. The ambition to commission one's own home is beset by physical, procedural, and financial constraints. On closer inspection the idea of *het wilde wonen* is inspired more by nostalgia or self-interest than by a sense of commitment to the larger living environment and a desire for collectivity. These aspirations may be better met by collective private commissioning. The gradual increase in the number of collectively commissioned projects goes hand in hand with studies of and publications about the phenomenon, both in the Netherlands and elsewhere. They tend to focus on the distinguishing features of collective private commissioning with respect to the processes of planning, realisation, and management. Private involvement in the commissioning process can take on many different guises and differs greatly from country to country, depending on national building practices. In the Netherlands, cooperation results in competitive advantages of scale, which has long been the underlying principle of the housing market. But how is this tied up with the desire of those participating in the collective to realise a dwelling that reflects their personal wishes and requirements? Do the new processes that result from collective private commissioning spawn new dwelling typologies as well?

II Cooperative building

Collective commissioning is not a recent phenomenon, as is shown by the quite spectacular Etagehuis Westhove, built in Amsterdam some hundred years ago.[Fig. 6] A group of people living in Amsterdam's Grachtengordel, the crescent of canals, formed a collective building society and asked architect F. A. Warners to draw up a design for an apartment building on a plot beside the NoorderAmstelkanaal, part of the system of new canals designed by Berlage in his master plan for Amsterdam South. Those behind the initiative were looking for a home on what was then the edge of the city to escape the crowded and polluted canals in the city centre. The layout and size of the apartments were adapted to meet the residents' specific requirements. Warners designed the interiors of some of these dwellings as well.[Fig. 7, 8]

Incidentally, Warners also initiated the development of luxury apartment buildings himself, for which he founded the NV Amsterdamsche Maatschappij tot Exploitatie van Etagewoningen (The Amsterdam Society for the Development and Operation of Apartments). His projects stand out even today as the most carefully designed and well-crafted apartment buildings of the city. The combined role of developer/architect, however, was practically unheard of at the time and is still a rare phenomenon.

The unusually spacious and beautifully finished apartments of Etagehuis Westhove are exceptional, but elsewhere, too, private initiatives to realise custom-made homes through collective commissioning led to remarkable projects in the first half of the twentieth century. Paradoxically, it was the strict, centralised control over housebuilding and the funding structure associated with it that made these private initiatives possible. In response to the Woningwet, the Housing Law of 1901, private housing associations were established to meet housing needs that had been ignored by speculative builders or that could not be addressed by the housing corporations specialising in affordable, large-scale social housing. The most distinguishing features of these private initiatives are the dwelling types (in terms of floor plans and the way the dwellings are linked) and the inclusion of collective spaces, both inside and outside.

The Frisia homes in Amersfoort, a development of forty-nine terraced houses with some shared amenities, were conceived on the initiative of a group of retired teachers and servicemen. The project was realised between 1920 and 1922 following a design by architect Ary Henri van Wamelen.[Fig. 9, 10] The compact, relatively wide and shallow houses with large thatched 'country house' roofs were conceived as an affordable alternative to detached houses and were to accommodate a community of 'like-minded people'.

In 1908, a number of high-ranking civil servants in Amsterdam founded the Corporation De Samenwerking, which set out to develop better quality housing for both themselves and other middle-class people looking for accommodation. The success of this initiative led to several follow-up projects, of which the Harmoniehof, realised between 1919 and 1922 following a design by Jop van Epen and Meindert Lippits, is the best known.[Fig. 11] Two elongated, rectangular blocks flank a public garden, while two substantial townhouses, each consisting of two semi-detached houses, are at either end of the green space. The blocks boast a variety of ground-floor and upper-floor flats, each of which has a front door on the street. The spacious dwellings all have a living room[Fig. 12] consisting of two spaces connected by sliding doors, and two to four bedrooms. The dwellings are linked and stacked in unusual but ingenious ways to reduce the

The People

2

3

5

1 Apartment at the end of Borneo Eiland.
2 Carel Weeber's 'Het Wilde Wonen' pamphlet on individual commissioning.
3 Cover of the 1965 portfolio of design examples for private commissioning of affordable individual houses, published by the Ministry of Housing.
4 The row of privately commissioned townhouses on Borneo Eiland.
5 Homerus Kwartier, Almere.
6 Front facade of Westhove, a collectively commissioned luxury apartment building in Amsterdam South, design by Warners.
7 Interior design for one of the very large apartments in Westhove.
8 Typical floor plan of Westhove with four apartments on one floor, ranging from 400 to 600 square metres.
9 The Frisia Woningen in Amersfoort, design by Van Wamelen.
10 Facades of the Frisia Woningen.

Cooperation and Customisation

6

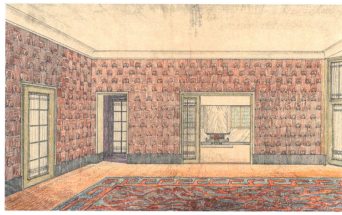

7

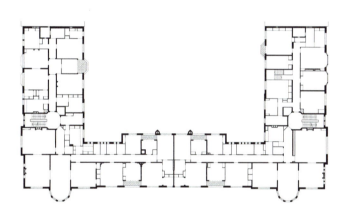

8

9

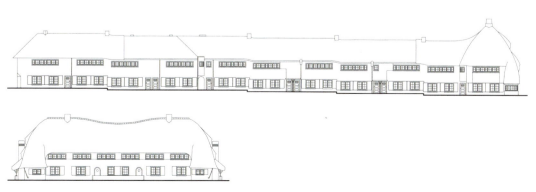

10

problem of noise between bedrooms and living rooms in homes with a traditional wooden floor construction. All this has resulted in homes that have retained much of the quality of the traditional townhouse, accessed from the ground level. The three-storey blocks with their projecting roofs and alternating bay windows appear as spacious terraced houses, while the semi-detached houses flanking the public garden look like large individual villas.[Fig. 13]

Although the post-war housing shortage led to industrialisation of the housing sector and great uniformity, the ideal of the custom-made home persisted. The establishment of the Huis en Wijk (Home and Neighbourhood) housing association in Eindhoven recalls the Amsterdam Corporation De Samenwerking of fifty years earlier. In this case the initiative came from a group of Philips employees, who thought the housing market in Eindhoven at the time was below par. They asked architect Jaap Bakema to come up with a design for a new neighbourhood for a thousand families: 't Hool, as already seen in chapter 2 (see p. 52).[Fig. 14, 15] The performance and spatial quality of the dwelling itself was to be the primary focus, not the location or the application of expensive construction materials. These requirements enabled Bakema to bring many of his existing ideas together in a development characterised by a great cohesion between public, collective, and private spaces and boasting a wide variety of dwelling types. Bakema and the project architects Jan Stokla and Gerard Lans proposed an extensive catalogue of fourteen dwelling types within an 'ideal' layout of smaller clusters separated by collective and public greenery with a high wall of flats as its northern boundary. The different dwelling types offered a great deal of choice in and of themselves, but there was further differentiation within the types. Most noteworthy in this respect is type seven, *de groeiwoning*, the growing house. These dwellings, with the sculptural exterior typical of Bakema's architecture, could be enlarged via both vertical and horizontal additions and extensions. The quirky sculptural quality of the design meant that instead of ruining the overall picture, such extras would enhance it.[Fig. 16, 17]

The split-level layout produced a house with a remarkable spatial quality, in which the most important rooms are grouped around a higher living room with access to the garden. Equally special is the interlocking parcellation, with its resulting wide garden facade and narrow entrance facade. The alternation of front and rear elevations effectively does away with a wall of rear facades, so that a block of *groeiwoning* types can be positioned within a fully public green space, comparable with Rietveld's houses in Reeuwijk.

III Individual and collective

The examples described above appear to be paradoxical: collective commissioning as a means of realising a diversity of individual housing requirements. Hans Ruijssenaars's design for eleven clustered dwellings in Leusden, commissioned by the future residents, put the collective's individual requirements at the forefront. In the early 1970s the village of Hamersveld near Amersfoort was renamed Leusden, before being rapidly extended with interminable plots of identical terraced houses made of brick and tiled roofs. The homes on Egelwier seem to resist this trend. The homes have the same basic structure, which is then adapted each time in a different way to create unique, customised units. The dwellings are two or three bays wide. At right angles to the constructive bays is a second three-part zoning. The front zone contains the entrances, kitchen, storage spaces, and/or garages; the middle features a light shaft in the roof; and the rear zone has a sunken ground-level floor. Bigger and smaller voids connect these zones and flood them with daylight. The clear spatial organisation and the structural design make it easy to vary the layout and the position of kitchens, voids, and staircases in each dwelling without a loss of overall cohesion and identity.[Fig. 18-20] The collective initiative behind this project put individual elaboration centre stage. The project features no collective spaces, but by operating as a collective, the clients were able to realise their individual wishes. The terraced house typology ensured the project was within budget and in accordance with the planning rules of the expansion of Leusden.

In the 1970s new ideas started to appear. Ideals regarding collectivity were less about collective commissioning with the aim of owning a home designed to one's own specifications than about cohabiting in a community and sharing facilities. The underlying principle here is not home ownership; instead, private initiatives for this kind of communal living are picked up by existing housing associations and often realised in the form of clusters of (subsidised) rental homes. This living arrangement became known as *Centraal Wonen* (Cohousing).

The first project to be built under this name, though via a private initiative, was the Wandelmeent in Hilversum. The project, realised in 1977 in Hilversumse Meent, a large suburb of Hilversum, is still regarded as one of the most successful cohousing projects in the Netherlands.Fig. 21 Wedged in between the 1970s *woonerven* full of single-family houses, the Wandelmeent is made up of fifty varied rental homes. They are divided into ten clusters, each of which has some shared facilities: kitchen, storage/laundry space, and garden. There are also some shared facilities for all the clusters together, including a space for people to get together, a work room, guest rooms, a sauna, and a youth club.Fig. 23 The project was designed by Leo de Jonge, a founding member of the SAR (see p. 100), and is a good example of a modular configuration. The clear articulation of the boundary walls in the exterior and the rhythm of the curved roofs reflect the repetitive, Mediterranean-inspired, low-rise, high-density housing clusters popular among the post-war modernists.

The units are based on a repeated module of approximately 23 square metres,Fig. 22 which in *Centraal Wonen* terms was known as *een vlakje* (a patch). Wandelmeent contains units ranging in size from two to five such patches or segments. The owner, housing association Het Gooi, leases the development to the Stichting Centraal Wonen (Cohousing Foundation), which manages the property and rents the units. Residents are not allowed to extend their modules, but when their housing needs change they can move to a larger or smaller unit (known as 'upscaling' and 'downscaling', respectively). The design of the houses also allows for easy conversion into standard single-family dwellings, though this has not happened yet.

IV Inclusive or exclusive

One of the defining characteristics of the Wandelmeent is its explicitly stated aim of achieving a mix of residents in a proper reflection of society. This is true of many of the later *Centraal Wonen* projects, especially those developed in the 1980s. In the 1990s, on the other hand, we start to see an increasing number of initiatives from more specific groups of residents. Again, housing associations were prepared to act as intermediaries.

Private commissioning in the true sense of the word made a comeback too. In Amsterdam, the continuous housing shortage made it difficult for many people to find suitable accommodation, prompting various initiatives by groups of private individuals. Collective commissioning makes it particularly attractive for architects to initiate projects themselves, since it enables them to pass any development risk on to the collective of clients rather than shoulder it themselves. BO1, part of the Borneo Eiland Sporenburg scheme in the Amsterdam Eastern Docklands area, is a clear example of this. This compact urban block, a project of CASA architecten at the entrance of the former harbour pier, is an attempt to create distinctive individual homes within the straitjacket of the conventional structure of load-bearing interior walls with narrow bays. Their exteriors mask both the differences within and the existence of some collective spaces, merely showing the outside world a neutral face.

→D05 The project at the very end of Borneo Eiland was developed in the regular way by a commercial builder. However, the three apartments at the end of the long strip of townhouses were customised according to the buyers' wishes. This small-scale customisation project led to three completely different layouts within almost

120 The People

11

12

13

121 Cooperation and Customisation

14

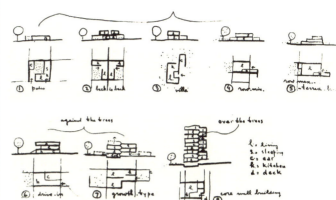

15

16

17

11 Harmoniehof in Amsterdam, intricate *boven-benedenwoningen* typology facing the central collective green space. Design by Van Epen and Lippits.
12 Interior view of one of the dwellings of the Harmoniehof, belonging to architect, publicist, and critic Mieras.
13 Ground-floor plan of the Harmoniehof.
14 View of 't Hool in Eindhoven.
15 Sketch by Bakema for different dwelling types to be implemented in the design for 't Hool.
16 Sketch of the growing house interior, 't Hool.
17 The growing house type, designed for 't Hool.

18

20

19

123   Cooperation and Customisation

21

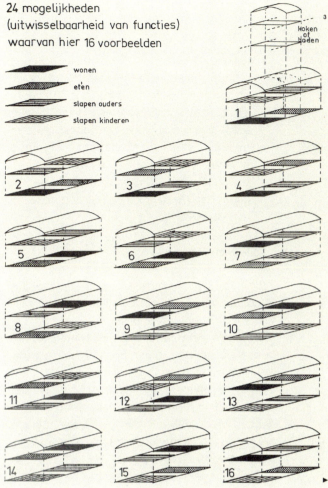
22

23

18   View of the Egelwier project in Leusden, design by Hans Ruijssenaars.
19   Ground-floor plan of the Egelwier project, eleven different plans within one continuous structure.
20   Interior of one of the Egelwier houses.
21   Community life in the Wandelmeent project in Hilversum, design by Leo de Jonge.
22   Diagram of the flexible layout of the Wandelmeent dwellings; there are twenty-four different options.
23   The collective living room of the Wandelmeent.

identical envelopes. The initially required standard plan, with three bedrooms, was each time transformed into variations of an open loft plan. Typically, the process to achieve this was so exceptional for the builder that in many instances the standard finishes were already being made before the (sub)contractors realised that the client had demanded something non-standard.[Fig. 24-28]

V Standard and exception

Within the Dutch context, the paradoxical aim of collective private commissioning to achieve greater differentiation through a joint effort has resulted in some remarkable dilemmas. In other countries, whether close by, such as Belgium, or far away, such as Canada and the US, collective private commissioning is usually a response to a highly individualised housing sector. There, the collective and connecting elements are at the forefront of collectively commissioned projects.

In Denmark, with its long tradition of collectivity within the living environment, the relationship between the collective and the individual seems to be self-evident. From early examples of the collective apartment building dating back to the eighteenth century, as shown in Hans Erling Langkilde's 1970 book *Kollektiv Huset*, collective housing extended to suburban housing complexes where individual houses were customised to the occupants' wishes while also provided with collective amenities.[Fig. 29] The German *Baugruppen*, or building groups, are another example of private collective initiatives, gaining more and more ground since the 1990s as the building activities of housing corporations were slowing down in favour of commercial developments. The *Baugruppen* realised often inventive projects, with an intelligent mix of living and working, but also contested signs of gentrification in existing neighbourhoods, which were slowly becoming unaffordable for the people already living there.[Fig. 30]

The collective initiative in the Netherlands, unlike that in other countries, is usually a reaction to standardisation and scale in the housing sector. The projects tend to be driven by the desire for custom-made solutions, individual expression, and profit. Communal facilities are not necessarily part of these initiatives. It is difficult to move away from the typical Dutch situation of standardised construction methods and fixed floor plans to its opposite: differentiated and flexible dwellings, using easily adaptable construction methods. And it seems to be even harder to find an architectural expression that deviates from the usual repetition, the 'state architecture' (Carel Weeber's term for large-scale, state-controlled social housing projects), or from a fashionable, forced individualisation of the exterior shell.

The 2009 report by the VROM Raad (Governmental Council for Housing, Spatial Planning, and the Environment), titled *Wonen in ruimte en tijd, een zoektocht naar sociaal-culturele trends in het wonen* ('Dwelling in space and time, a search for socio-cultural trends in living'), identifies as the key trend for the near future the wish to share one's living environment with like-minded people, so that various social groups can live, if not together, at least side by side in relatively small clusters and in a durable way. The report's observations on communality and scale tie in well with the opportunities afforded by collective private commissioning: the development, with like-minded people, of our own homes and of a communal in-between space by way of transition to the outside world. The examples described of collectively commissioned neighbourhoods and buildings shed light on the possibilities and impossibilities of collective private commissioning. Developments on the scale of a neighbourhood such as 't Hool in Eindhoven (1,000 homes) seem no longer possible today. Such a large scale is not compatible with the ambition of bringing together cohesive groups of residents, nor is it relevant in an era when the large-scale expansion of cities is no longer on the agenda. What we need is a scale that is consistent with the new focus on the existing city and the existing housing stock. Besides, society has become so diverse that it is neither feasible nor desirable to expect a project to reflect society

Cooperation and Customisation

as a whole. This is why projects that focus on a cohesive group of residents are relevant, while the ideal of the broad social mix propagated by some of the older projects may well be obsolete.

At any rate, we can say that collective private initiatives have always been a catalyst for stepping away from conventional housing and developing new, custom-made solutions for a wide range of residents. This might be a good time to embrace the experimental character of many a collective housing project. The question is more relevant than ever: How can we use modest means to achieve greater differentiation in the housing market and cater to the specific requirements of future residents? How can we develop structures that will enable different spatial and programmatic elaboration, including growth and change at a later stage, even in affordable housing?

→S1 To address these questions, the typological studies for Strandeiland, the latest extension of the new Amsterdam housing archipelago IJburg, focus on the parcellation strategy. By introducing a medium scale in both the plot sizes and the tender strategies, possibilities are created for projects initiated by private collectives. In this way the city seeks to create a stronger diversity in the future population of Strandeiland, and an attractive variety in the types and architectural expressions of the buildings that together will be positioned in a typical Amsterdam grid of long and narrow building blocks. The idea is that the strong rigidity of a straightforward urban grid structure can accommodate an extensive variation in housing types without losing control and cohesion.^{Fig. 31-33}

Whether collective private commissioning offers a way out of the current dilemmas in the Dutch housing market remains to be seen. Perhaps it is inevitable that affordable housing, especially in the existing city, continues to depend on project-based developments and the intervention of professional commissioning bodies. But even if collective private commissioning is not a magic formula, the approach does play an unmistakable role in facilitating experimentation and has produced some inspiring results as far as the balance between differentiation and cohesion is concerned. These initiatives are valuable because they can point the professional developer and corporation in the right direction, towards the demand for decent and affordable homes, and away from a uniform standard, not through the illusion of visual differentiation and expensive options, but through structural variation and flexibility.

126 The People

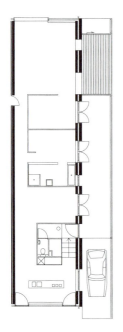
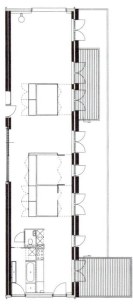

25 ↑ D05

26 ↑ D05

28 ↑ D05

27 ↑ D05

24 ↑ D05

24 The three different layouts of the end apartments on Borneo Eiland (D05).
25–27 Interior views of the Borneo Eiland end apartments: ground level, first floor, second floor (D05).
28 Exterior view of the Borneo Eiland end apartments (D05).
29 Hans Erling Langkilde's study *Kollektiv Huset*, on collective housing in Denmark, showing the collective living space of Utzon's Fredensborg housing.
30 Baugruppe project in Berlin.
31 Study of the parcellation and housing typologies for Strandeiland, part of IJburg in Amsterdam: small clusters of units, repeatable and adaptable to different positions within the Strandeiland grid structure, allowing for collective commissioning (S01).
32 IJburg study sketch.
33 IJburg study: test design for one of the blocks within the Strandeiland grid structure (S01).

127 Cooperation and Customisation

29

30

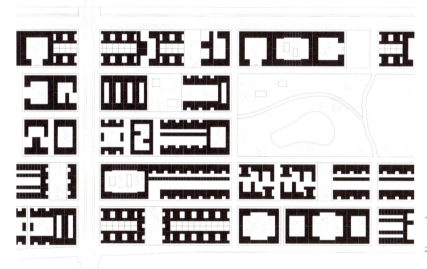

31

↑S01 32   ↑S01

33   ↑S01

5 Space and Material
Seven Elements of Housing Design

The character and the identity of our cities depend on the way housing is designed and built, much more than any other type of building. As Berlage wrote in his pamphlet 'Normalisatie in Woningbouw':

> Stedenbouw is met huizenmateriaal ruimte scheppen (Building cities is creating space with houses as material).

The definition of the open, public space is determined by how houses shape the built structure of our cities. The clear contrast between the densely built structure of Dutch cities, where the house always formed a part of a larger, closely knitted building block, and the open structure of villages, formed by linear or more random clusters of free-standing houses and farms, has been lost in the twentieth century. The ubiquitous suburbs of the last hundred years present a compromise between these two distinct contexts, resulting in an undefined repetition of housing clusters without the character of the clearly articulated urban space of the city or the continuous intertwining of buildings and landscape of the village.

In whatever context, it is essential when designing housing to look for a coherent structure that either enhances the urban character or, in a suburban area, introduces the open green space or continuing landscape as an essential defining element of the living environment. This demands a careful anchoring of the project in its surroundings. The architectural form and articulation of the project should express this anchored and situated continuity, not seeking to stand out, but instead to blend in. To quote Steen Eiler Rasmussen:

> Ein Bauwerk soll nicht das Denkmal einer besonderen Architektenpersonlichkeit sein. Es gehort zum Leben des Alltags und muss sich ganz naturlich, ohne Aufdringlichkeit seiner Umgebung einfugen (A building should not be the monument of an architectural ego. It belongs to everyday life, and should fit, without intrusiveness, in its surroundings).

Seven Elements of Housing Design

A first example of this approach can be seen in the project for the Haarlemmerplein in Amsterdam's historic centre (D01). The building fills a vacant site that was left abandoned for thirty years after the demolition of a block of seventeenth-century houses to make space for a central access road that was never built. The square was one of the main entrances to seventeenth-century Amsterdam, bordered on three sides by modest townhouses, and on the side facing the open land by a gate and the city walls. The new building restores the original outline of the square. A typology of narrow and deep loft apartments around three small, protected courtyards helps to minimise the noise of roads and railways while bringing back the original parcellation of narrow townhouses that used to stand here. The design seeks to create a quiet background to life on the square. The brick facades and white plasterwork in the courtyards refer to the original patterns of material and finishes of the historic centre. The white stucco window surrounds create a visual link to the eclectic late-nineteenth-century houses that were built on the site of the former city walls. In the spring the building disappears behind the leaves of the trees on the square, becoming visible again in autumn.

← D01

I The Street and the Square

→ D32

On Java Eiland, the second phase of the urban regeneration of the former Eastern Docklands of Amsterdam reintroduced the individual canal house (D32) as part of the new urban fabric. Young architects just starting out were asked to design a canal house that could be repeated several times in different combinations. The brief contained a few challenges. All individual and differently designed houses had to be built in one continuous concrete tunnel structure, following the standard of housing construction developed during the period of industrialisation of housing production in the 1960s. A series of collective workshops aimed to find the right balance between uniformity and individual expression. An interesting and important element of the master plan was the different levels of the quays: the main north and south quays of Java Eiland were placed on a higher level than the quays of the new transversal canals. The land on which the canal houses were to be built was on the higher level of the main quays. The front door of the canal house could therefore be made accessible by an outside stair on the *stoep* in front of the houses, recreating another typical aspect of the traditional canal house.

Seven Elements of Housing Design

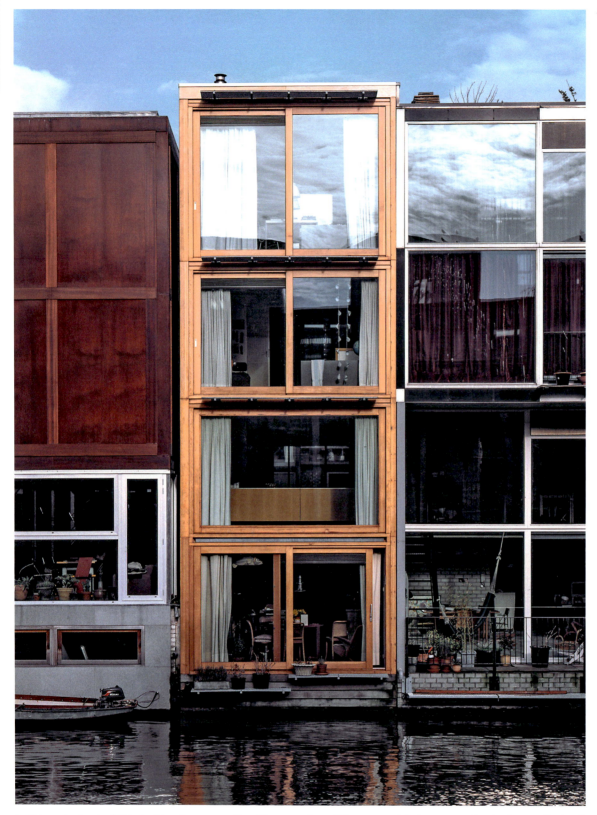

In the next phase of the docklands regeneration, Borneo Sporenburg, individual houses were planned for one strip of land. In this case, however, the structural design – that is, the material and design of the load-bearing structure – was left free as well. This resulted in wide architectural variety, all new interpretations of the traditional townhouse. The project (D30), designed for Scheepstimmermanstraat, has a plot 3.8 metres wide and 16 metres deep. The front doesn't face a canal, but a narrow street, whereas the back is on the water, a way of building that goes back to the early medieval Amsterdam. Like its historical precedents, the house has a *souterrain*, or a half-sunken lower level with the kitchen accessed by steps from the street, and a *bel-etage* level, with the formal front door raised above street level, here accessed by a ramp.

I The Street and the Square

↑ D36

The earliest built project of those discussed here is an apartment building on a street at the edge of the historic town centre of the city of Nijmegen. The project (D21) occupies a space made available by the demolition of a former school building. The surrounding buildings in the slightly curving street form a mix of very different functions and building periods. The site itself is bordered on one side by a former synagogue that escaped the large-scale devastations of the centre of Nijmegen during the Second World War, and on the other side, by a typical 1960s apartment building from the period of post-war reconstruction. In scale and use of materials the project mediates between the two, connecting the different fragments of time in a more homogeneous street front. Moving the car park to the roof and the bicycle storage to a basement level allowed the street level to be used for living and working. The commercial spaces are accessible directly from the street while the ground-floor dwellings are raised above, accessed by a platform, mediated by a garden zone that creates privacy between the dwellings and the street.

↓ D21

Seven Elements of Housing Design

The projects near Delflandplein (D07), on the Slotermeerlaan (D06), and on the Nierkerkestraat (D10), all built in the post-war Western Garden Cities of Amsterdam, create new street fronts, replacing the closed, storage-filled plinths of the former housing from the 1960s with a more open and transparent connection to the public space. The Delflandplein project has an alternation of entrance lobbies, commercial spaces, and neighbourhood healthcare facilities. The Nierkerke buildings face the main road, the Baden Powellweg, with entrance lobbies and units that have extra ceiling height to allow for a combination of working and living. The more peripheral location of Nierkerkestraat made it impossible to have commercial or neighbourhood services in the plinth. The project on the Slotermeerlaan, on the contrary, is in the centre of the Slotermeer neighbourhood and has social and cultural amenities on the first two floors, clearly expressed in the plinths of the street facades.

← D06
D10

← D07

137 I The Street and the Square

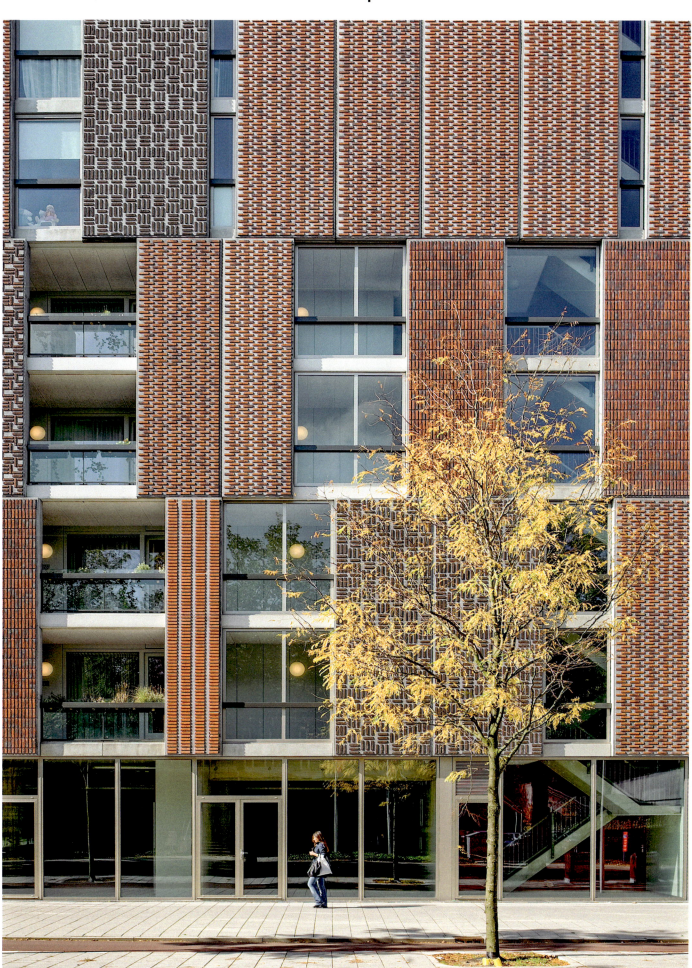

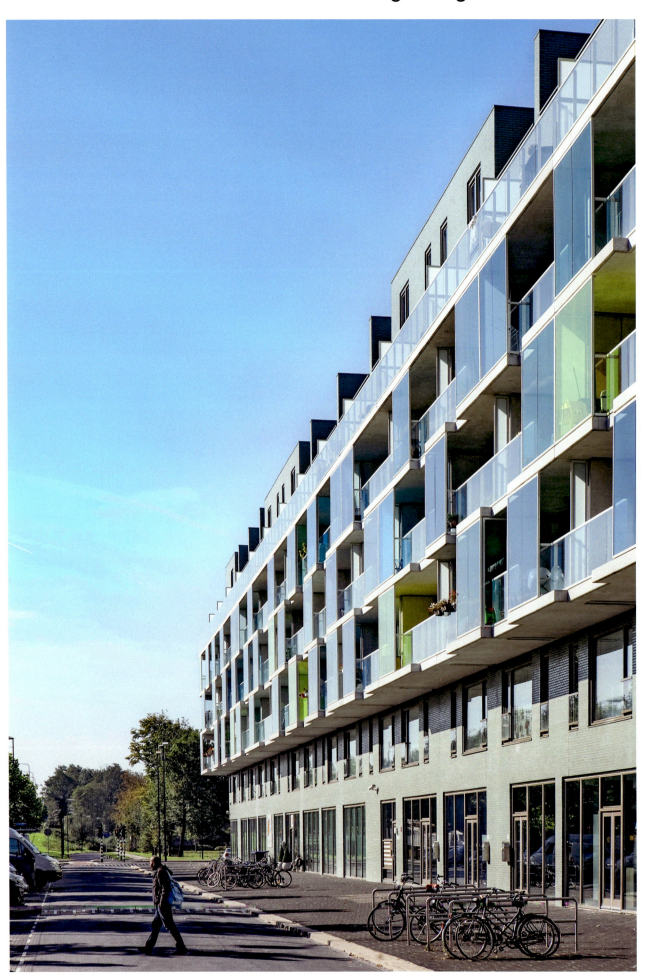

← D13

I   The Street and the Square

Another project that is part of the major interventions and renewal of the Western Garden Cities is the buildings on the Laan van Spartaan (D02). The street facade facing the Erasmusgracht, a canal connecting the garden cities to the earlier western extensions of Amsterdam, had to address the issue of traffic noise coming from the A10 ring road that crosses the Erasmusgracht immediately east of the project. Lamellas with a perforated steel cladding, hiding insulation material, were placed perpendicular to the facade to reflect and absorb the noise, resulting in a facade with a brise-soleil design suggestive of Oscar Niemeyer, though in fact it is effectively a brise-bruit solution. By changing the angle of some of the lamellas, this analogy is made clear to the passing observer. The lower two floors did not require the added sound insulation, and open towards the street and the canal. The adjacent buildings designed by others use the same lamellas in different configurations, creating a continuous street front that reveals the different designs when seen from a frontal view.

The Karspeldreef project (D13) is a typical case of the Bijlmermeer, now called Amsterdam South-East, the other major post-war urban renewal area of Amsterdam. The building replaces one of the original parking garages with ground-floor shopping centre that served as a connection between the elevated road system and the large honeycomb slabs. The road has been brought back to ground level, and the garage is gone. A plinth with a series of entrance halls and social facilities introduces a traditional street connection. The south-facing street facade has an elevation of a two-storey plinth, three floors with meandering balconies and colourful glazed screens, and two top floors with setback loggias, resulting in a sculptural expression of a rather straightforward building whose first objective was to provide affordable housing and a shelter for homeless people.

↑ D02
↑ D13

↓ D16

Casa Parana (D16) in the post-war neighbourhood of Overvecht in the city of Utrecht has an even more dominant social programme. A transparent ground floor gives space to a series of social workspaces, including a café and a bike repair shop. The workspaces create a clear spatial and functional connection between the surrounding neighbourhood and the building itself, which is inhabited by those who face urgent problems and need shelter, and those who help to bring lives back on track. Cut-outs in the main volume provide outside spaces to all floors, making another visual connection between the building and its residents on one side, and the street and neighbourhood on the other.

Seven Elements of Housing Design

→ D28

Not far from Casa Parana, closer to the centre of Utrecht, a series of outdated 1950s free-standing apartment blocks have been replaced with a more traditional pattern of terraced housing (D28). A 600-metre-long street facade of terraced houses along the Talmalaan ends with a five-floor apartment building with small studios. Behind the long line of terraced housing, smaller groupings form clusters of townhouses alternated by collective green squares. The length of the Talmalaan is emphasised by the repetition of the terraced houses, and the vertical or horizontal bands in the brickwork of the top floors. The smaller clusters behind have a more individual articulation due to the variations in the brickwork, now from top to bottom, and changing from each unit to the next.

The long rows of houses facing the Talmalaan have the main living space on the first floor, indicated by the large protruding bay windows. The ground floor has a workspace facing the street, accommodating all kinds of work at home and creating an active street level. Small private front gardens and larger collective strips of greenery create distance from the busy Talmalaan. The houses in the clusters behind the Talmalaan have the main living space on the ground floor, connecting to the more quiet streets and pocket parks in between.

The IJburg terraced housing (D26) project follows a similar typology of townhouses with a living room on the first floor, a workspace at street level, and ground-floor parking at the back. Here a *stoep* is introduced to create a threshold space between the house and the street. Each house's *stoep*, used by many for potted plants and benches, is differentiated from its neighbour by a raised element.

← D26   → D28

Seven Elements of Housing Design

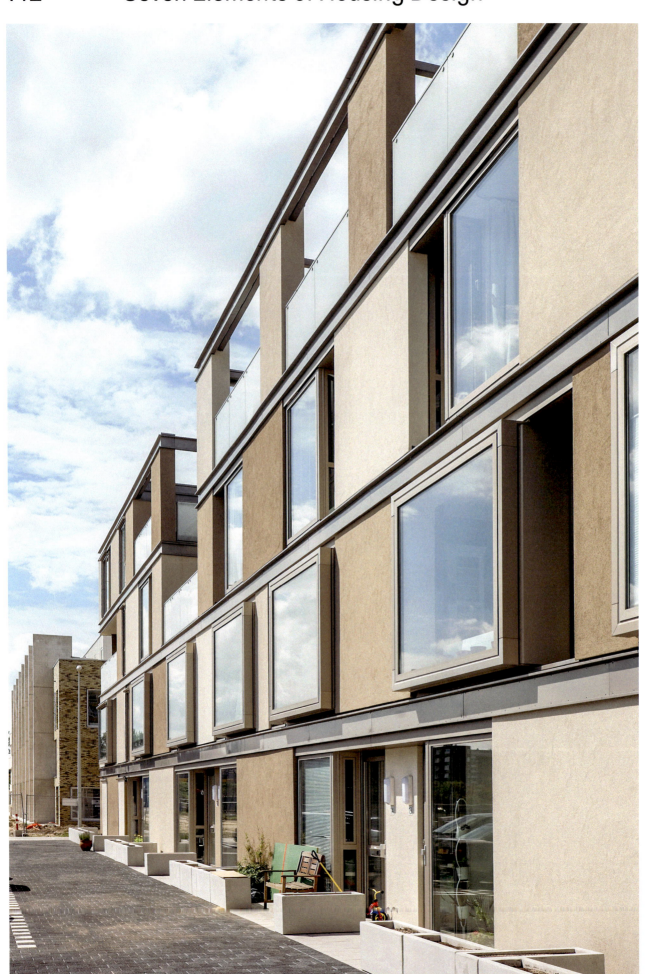

← D02

I The Street and the Square

The same can be seen in the high-density, low-rise part of the Laan van Spartaan project (D02) in the Amsterdam Western Garden Cities. The three lower floors form one unit, only facing the street. Another house stands at the back, accessed from a raised inner courtyard, with a roof terrace on top of the street-facing unit. The street-facing unit's main outdoor space is the *stoep*, which is very well used and full of plants and garden furniture.

In the more suburban surroundings of the Noorderplassen area in Almere, the new town on Flevoland, east of Amsterdam, the *stoep* is introduced along the main road of the area. Along the quieter side street, the terraced houses have a small front garden, in line with the suburban, garden-city character of the development (D27).

→ D27

144 Seven Elements of Housing Design

In the design for a new neighbourhood of 650 terraced houses (D29) in the Ypenburg Vinex area between The Hague and Delft, different ways to connect the house with the street are explored. Front gardens in this Vinex garden city are dominant, but in more secluded inner streets and courtyards the connection is more direct between house and the shared space in front. Cars have been moved out of sight as much as possible. Parking areas are located between the back gardens, in the back of the house itself (as in the IJburg and Talmalaan housing), or in covered carports.

← D29

↓ D29

145 | The Street and the Square

The study for Strandeiland (S1), the new island of the IJburg development in Amsterdam, sets out the rules for the housing within the urban master plan that is based on a very regular grid of streets, interrupted by green squares. The aim is to create a pattern of housing blocks, built from a variety of types – apartments, townhouses, and *boven-benedenwoningen* – in a relatively high density, following the Amsterdam identity of long streets with a continuous line of four- to five-storey buildings. A set of rules directs the development towards a varied alternation of streets, entrance courts, and green inner courts, with elements such as bay windows, *stoeps*, small front gardens, and external stairs creating a strong connection between the individual houses and the continuous pattern of streets and squares.

↑ S1

Seven Elements of Housing Design

← D17

The Langebrug student housing (D17) is located in the historic heart of the old university town of Leiden. A large gunpowder explosion occurred on the site in around 1800, and it was filled in with a succession of buildings that fell victim to either demolition or fire. The project for student housing made it possible to restore the medieval pattern of narrow back alleys connecting the main streets and canals of the city. By reintroducing these vanished connections, a finer urban fabric could be integrated, dividing the site into four plots. One plot facing the main street on the western edge of the area, called Langebrug, still contains a few surviving fragments of a burned-down, nineteenth-century church that was transformed into a fire station in the last century. These remains were carefully integrated into the new structures, and the surviving hose tower was preserved as well. The street facades on Langebrug are of brick, with the main entrance halls placed in prominent positions. The back alleys translate the patterns of brick garden walls and white-plastered back and side facades of the surrounding historic fabric into a new, layered composition of space and material.

I The Street and the Square

↑ D17

Seven Elements of Housing Design

↑ D24

The urban regeneration of Thamesmead South (D24) in London is based on a complete restructuring of the former neighbourhood centre and linear spine block along the main access road, the Harrow Manor Way. The original elevated brutalist megastructure could sadly not be salvaged. Unlike the renewal of the Amsterdam Garden Cities, where the existing structure of tree-lined roads provided a firm base for the new architectural interventions, here in Thamesmead an entirely new system of roads was needed to replace the failed first-floor pedestrian network. The project therefore started with the design of a new network of roads, squares, and courtyards on the ground level. A few, very unfortunate earlier attempts at renewal had to be incorporated in the projects, as well as some renovated surviving tower blocks. The main design concept was to create a new public realm, defined by clusters of buildings that would have a clear and active connection to the new streets. Parallel to Harrow Manor Way a new spine road was proposed, meandering from the Abbey Wood railway station to Southmere Lake, connecting a series of public squares of different shapes and sizes. The new route culminates in a new central civic square, lined by shops and amenities. The first built cluster of the Thamesmead South master plan connects a new apartment tower, three terraces of townhouses, and two existing tower blocks into one ensemble with fronts to all sides. The central courtyard is a collective green space on top of a parking garage. Entrance patios and stairs make the green courtyard visible from the street and accessible for the new and existing residents of the ensemble.

149   I   The Street and the Square

↓ D24

Possibly one of the greatest challenges of housing design in an urban context is how to reconcile the need for privacy inside the dwelling with the immediate presence of public space outside. The introduction of an in-between space, which can take on many different shapes and sizes, is the obvious answer. The traditional Dutch *stoep*, the privately owned, narrow zone between the street and the house, is the most enduring form of this threshold space. For the individual and terraced house, a *stoep* can be an extension of the private space, shielding the inside by creating distance, while also allowing visual connections from the interior to the street.

However, when designing and building clusters of apartments in a dense urban context, the in-between needs to be larger to accommodate a space of transition for all residents. A courtyard as an interface between street and building provides a possible answer and can be extended into another transition space, the interior entrance hall of the residential building. In this way a sequence of spaces between the public and private realms can anchor the building, preventing it from being closed off from the public space, which could lead to disconnection and loss of a contribution of the building to its surroundings. The courtyard can be open to the street or square itself or surrounded by the building volume, connected to the streets with large openings, gates, and passages. The courtyard also acts as a space of transition for an individual house, either between the street and the house or between different parts of the house, providing privacy inside as well. On the scale of the single house, the courtyard then becomes a patio, a partially opened or completely secluded exterior space that can be used as an outdoor living space. The courtyard and patio, when planted with trees or designed as a garden, can create an attractive environment in a high-density urban setting. In such conditions, a collective green space is a necessary part of a residential building, an alternative to private gardens, offering an outside space for all residents that can be characterised by a milder microclimate during the different seasons.

Seven Elements of Housing Design

← D01

The entrance court of the building on the Haarlemmerplein in Amsterdam (D01) creates a threshold between the busy inner-city square and the collective entrance hall. It allows for a clear articulation of the residential entrance, which would otherwise be lost between the shopfronts on both sides. The court is marked off from the public space with a transparent steel fence, comparable to some beautiful historic precedents in the city. A tree and a large planter surrounded by a curving bench create a small green space in this dense urban environment dominated by brick paving and traffic. A similar entrance court was introduced in the early project for an apartment building in the town of Emmen (D23). As in Amsterdam, the building is surrounded on all sides by public space in an urban context. The entrance patio is defined by brick walls and transparent wooden fences, and a path leads from the wooden entrance gate via a garden to the main entrance, and via a sunken ramp to the storage basement.

→ D23

II The Courtyard and the Patio

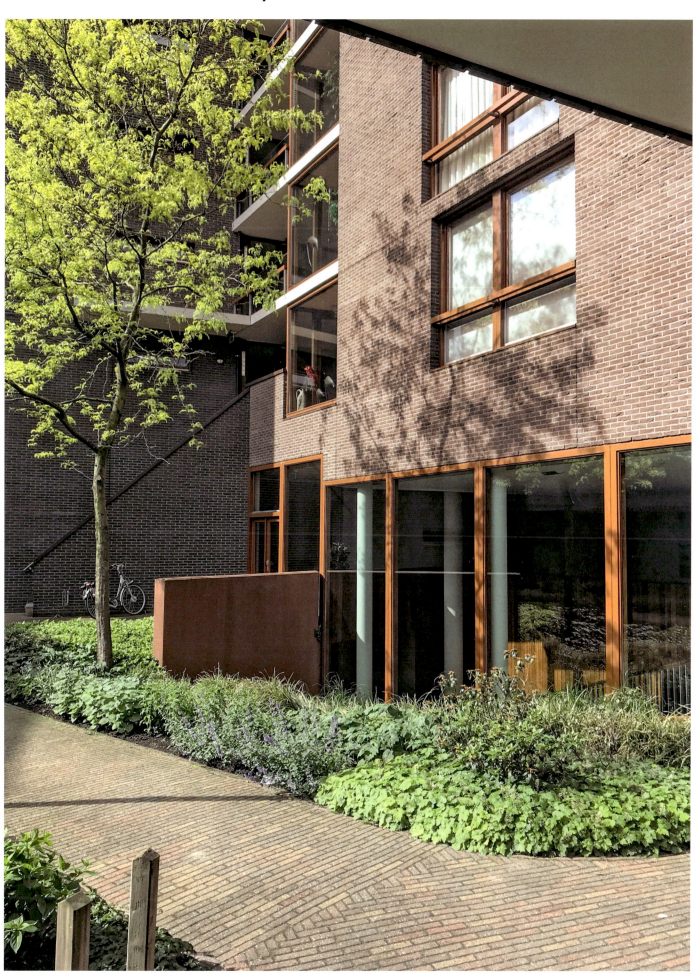

The housing project along Leaf Street close to central Manchester (D25) is also surrounded by roads. The continuous, meandering shape of the project, containing both apartments and townhouses, defines a series of partly open courtyards. The first one, an entrance court, is the access from the city centre via Hulme Arch Bridge and has the character of a garden square. The second courtyard, facing Leaf Street, is a quieter neighbourhood pocket park where children can play. These public spaces are connected to each other via large gates cut out from the building volume. These connecting gates also give access to the apartments' collective entrance halls. A third courtyard provides space for private gardens for the townhouses.

D25 →

← D25

II The Courtyard and the Patio

The courtyard opening towards the street is an excellent means to increase the number of residential units that have a direct connection to the public space that surrounds the project. This is shown in the previous projects, and again introduced in the studies for the new island of IJburg in Amsterdam (S1). Courtyards facing the streets of the projected rigorous grid pattern maximise the number of front doors in the public space and create variety and rhythm in the continuous street facades of the long perimeter blocks. Fenced gates make a visual connection from these publicly accessible entrance courts to the collective inner courts that provide a secluded green space for all the residents.

→ S1

II The Courtyard and the Patio

In the built project on Haveneiland in IJburg (D12), an interior street, as a variation of the courtyard, was introduced to maximise the number of units directly connected by a private front door to the ground level. This street connects terraced houses and maisonette units to the surrounding public space and the large green garden courtyard shared with the neighbouring buildings. The interior street was carved out of the building mass, partly covered and partly open to the sky. The entrance hall of the upper-floor units is positioned where the two interior streets connect, the stairs winding their way upwards from here.

→ D12

← D12

← D27

The entrance courtyard can also be used as an in-between space for individual dwellings. The entrance patios of the Noorderplassen project (D27) in the new town of Almere close to Amsterdam create a clear border between the house and the street. A wooden fence and door allow for a glimpse of the private patio, where at the same time a generous window looking onto the street keeps a direct visual connection between the interior of the house and the public space.

II The Courtyard and the Patio

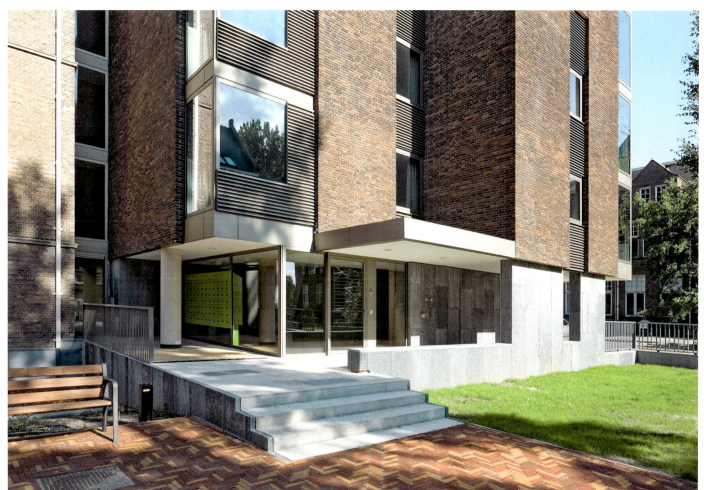

↑ D18

↓ D18

The Boerhaave project in Leiden (D18), housing for academics working at Leiden University, is an addition of a slender apartment tower to the former Anatomy Laboratory, converted into housing. The tower and the existing building give shape to a courtyard that opens on one side to the surrounding green campus. Here the entrance to the new building was positioned in the courtyard, turning it from an unused backyard into an active central green space for the residents.

160   Seven Elements of Housing Design

The collective green courtyard played a central role in the design of several projects that were built as part of the large-scale urban regeneration of Amsterdam's post-war Western Garden Cities. To avoid the issue of undefined – and therefore uncared for – green in-between spaces that was a major problem in the existing repetition of *wooneenheden*, the new courtyards needed to be closed off as collective green spaces accessible only to the residents. However, to maintain the original intention of one continuous green park-like space, the designs made the new green courtyards clearly visible from the streets and created in some of the projects publicly accessible routes through the courts. The new building block on the Nierkerkestraat in the Osdorp area (D10) was set up as a cluster of five individual buildings, thus avoiding a closed perimeter block. The lower level of the in-between space was made accessible for the neighbourhood as a whole, while the raised part is a collective deck garden for the residents only.

↑ D10

↓ D07

The courtyard of the Delflandplein project (D07) has been made visible through a large, covered porch. The garden is on the first-floor level, covering the ground-floor parking garage. Its more secluded position was necessary as it is used as a protected garden for elderly residents.

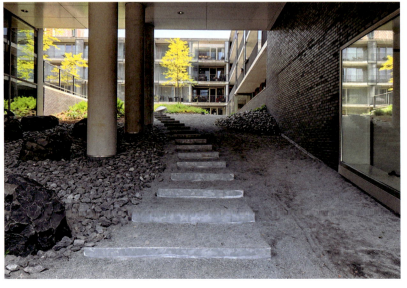

→ D09

II The Courtyard and the Patio

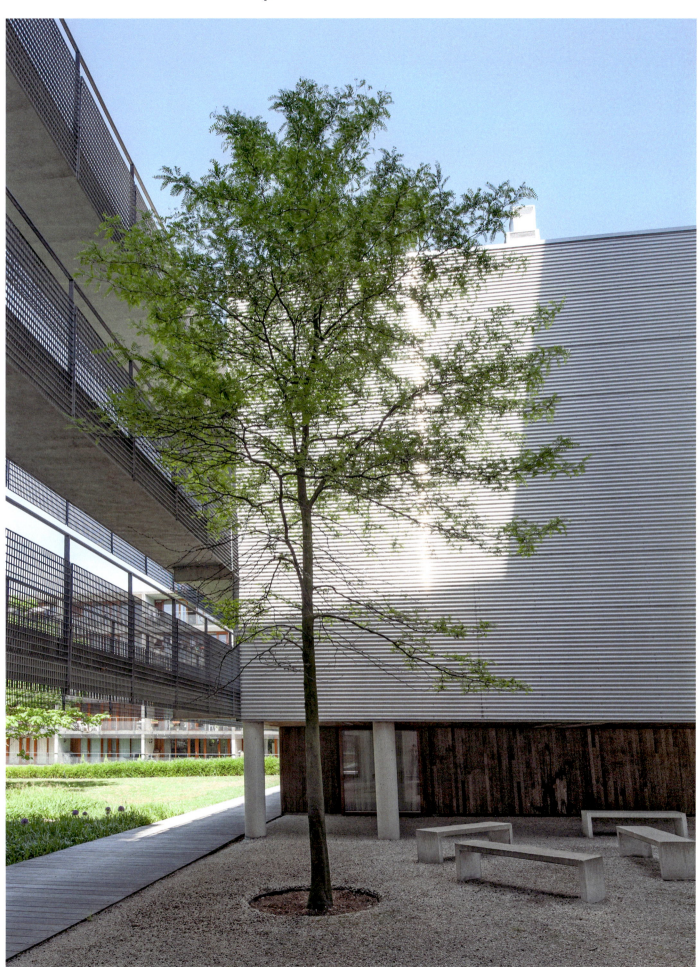

162 Seven Elements of Housing Design

The courtyard of the U-shaped building in Osdorp next to the Sloterplas (D09) opens on all sides via open porches and transparent entrance halls to the lush green surroundings. On the side of the lake, an open outside 'room' offers a collective space for all residents. A diagonal path crosses the courtyard, leading the way to the lake and the park.

↑ D09

→ D09

II The Courtyard and the Patio

← D15

The three buildings that form the Huizen project (D15) are clustered on a generous plot. In between the buildings and the surrounding garden wall, there are green courtyards, all planted in different ways with trees and perennials. The courtyards together introduce a large, uninterrupted green space. The project aims to show an alternative to the ubiquitous terraced housing with private and fenced-off front and back gardens that completely dominates the large suburban neighbourhoods of this former fishing village close to Amsterdam.

→ D15

Seven Elements of Housing Design

A series of connected courtyards is further explored in the proposal for the regeneration of the Maria Hilf Hospital grounds in the German city of Mönchengladbach, close to the Dutch border (S2). Existing buildings of the former hospital on the site are connected to new structures to create an intricate pattern of courtyards leading to an open terrace with a view of the town.

↑ S2

II The Courtyard and the Patio

← D11

The Berkenstede care home in Diemen (D11) can be interpreted as a miniature version of the concept of connected courtyards as a main structuring device for a high-density residential project. Four tower pavilions, each catering for different kinds of care for the elderly residents, are positioned between a number of courtyards and patios. The green undulating roof of the ground- and first-floor shared facilities is visible from the patios. Both elements – the patios and the green roof – create a connecting green landscape that provides either intimate or more outward-looking exterior spaces for the vulnerable residents.

→ D11

Seven Elements of Housing Design

↓ D30
↓ D36

→ D37

The patio in Villa 4.0 in Naarden (D37) brings the beautiful natural surroundings into the heart of the house. It contributes to the transparency of the interior spaces while acting as a sound buffer between the main living hall and the workspace. The swamp oak in the patio provides shade in the summer, and, as it turns a beautiful red in autumn, brings the change of the seasons into the villa's interior.

The patio as a protected outside space that directly connects the interior to the outside and brings greenery into the heart of a dwelling is further explored in a range of projects of very different scales. The minimal affordable low-rise housing in Oosterhout near the city of Nijmegen (D30) is inspired by the typical 1960s and 1970s experiments with patio houses in both Europe and North America. The narrow, tube-like ground-floor units receive daylight from the entrance patio and terrace patio at the back, and in the heart of the house through a small, internal garden patio. In a completely different, urban context, a patio in the canal house on the Scheepstimmermanstraat in the Amsterdam Eastern Docklands (D36) brings daylight and fresh air to all levels of a very narrow and deep four-storey structure. The patio contains an outside stair to connect the upper level to the hidden roof terrace.

→ D37

II The Courtyard and the Patio

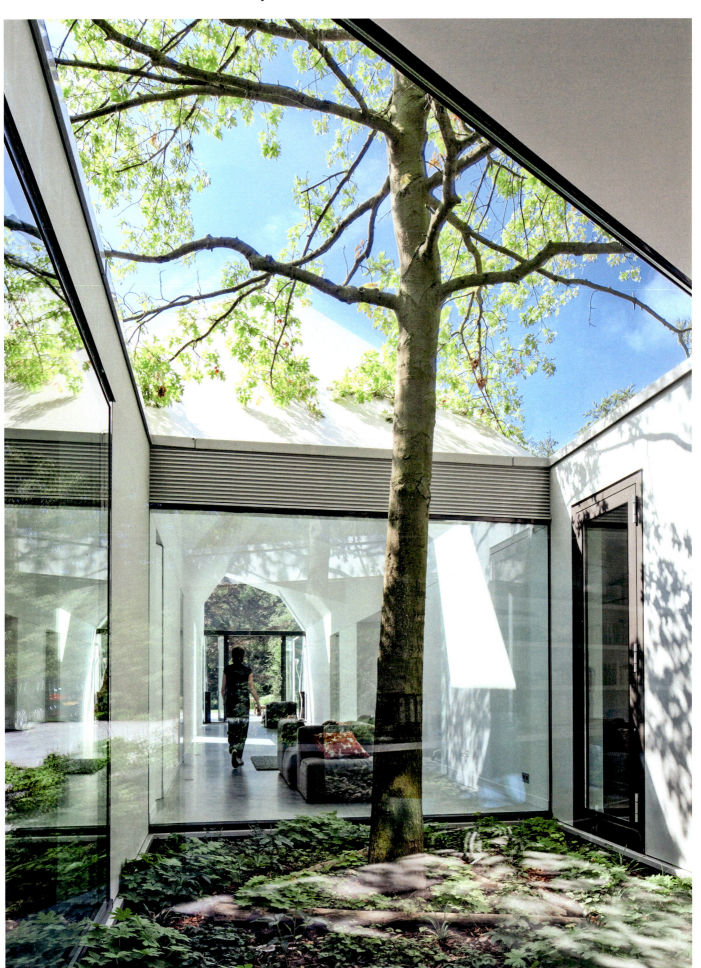

II The Courtyard and the Patio

↑ D40

↑ D40

The two patios of the residence in Addis Ababa (D40) bring all properties of the patio to this project for the Netherlands Embassy compound in Ethiopia's capital city. The covered entrance court, or patio, forms a threshold between the house and the surrounding landscape. It is an inviting gesture to all visitors who arrive by car via the winding access road, or on foot via the stairs from the upper-level path. When entering the reception spaces, one's eye is directed towards the second patio. This garden patio slopes down, affording a view through the dining room at the other side of the patio to the surrounding hills.

The plants bring the garden into the heart of the house and hide a series of steps that lead downwards to the private living spaces of the lower level of the house. Seen from the other side, inside the dining room, the patio leads the eye over the planting back to the entrance court, thus giving a clear sense of orientation, and emphasising the leading design theme of the project: the interweaving of the interior spaces and the outside gardens.

← D40

The first garden suburbs were based on the idea of connecting housing with collective green spaces and the surrounding landscapes. This principle was lost during the twentieth century in the suburban developments, resulting in often poor and characterless environments dominated by endless repetitive housing patterns and parked cars. To give suburban housing a quality and identity of its own compared to housing in urban conditions, the connection of the house and open, green space is crucial. Green in-between spaces that connect to larger open spaces and clear borders between private outside spaces and the larger public green spaces are essential components of a suburban development. A succession of private gardens, collective greens, and public park spaces can create a layered outdoor environment that will result in a very different but equally attractive living environment compared to the livelier atmosphere and proximity of services in urban conditions.

For the individual house in a more open or rural setting, the surrounding landscape can and should create privacy and connectivity at the same time. Careful positioning in the site, planting or replanting of existing greenery, and a precise use of a site's topography are all inseparable components of the architectural project.

III The Park and the Garden

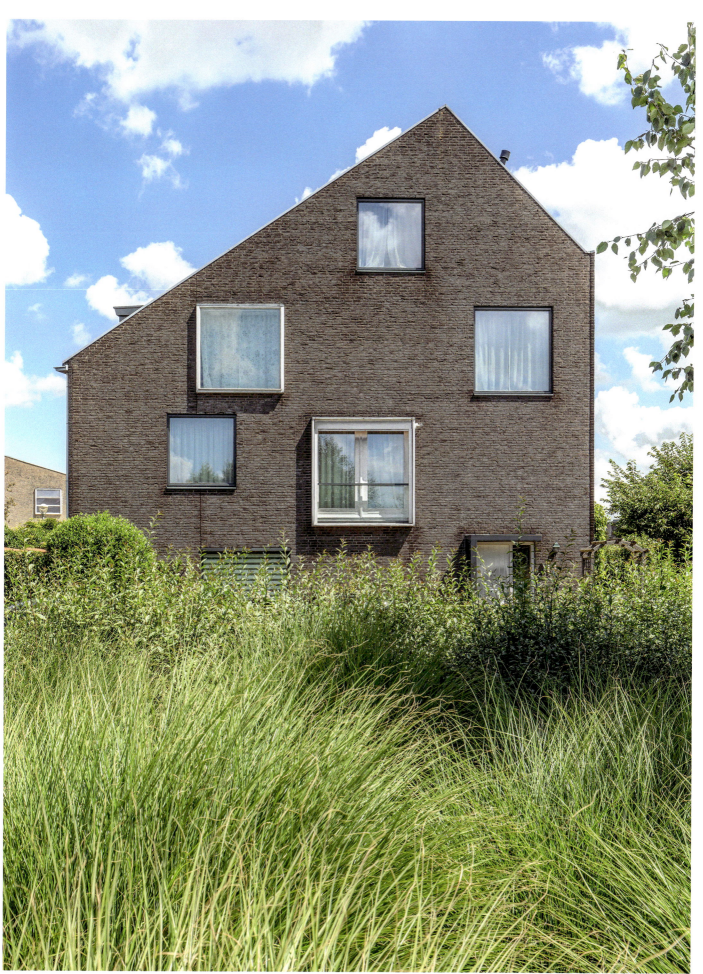

172   Seven Elements of Housing Design

In three low-rise neighbourhoods in a suburban context, different strategies from earlier garden-city models were explored to maximise the integration of the landscape in the residential areas. The Vinex project in Ypenburg near The Hague (D29) introduced the idea of the close, as seen in early-twentieth-century English garden cities. The low-rise terraced housing is in long, linear, and meandering volumes. The open green landscape is part of the neighbourhood, and the terraced housing starts to fold itself around a number of green fingers. In this way, a series of closes, opening towards the larger open space, are created.

→ D29

← D29

III   The Park and the Garden

The Grootstal project in Nijmegen (D31) finds inspiration in the garden-city projects in Frankfurt, built under the leadership of Ernst May in the interwar period. The parallel placement of blocks of terraced housing with collective green spaces in between, realised in Frankfurt's Westhausen Siedlung in a most radical way, is the underlying principle of the Grootstal project. It is, however, made much softer and less repetitive by occasionally mirroring the entrance orientation of the dwellings, and varying the distance between the blocks, thus creating in-between spaces with different characters.

→ D31

← D30

In the Oosterhout project near Nijmegen (D30), the built area is condensed by introducing a patio typology for the small affordable units, leaving space for a large, central green landscaped area that is bisected by a rainwater-collecting wadi. The low-lying wadi and the green area sloping up to the housing create a subtle valley landscape bordered by the garden terraces of the dwellings. The clustering of the units can be seen as a reinterpretation of the mat-building ideas of Team 10 and others in the decades after the Second World War.

Seven Elements of Housing Design

The Funenpark (D03), in the centre of Amsterdam, introduces the idea of a direct connection between the residential buildings and an open, green, landscaped space in a very different, highly urban context. Two quite different projects have been designed to fit in the master plan of architect Frits van Dongen. The six-storey *palazzina* takes advantage of its position in the centre of the cluster of buildings to open on all sides to the surrounding collective green space. The continuous park on the western edge has a much stronger public character. Here the units of the two triangular *palazzinas* have been raised above the ground level to create a clear boundary and privacy for the residents. Generous loggias and cantilevering balconies provide a strong connection between the apartments and the park.

III The Park and the Garden

↑ D21

The introduction of green spaces and trees, or the preservation of them, is of crucial importance in any project. This was the starting point for the design of the apartment building along the Gerard Noodtstraat in the centre of Nijmegen (D21), which was awarded through the 1991 Europan Competition. The presence of a great red beech tree in a neighbouring garden triggered the idea of making a garden between the existing garden walls of the houses on the other side of the urban block and the new building. The tree became visually a part of the new garden, a collective outside space for all residents. Height differences were introduced to give access to the sunken bicycle storage space and create a small, visually interesting park. The main consequence of the introduction of a garden was that another place had to be found for the required parking spaces that were originally planned by the city to be positioned in a paved backyard. It was decided to locate the parking spaces on the roof, as further explored in the 'Roof' part of this chapter.

↖ D04

The collective garden in an urban context was also the main structuring element of the Zuiveringspark project for apartment buildings in Slotervaart, part of the Amsterdam Western Garden Cities (D04) and the result of another successful competition entry. Here the idea was triggered by the presence on the site of remaining structures of the former sewage treatment plant that had been moved to a site outside the city. It was proposed to keep as much of these structures as possible. The clusters of square basins were filled with earth and turned into collective gardens, as was the space in between the circular concrete water tanks. A second idea was to condense the required built programme, resulting in a tower of eighteen floors and a seven-storey slab structure, opening up space for a public pocket park that forms the heart of the new residential area and makes a connection with the vast park surrounding the Sloterplas, the central lake of the Western Garden Cities.

→ D04

177 III The Park and the Garden

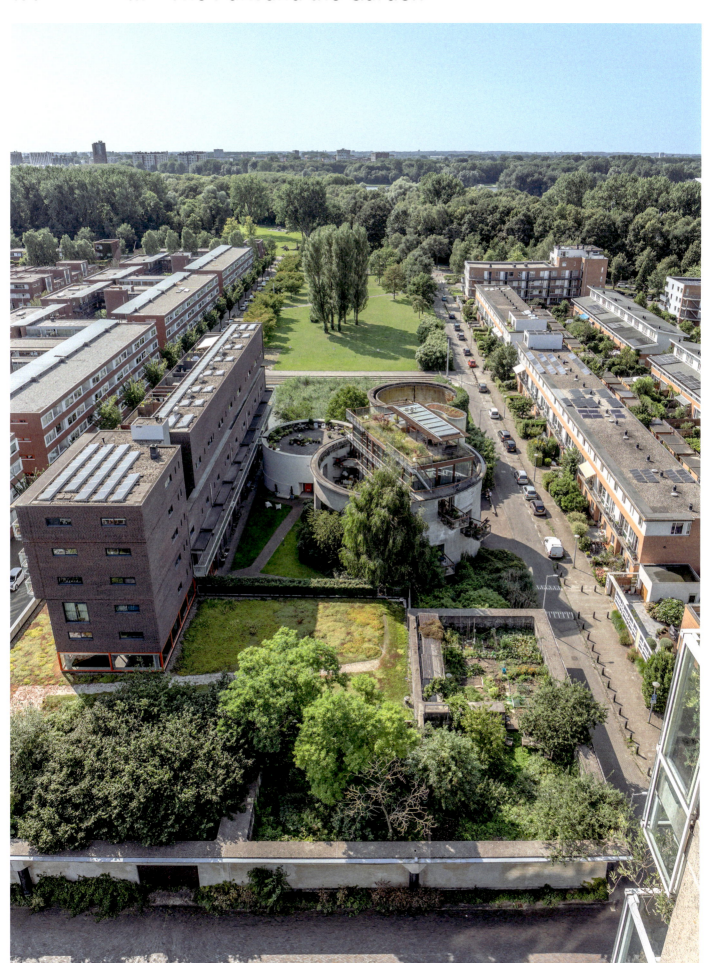

178   Seven Elements of Housing Design

← D08

The design of the Bouwmeester housing project in another part of Slotervaart (D08) is also based on the idea of creating a succession of green spaces. Several buildings with apartments for the elderly, including some cooperative groups, are situated around a large central green garden. Smaller courtyard spaces are positioned immediately next to the ground-floor communal living rooms, creating an in-between space between the dwellings and the central garden. These spaces are taken care of by the residents themselves, who turn them into gardens full of flowers.

III The Park and the Garden

↑ D40

The brief for the embassy compound in Addis Ababa (D40) asked for a chancery, a residence for the ambassador, the renovation of an existing house for the deputy, and three more staff houses, next to a couple of service buildings. The compound is a remarkable park area of 5 hectares, a rare surviving part of the original natural landscape in the rapidly growing city. It is reflective of the beautiful church forests on the high-altitude plains north of Addis Ababa, which remain green fragments in a land plagued by erosion caused by intensive agriculture. Preservation of the natural quality of the compound was obviously the main starting point of the project. The brief led to some concern among the staff as they feared that living and working in one compound would greatly affect their privacy. In the proposed master plan, however, it was shown that by making use of the existing trees and the pronounced height differences of the site's topography, privacy could be created between all the individual buildings.

The residence is hidden from view of all other houses by positioning it in the valley that slopes down steeply on the edge of the compound, looking towards the hills west of the city. A cantilevering terrace, hovering over the valley, connects the private living spaces to the natural gardens, whereas the formal reception space on the upper floor opens towards a wide lawn used for open-air gatherings. As in the adjacent chancery, visually separated from the residence by the higher ridge in the heart of the compound, cut-outs of the main building mass reinforce the connection between the buildings and the landscape, as do the patios described in the previous part of this chapter (see p. 169). The three staff houses also take advantage of the site's topography. They are placed on the sloping northern edge of the site, in a stepped section, so that each house looks over the roof of the next one towards the hills. The roof of one house serves then as an extension of the garden of the next house.

Seven Elements of Housing Design

Villa 4.0 near Naarden (D37) is positioned in a remarkable artificial landscape of irregular drainage canals and low-lying meadows and the remains of the higher, now overgrown sand dunes, left there after the retreat of the last ice age. The area has been transformed once more in the last hundred years by the building of villas and country houses for well-to-do citizens escaping nearby Amsterdam. The open and transparent character of this radical rebuilding of an existing 1960s house was made possible by a similar careful rebuilding of the landscape. Following a design by landscape architect Michael van Gessel, existing trees were replanted to create both privacy and better views to the open areas surrounding the plot.

← D37

III The Park and the Garden

→ D39

This strategy was followed in a comparable way for the House on the Lake (D39) project in the Cotswolds in England. The house is positioned on the edge of a small lake, made by filling an old stone quarry. To ensure privacy for the fully glazed volume, as desired by the client, small artificial hills planted with trees and shrubs hide the house from view of the neighbouring houses and the access road. A diagonally placed access bridge cuts through the trees to the villa's entrance. Towards the lake, the villa is fully exposed, as nothing will be built on the opposite side of the water, affording a panoramic view from all main living spaces. As in the two previous projects, the built volume and the surrounding nature stand in sharp formal contrast, but merge at the same time into one continuous inside-outside space.

← D39

The hall is a focal point of any house and apartment building as it is where the members of the family, the larger household, or residents encounter one another. It is the communal space, the place where guests are welcomed by their hosts. It is a distributor, the space that leads to the more private spaces of the house, set apart for a specific function, or in a cluster of dwellings, leading to the individual apartments. The hall has gradually lost its importance, reduced to a corridor or lobby that only gives access to the individual spaces of the house or the individual apartments but doesn't allow for any life or activity. The hall needs to regain its central place as the communal space shared by all and as a point of transition between the public outside world and the private interior. The architectural design of the house should allow for an optimal freedom for the inhabitants to appropriate their own private space, but should carefully plan and detail the hall as a place that is welcoming for all.

IV The Hall

← D21

To emphasise the hall as a place of transition, as a meeting point of different spheres, of the inside and the outside, in many projects the hall has been placed next to open porches or gates that connect to courtyards and gardens. In the project for the Gerard Noodtstraat apartments in Nijmegen (D21), the two main entrance halls are positioned next to open gates to the garden at the back. By giving the halls fully glazed facades and by winding the stairs going up to the apartments in all directions through the hall and the gates, there is a clear experience of the transition from the street to the residences, with views in all directions.

Seven Elements of Housing Design

← D09

The entrance halls of the Oeverpad (D09) and the Delflandplein (D07) projects, both in Amsterdam's Western Garden Cities, repeat this concept, forging clear links between the interior and the exterior with views of both the surrounding public space and the collective courtyards. The entrance hall of the Oeverlanden apartments and care home in Purmerend (D14) connects visually to the street running straight through the building, making the passage through the project both interesting and safe, with the brightly illuminated hall spreading its light to the outside passage during the evenings and overnight.

↓ D14

↓ D07

IV The Hall

The entrance hall of the eighteen-storey tower in the project on the former sewage treatment plant in Slotervaart (D04) is designed as a two-level, 9-metre-high lobby that connects the ground floor to the first-floor collective garden in the adjacent deposit basins. The hall of the Berkenstede care home in Diemen (D11) has been enlarged to form an interior street, lined by collective facilities that are interrupted by patios and outdoor terraces to bring in daylight. A number of large circular roof lights pierce through the undulating roof to provide even more light. The street opens again to the outside at the end, thus providing a publicly accessible passage, or arcade, for both the residents and those living in the surrounding apartment buildings.

→ D04

← D11

Seven Elements of Housing Design

← D06

↓ D16

In two mixed-use buildings with residential units for specific groups, the hall is made into a place where the different programmes meet both functionally and visually. The Honingraat Building in Amsterdam Slotermeer (D06), a multifunctional social-cultural centre combined with elderly housing, has a central hall going up four floors that brings together all parts of the programme: a branch of the Amsterdam Public Library, a family health centre, a maternity practice, a youth centre, a neighbourhood social meeting centre, a café, and apartments for elderly people. The hall opens towards a central patio with trees that is visible and accessible also from the library and the health centre. The white, vaulted space together with the patio provides a light and cheerful collective heart for the building as a whole.

Casa Parana in Utrecht (D16) is an exceptional community project. On the ground floor, social amenities and workplaces provide both employment and services to the vulnerable residents and the neighbourhood. Here the entrance hall is the principal connector. It leads to the wide corridors of the upper floors that are all provided with daylight, coming in through the carved-out parts of the built volume and through the glazed partitions of the shared facilities on each floor.

IV The Hall

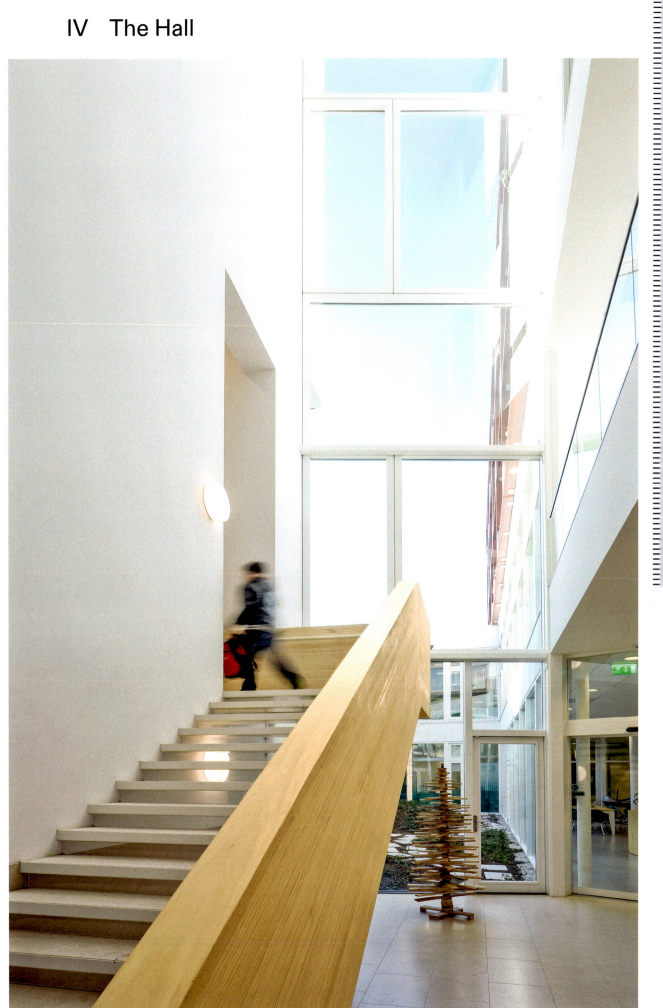

→ D06

Seven Elements of Housing Design

↑ D34

As previously stated, the hall's historic importance as a main living space was reduced to a minimal corridor limited to giving access to individual spaces. This is very much clear in the typical Amsterdam townhouses built around 1900, where even the spacious middle-class townhouses in the affluent Oud-Zuid, or Concertgebouw, neighbourhood suffer from such cramped and dark, rather uninviting access spaces. Several interior refurbishment projects in this area of Amsterdam presented an opportunity to address this issue. The first one is a *benedenhuis* on the Valeriusstraat (D34). The house has three levels: a half-sunken basement, or the *souterrain*; a ground floor 1 metre above street level, the *bel-etage*; and a first floor. The *bel-etage* entrance and the first-floor corridor in the narrow bay of the house suffered from lack of daylight and space to move, and the *souterrain* could only be accessed through a steep set of stairs hidden underneath the stairs to the first floor. The refurbishment radically redesigned the layout of the narrow bay. The floor of the *bel-etage* corridor was removed to make an open stair towards the *souterrain* that contains workspaces and a guest room. The floor of the first-floor corridor was partly removed as well, repositioning access to the first-floor spaces via a new layout of the wide bay. With these interventions, the three dark corridor spaces on each level were transformed into one continuous three-storey hall with daylight coming through a series of interior windows placed in the former door openings.

↓ D34

IV   The Hall

The second project is a house on the nearby Van Breestraat (D33), a single townhouse of five floors with the conventional narrow bay/wide bay floor plan. By repositioning the stairs leading to the top floor, daylight now penetrates via a large skylight to the first and second floors. Adding glass partitions in the corridors on these levels brings still more daylight and visual connections. The very cramped ground-floor entrance space was transformed into a generous hall, with visual connections to the large kitchen and stairs to the basement. The design's changes to the vertical connections evolved the house from a succession of dark and winding stairs to a trajectory filled with daylight and changing views.

← D33

↓ D33

190 Seven Elements of Housing Design

IV The Hall

The transformation of Villa 4.0 (D37) offered other possibilities to create a central living hall as the heart of the house. Previous additions to the 1960s bungalow had turned the entrance hall into a dark and disorienting place. The refurbishment opened the middle part of the house again, making within the existing structure a new central space leading to all parts of the house. The result is a large living hall in the tradition of English country houses, which has views in all directions and receives additional daylight from the three large sculptural skylights. During the day the sunlight coming in through the skylights moves around on the walls and angled ceilings, changing the impression of space and light. The new hall is now central to the house's activities: a playground for the children during the day, and a dining hall and dance floor for large parties at night.

D35 →

More radical was the intervention to a corner house on the Dufaystraat (D35). The house was originally a *winkelwoning*, a house typically situated at the intersection of two streets with a shop at the front on the street and a split-level section with two floors of private living space at the back. In the redesign, the floor of the shop was removed to create a large living hall on the lower level. The higher level now opens as a mezzanine to this double-height hall. The large original shop window provides abundant daylight to the hall and the living spaces at the back.

← D37

← D37

The new _achterhuis_ on the Oude Delft canal in the city of Delft (D38) afforded a chance to create a living hall from scratch, without the restrictions of an existing structure. A new entrance hall with stairs leading to the first floor is reached via a long and narrow corridor through the existing _voorhuis_ facing the Oude Delft. The entrance hall and stairs are then connected by glazed doors and a huge interior window to the central living hall, a 4-metre-high space in the centre of the house that opens via large glazed sliding doors to the courtyard garden. Two lower interior spaces are connected to the hall: an intimate sitting nook, and a kitchen and dining space stretching out into the garden.

↓ D38

↑ D38

IV The Hall

→ D38

194 Seven Elements of Housing Design

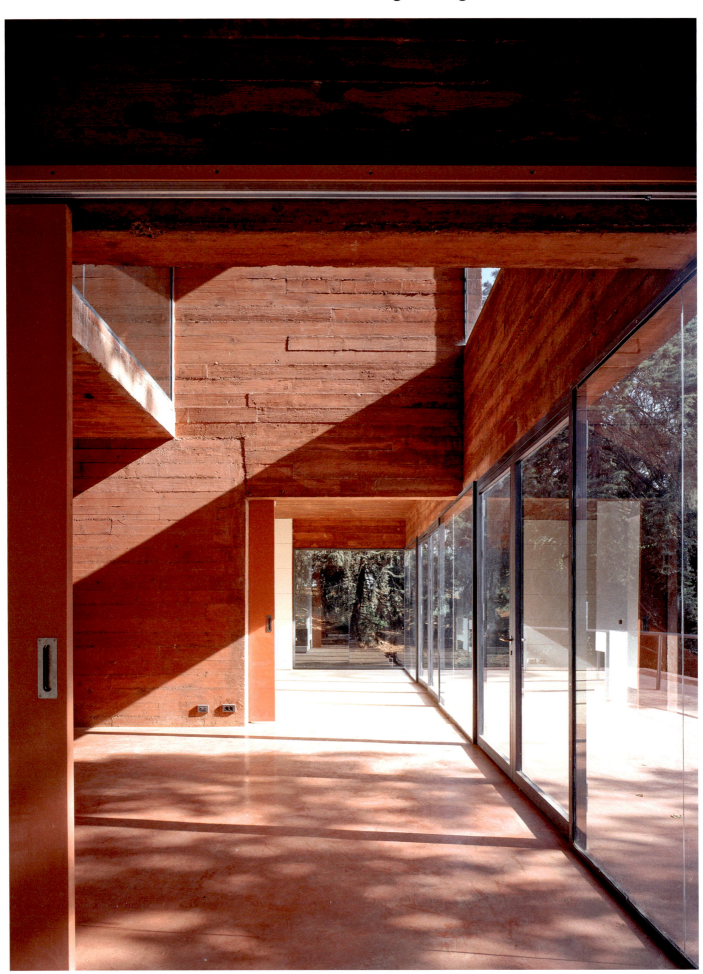

IV   The Hall

↑ D40

The hall as the main place of meeting and core of the house was further explored in the design of the residence in Addis Ababa (D40). The formal reception spaces on the upper level of the residence form an enfilade of spaces; after entering through a smaller access lobby, guests arrive in a reception hall where introductions are made, informal exchanges take place, and one can enter the garden. The reception hall continues into a sitting room where more informal exchange can continue around the fireplace or near the patio garden. The salon opens then to the dining room where the formal dinners take place. On the lower level is the actual living hall, the central living space for the resident family, which opens towards a garden terrace and the other living spaces: a small sitting room, a dine-in kitchen, and the two clusters of bedrooms. The living hall, open to the garden terrace and a view of the distant hills, is a double-height space, with an interior window providing a connection with the dining room, the heart of the formal upper floor.

↓ D40

The fireplace symbolises the heart of the house, the place to come together, to turn one's back on the world and retreat into the intimacy of the dwelling. The combination of the centripetal hearth – the intimate space, the place of ultimate privacy – with the centrifugal movement experienced through the connections between the interior and the exterior of the house is a most powerful architectural motive.

197 V The Fireplace

The interior of the top apartment at the end of the Borneo Eiland housing in Amsterdam's Eastern Docklands (D05) demonstrates the centrality of a fireplace, with one situated immediately next to the picture window that frames the view from the living space to the IJ river. A long bench next to the hearth affords a simultaneous view of both the fire inside and the water outside. The cantilevering glass veranda that faces the quay in front of the apartment acts as a screen between an outside observer and the viewer inside.

↑ D05

→ D04

Seven Elements of Housing Design

← D04

To create an intimate unobserved space in the 'glass house' top-floor unit of the dwellings in the large circular concrete drum of the former sewage treatment works in Slotervaart (D04), an interior hall with a fireplace was designed with light coming in only indirectly or from above. A similarly intimate inglenook fireplace was made as an annex to the interior street of the Berkenstede care home (D11). Residents can sit here unobserved but have a view to the outside pond and terrace and to the old heart of the village of Diemen across a canal.

↑ D11

↓ D34

→ D33

New fireplaces take central positions in the rebuilt interiors of the houses on the Valeriusstraat (D34) and Van Breestraat (D33) in Amsterdam Oud-Zuid. The corner fireplace of the first house makes the fire visible in all parts of the main living space and the kitchen.

V The Fireplace

The panoramic views from the House on the Lake (D39) are mirrored in the open, see-through fireplaces in the centre of the house.

↑ D39

→ D39

200 Seven Elements of Housing Design

The wide-open fireplace in the fully glazed new wing of Villa 4.0 (D37) anchors the glass pavilion to the ground and gives the conversation pit a focus point away from the vast expanse of the garden outside.

← D37

V The Fireplace

In the much more introverted living spaces of the Addis Ababa staff houses (D40), the fireplace has a central position as well. A circular skylight right next to the fireplace enhances the centripetal effect of its position, creating a heart for the large living space. In the completely rebuilt historic house for the deputy ambassador on the opposite side of the embassy compound, the stones of the old fireplace were kept and it was rebuilt in its original spot in the main living room. Though the climate here during the day is mild, the city, positioned 2,500 metres above sea level, can be chilly in the evenings, meaning that the fireplace has always been the best place to come together and be comfortable.

→ D40

Walls define spaces. They separate one space from the other, and they also connect spaces, reaching from inside to the outside, or moving upwards to define vertical connections. The wall is the physical anchor of the project to the site and to a wider context. It can relate to the site's geography or to the built surroundings, or introduce a completely new notion of place.

Connecting individual houses or buildings with continuous walls creates the possibility to collect fragments into a larger structure, defining urban spaces, or creating clear boundaries between public, collective, and private spaces. Strategically placed openings in walls give the passer-by a glimpse of the other side without having to enter it, while giving on the other side of the wall a protected view of the outside world. Walls are not only anchors of space. They can also be anchors of time. Keeping existing walls in new projects can create a strong sense of layering, palimpsests of occupation over time, signs of permanence and of change.

VI   The Wall

→ D31

The green spaces between the terraced houses of Grootstal in Nijmegen (D31) lead to a larger open green space that runs through the entire neighbourhood. To mark the transition from the well-maintained green in-between spaces to the wilder, so-called ecological zone, a curving, fragmented garden wall was erected from leftover and second-hand bricks. After more than twenty years, the walls are almost completely overgrown, obscuring the original reference to the city wall that defines the border between the houses on one side and the wilderness on the other. The overgrown, 'wild' nature of the wall and how it connects the housing development and the green space draws references to London's Hampstead Heath and the Hampstead Garden Suburb, still probably one of the most inspiring garden cities.

↑ D30

More subtle is the continuous low brick wall that defines the border between the patio housing and the central green valley in the Oosterhout project (D30). Together with the green hedges that separate the individual garden patios and the trees and shrubs on the patio terraces, the walls create a layered and soft transition between the private space and the public central space.

VI The Wall

→ D15

Garden walls bind the three blocks of apartments and townhouses together in the Huizen project (D15). The walls have a stone cladding on the outside in a continuation of the building facades and large openings with transparent steel fences and wide entrance gates. On the north and east side of the project, the clusters of housing are bordered by water. Here the wall is lowered to form a balustrade that continues downwards until it reaches the water level. The continuity of facades, garden walls, and balustrades on the water's edge gives the project a clear unity and strong identity in the sea of individual low-rise housing.

VI The Wall

The ability of a continuous wall to both unify and separate is a starting point of the design of the staff houses in Addis Ababa (D40). The existing compound wall along a small unpaved side street is offset by another new wall in the same grey volcanic stone. In between these two walls are the three staff houses and their gardens, each house and garden successively on a higher level than the previous one. The external wall remains the main line of security; the internal wall is opened to give access to each house's garage and service spaces and, via a steel gate and steps, to the main entrance facing the private garden. The internal wall follows the slope of the terrain, making gradually visible the horizontal line of the houses' roofs behind the wall.

↑ D40

← D40

208 Seven Elements of Housing Design

A sketch for housing in the Lo Recabarren master plan in Santiago de Chile (S3) picks up the idea of the connecting boundary wall once more. The houses stand right behind the walls, which are inspired by the old *pirca* (drystone) walls found on the site, a former plantation between the city and the foothills of the Andes.

← S3

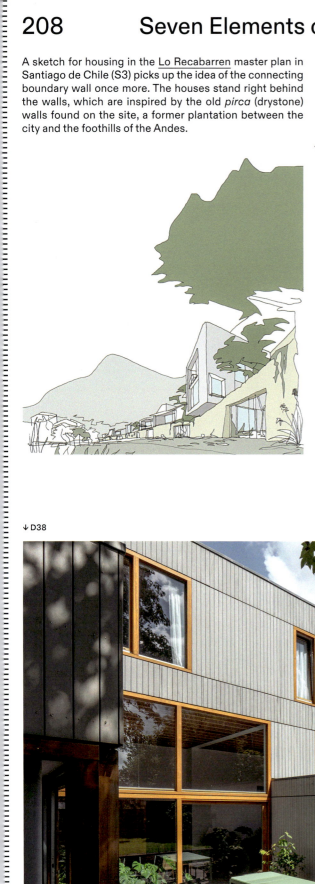

Preserving and reusing existing walls is an important tool to anchor a new project in its existing context. The new *achterhuis* in Delft (D38) is built between old garden walls, creating a walled backyard that is reminiscent of the paintings by Pieter de Hooch of seventeenth-century backyards in Delft. The reinstated back alleys of the Langebrug student housing project in Leiden (D17) show the same result; merging the old garden walls with new walls and buildings makes the existing and the new inseparable and firmly anchored to the site.

↓ D38

VI The Wall

↑ D17

→ D17

210   Seven Elements of Housing Design

Two very clear demonstrations of the possibilities of this design principle are the two housing projects in, respectively, Slotervaart Amsterdam and Hengelo.

↑ D04

↓ D04

The retained sewage treatment structures in Slotervaart (D04) keep the history of the site alive and create at the same time a rather unique identity for the new housing project. The square retaining basins are now the garden walls of the two collective gardens. Beautifully crafted steel gates, by the artist Peter Schoutsen, mark the openings in the walls and allow a glimpse of the gardens inside from the in-between paved square. Most attention is, however, drawn by the high circular concrete wall of a former water tank. It acts now as a 'holder' and a screen for a small apartment building inside the cylinder, built on the existing foundations. The heavy steel reinforcement of the concrete walls allowed for large openings without new structural interventions. The new building's rectilinear footprint inside the cylinder leaves open two crescent-shaped patios that bring light to the apartments. New balconies cantilever out from the circular wall, allowing the inhabitants to view the old structure not only from within but also from the outside, without leaving their home.

VI The Wall

↑ D22

The Buigerij apartment building in the industrial town of Hengelo (D22), near the German border, is built within the preserved shell of a typical twentieth-century industrial shed. The shed has a steel structure with brick infill and was built to accommodate a steel-pipe-bending workshop, hence the name Buigerij. The south facade of the shed was removed to make a new facade for the housing block, though the new one follows the idea of the steel frame with brick and glass infill. An internal courtyard was created by leaving open a 4-metre-wide space between the new structure and the existing north facade, which, as with the east and west sides of the original shed, keeps their original structure and window frames.

↓ D22

The roof is too often an unexplored element in housing design. It can compensate for the space taken up by the building, as famously noted by Le Corbusier in his 'Five Points for a New Architecture'. The roof can become a garden or more prosaically a parking lot. It can become a sunlit terrace, a shared space par excellence. Possibly even more interestingly, the roof can become another 'ground level'. The roof of a residential building can be turned into a pattern of streets and squares, giving access to another cluster of dwellings.

Even the traditional pitched roof, so detested by the Dutch twentieth-century modernists, is a very rich component of the architectural vocabulary of housing design. The roofs can either create individual expression in a repetition of houses, or, on the contrary, bind dwellings together in one long and more grandiose gesture. The space underneath the roof is often neglected – most of the time it is a closed-off, though useful, storage room – but when opened to the lower levels of the house it can add a spatial complexity and interest that is lost in a simple repetition of standard floor-to-ceiling heights.

VII The Roof

→ D29

The roof as a unifying gesture is the most characteristic element of the design for 650 dwellings, almost all lowrise terraced housing, in the Vinex area of Ypenburg (D29). Positioning the ridge of the pitched, ceramic-tile-clad roofs at varying angles to the front facades creates an effect that the roofs gradually slope up, only to start sloping down again when the angle changes. The individual dwelling becomes a part of a larger composition of meandering blocks and roofs sloping in different directions. The height of the long blocks and the direction of the roof angles were chosen to enhance the urban layout of larger roads, smaller side streets, introverted inner courts, and the closes.

Designs of Dutch and English garden cities during the first part of the twentieth century employed this device of emphasising the larger scale rather than the scale of the individual house to create a sense of unity and collectivity.
The roofs were also used to add spatial interest to the interior of the houses. An example can be seen in the design of the houses surrounding the triangular close that opens onto the surrounding park. The steeply pitched roofs of the facades towards the close are punctuated by large vertical dormer windows behind which a cascade of stairs connects the three levels and makes the ridge of the roof visible in the interior from the ground floor.

→ D29

214 Seven Elements of Housing Design

← D31

The social housing in the Grootstal project (D31) has aluminium-clad sloping roofs, creating a distinct identity for the cluster of terraced housing blocks, and allowing for a mezzanine or storage attic in each dwelling.

The flat roofs of the equally minimally dimensioned patio housing of the Oosterhout project (D30) allow for a future extension on the roof level. The corner units already have first floors, the facades of which are clad with roof tiles. If new roof-level volumes are added, a similar cladding with the standard red ceramic roof tiles will make them blend in with the existing appearance of the housing clusters.

→ D30

215 VII The Roof

↑ D37

→ D37

Another clear example of how roofs create both a clear identity and an interesting spatial interior can be found in the Villa 4.0 transformation project (D37). The three folded skylights give a sculptural quality to the exterior and a vertical expression in the interior to what was before a rather bland and hardly noticeable flat bungalow.

216 Seven Elements of Housing Design

↑ D21

As mentioned, the flat roof allows for a range of possible uses. The roof of the Gerard Noodtstraat apartments (D21), which is also the car park, is a good example. Moving the cars to the roof allowed for a collective garden. In addition to serving as the car park, accessed via a hydraulic car lift, the roof is also a viewing platform. The residents arriving or leaving by car can enjoy the view over the city centre and to the Waal river and its iconic steel bridge.

↓ D20

VII The Roof

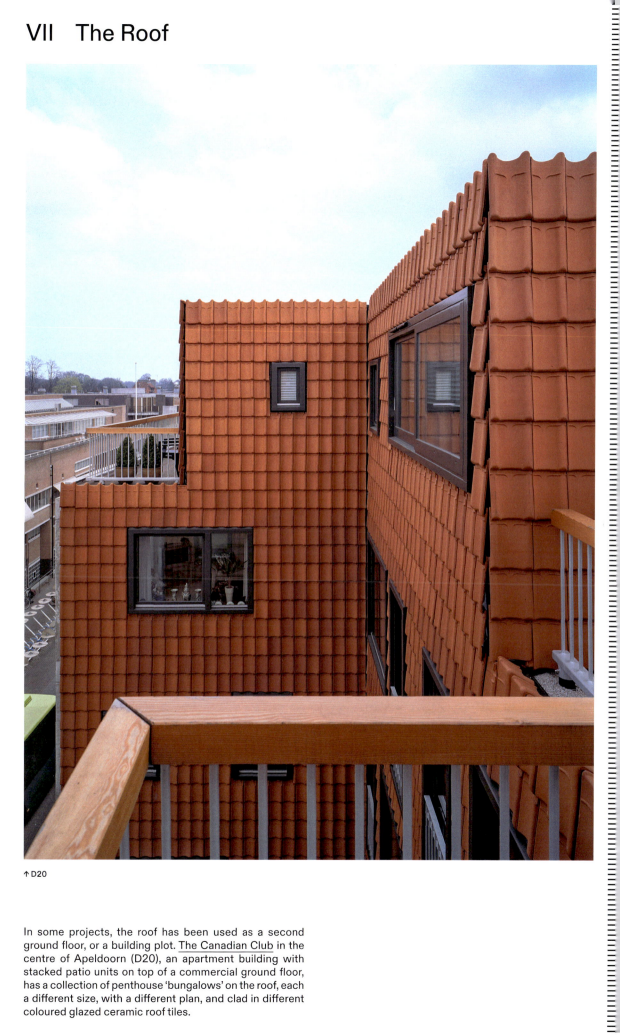

↑ D20

In some projects, the roof has been used as a second ground floor, or a building plot. The Canadian Club in the centre of Apeldoorn (D20), an apartment building with stacked patio units on top of a commercial ground floor, has a collection of penthouse 'bungalows' on the roof, each a different size, with a different plan, and clad in different coloured glazed ceramic roof tiles.

218 Seven Elements of Housing Design

↑ D12

The social housing building on IJburg's Haveneiland (D12) has eight free-standing or semi-detached maisonette units on an intermediate roof. Residents access their homes via a pedestrian 'street' on the roof lined with birch trees.

→ D12

219 VII The Roof

← D03

The same idea was further developed in the six-storey *palazzina* in Funenpark (D03). Here six free-standing maisonettes stand on the fifth-floor roof, their front doors connecting to a small 'square in the air', again provided with a tree.

→ D03

220 Seven Elements of Housing Design

A variation on this idea can also be seen in the Schokkererf project in Nagele (D19). The ground-floor volume with commercial spaces and a number of dwellings serves as a platform on which, in an irregular way with a series of setbacks, there are another two floors of apartments. The first- and second-floor apartments leave space open for large private and collective terraces, blending in with the small scale of the village of Nagele, repeating its characteristic architecture of flat roofs and expressive wooden window frames.

← D19

The roof is an obvious place to serve as an outside terrace. The five loft units in the annex of the Buigerij project in Hengelo (D22) have a sunken private roof terrace carved out from the original sloping roof structure.

→ D22

VII The Roof

↑ D16

Casa Parana in Utrecht (D16) has a large collective roof terrace as the tiny apartments of the building have French windows but no private outside space. Brick columns hide the ventilation pipes and carry a wooden trelliswork covered by climbing plants. Birch trees in planters complement the roof garden design.

The roof terraces of the top apartment of the Trommel project in Slotervaart's Zuiveringspark (D04) not only provide private outside space but also create a buffer, a privacy screen, between the fully glazed apartment and the dwellings in the nearby tower and slab apartment buildings.

↓ D04

The roof of the House on the Lake (D39) is another example of a private terrace, sunken in the main volume, as an outside conversation pit. A sliding-glass hatch avoids the addition of a staircase volume on the roof, keeping the simple lines of the building envelope undisturbed. The wide parapet acts as a balustrade and a frame for a series of photovoltaic panels.

↑ D39

← D39

VII The Roof

The roofs of the Addis Ababa chancery and residence (D40) show how flat roofs can also have a clear expressive quality and a meaning that goes beyond form and functionality. The two buildings become one when seen from above, only interrupted by the road on top of the ridge bisecting the elongated volume. As the roofs disappear in the landscape, the buildings seem to be 'extracted' from the earth. This is an intended parallel with the unique rock-hewn monolithic churches of Ethiopia, the most famous example being the Church of Saint George in Lalibela. The use of red pigmented concrete in the facades, the roof, and the interior, blending with the red soil, enhances the reference further. The flat roofs fill with water during the rainy season. When the water starts to evaporate, the concrete reliefs on the roofs become visible again, showing an Ethiopian cross motive on the chancery, and a Dutch polder pattern on the residence. The roof has become a symbol, connecting Ethiopia and the Netherlands.

↑ D40

→ D40

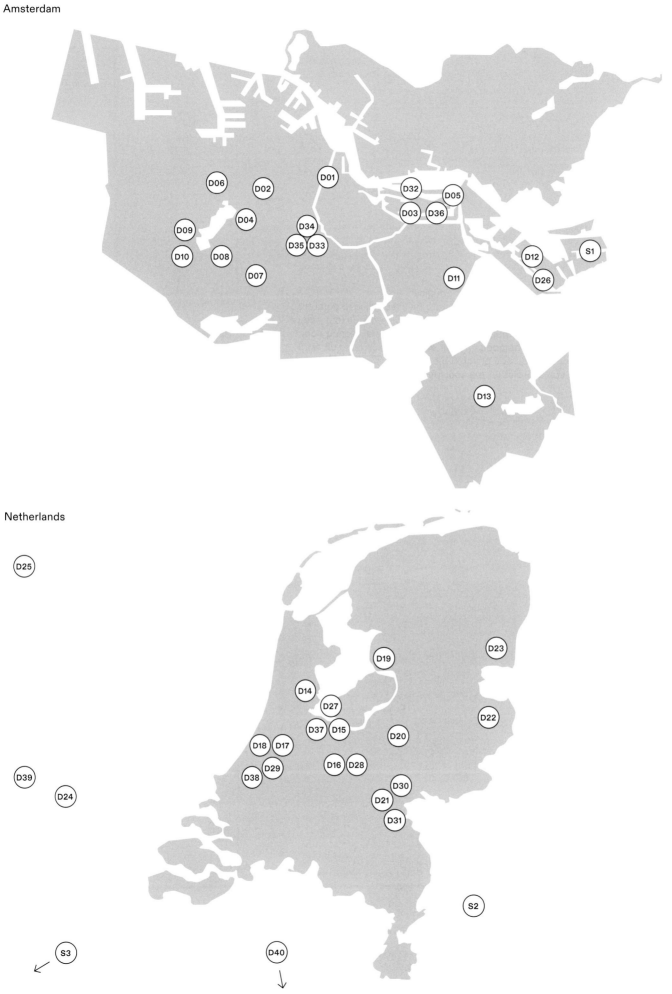

6 A Catalogue of Projects

Haarlemmerplein
Amsterdam

The Haarlemmerplein project is the result of a competition for the rebuilding of a building block on the north side of the seventeenth-century Haarlemmer Square, situated at the western end of the historic centre of Amsterdam. The square was greatly disfigured in the 1960s when the buildings on the north side were demolished to make space for a new major access road to the city centre, a brutal intervention that in the end was never realised. After thirty years of debate and several cancelled projects, a new building with seventy apartments, commercial space on the ground floor, and a four-storey underground parking garage, has been built.

The main design theme was to create a typology that reflected the former seventeenth-century parcellation of the city block into narrow plots, while also addressing modern concerns related to the noise of the railways and roads. The solution was a series of parallel structural walls based on the former plot dimensions, creating a series of long and narrow apartments, typical for Amsterdam. Three courtyards cut through the structure to provide light, giving each apartment at least one facade not affected by noise and most apartments a view of the square.

Architect	Dick van Gameren Architecten
Commission	2004
Construction	2006–2009
Client	Heijmans IBC Vastgoed, Almere
Contractor	Heijmans IBC Bouw, Hoofddorp
Structural engineer	ABT, Velp

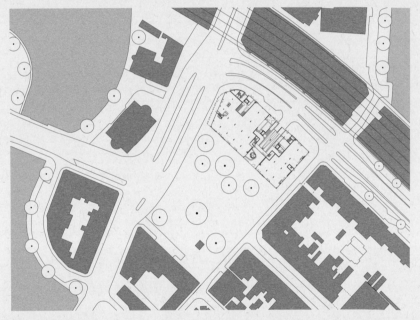

Site location plan

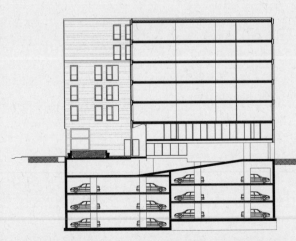

Section A

Section B

227 Apartments → 132, 152

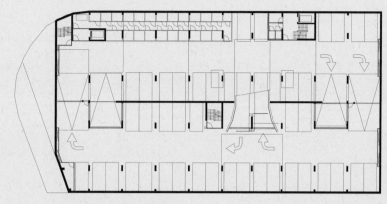
Parking garage level –1

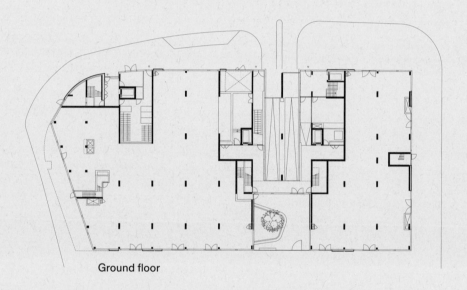
Ground floor

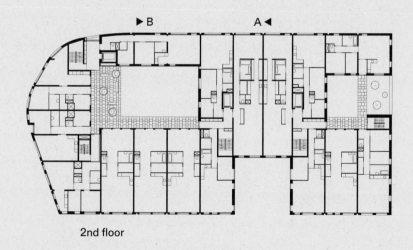
2nd floor

Laan van Spartaan
Amsterdam

The Laan van Spartaan project was planned on the site of a sports area in Slotervaart, part of Amsterdam's Western Garden Cities. The area lies next to the A10 ring road, making noise reduction in the new dwellings a major design challenge. The project consists of three large courtyard clusters, each composed of apartment buildings facing the Erasmusgracht, one of the major canals in the interwar AUP expansion plan, and of L-shaped blocks of townhouses that sit back-to-back, one unit facing the surrounding streets, the other facing the collective courtyard.

The project shows parallels with the way the housing was designed in the Berlage Amsterdam South extension plan. The firm Claus and Kaan Architecten designed the master plan and the unit plans; it was joined by two other architectural offices to design the facades that were then distributed evenly throughout all three clusters. For the facades facing the Erasmusgracht, all three architects used a sound-absorbing and reflecting louvre element especially developed for this project.

Architect	Dick van Gameren Architecten
Commission	2007
Construction	2011
Client	BPD Amsterdam
Contractor	UBA Bouw BV, Uithoorn
Structural engineer	Goudstikker - de Vries, Almere

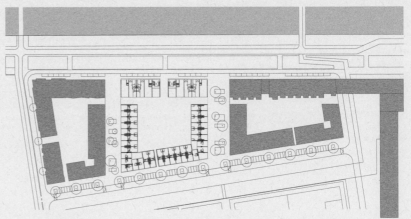

Site location plan

229 Apartments →139, 142, 143

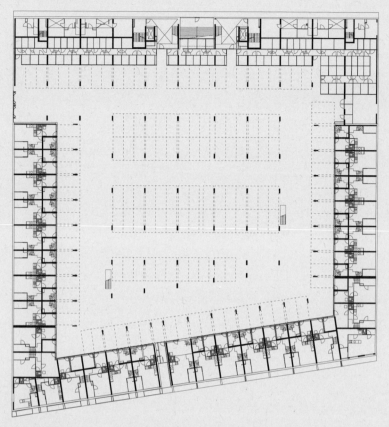

Ground floor

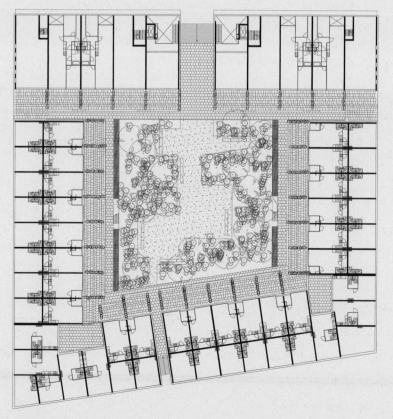

1st floor

Funenpark Amsterdam

Architect	Dick van Gameren Architecten
Commission	2003
Construction	2003–2009
Client	Heijmans Vastgoed, Almere
Contractor	Heijmans Woningbouw, Almere
Structural engineer	Berkhout Tros Bouwadviseurs, Alkmaar
Urban planning	Frits van Dongen / de Architecten Cie.

Three buildings were designed for the inner-city Funenpark project in Amsterdam to fit with the master plan by architect Frits van Dongen. A six-storey urban villa, or *palazzina*, stands out from the other urban villas in the inner area of the Funenpark project due to its varied programme. The building contains twelve four- and five-room maisonettes and ten smaller two- and three-room apartments. The twenty-two-unit block is made of up of thirteen different variations of the two basic types.

The six maisonettes at ground level each have an outside area bordering the green car-free space between the residential blocks. The other six family residences are detached houses located on the roof of the fourth storey. A small square on the roof, with trees and some small side alleys, connects these houses to the ground-floor access hall via two stairways and a lift. Each of the two storeys situated in between contains five apartments located on both sides of an interior passageway that stretches from facade to facade. The twelve larger family dwellings stand out due to the variety of brick colours and masonry bond patterns which emphasise their individual characters. The two intermediate storeys, on the other hand, suggest the communal character of an apartment complex; continuous glass fronts create a neutral filter between the city and the apartment.

On the edge of Funenpark, two identical triangular apartment buildings of three storeys each sit on a semi-underground storage level. Ten apartments and a maisonette are clustered around a central access core.

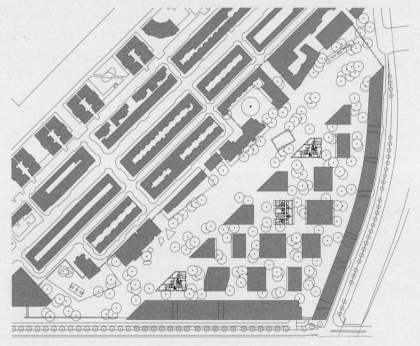

Site location plan

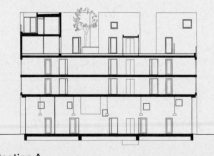

Section A

231 Apartments → 41, 60, 62, 65, 106, 108, 174, 219

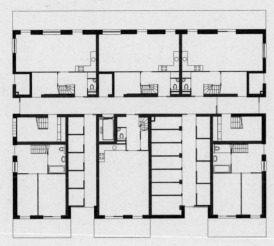

Ground floor

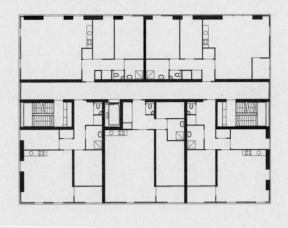

2nd & 3rd floor

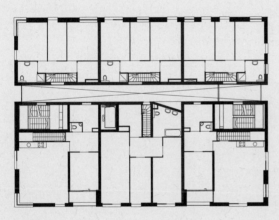

1st floor

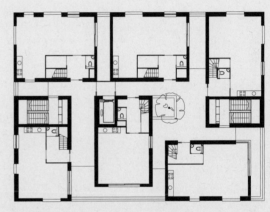

4th floor

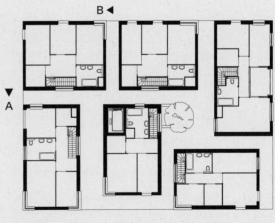

5th floor

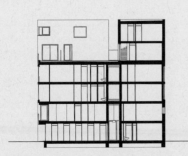

Section B

232 D03 Funenpark Amsterdam

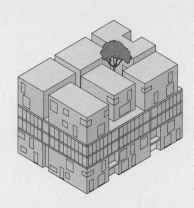

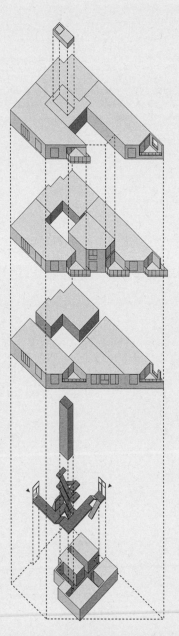

3 × apartment

3 × apartment
+ 1 maisonnette

3 × apartment
+ 1 studio

central entrance hall

basement

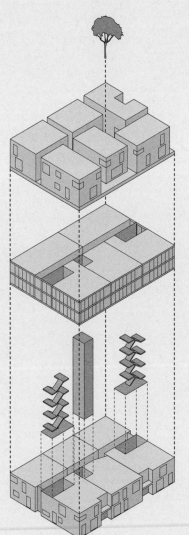

6 × maisonnette

2 × 5 apartments

6 × maisonnette

233 Apartments

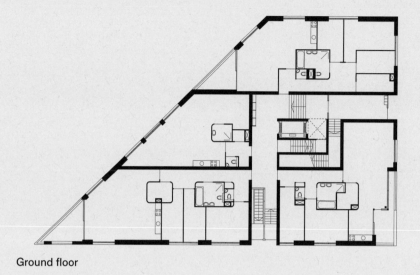
Ground floor

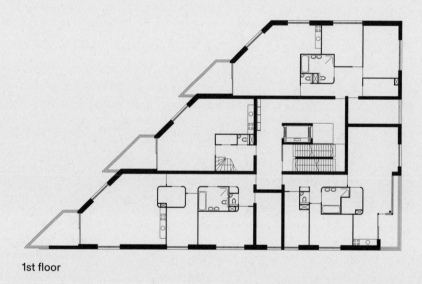
1st floor

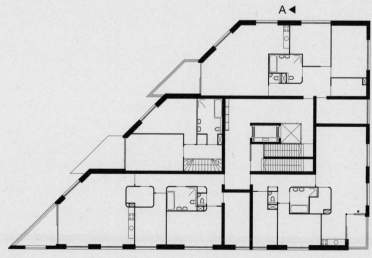
2nd floor

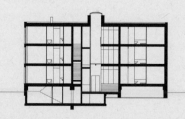
Section A

Zuiveringspark Amsterdam

With the transfer of the sewage treatment plant east of the central Sloterplas lake to a site outside the city, a large area within the Slotervaart part of the Western Garden Cities became available for a new residential neighbourhood. Several surviving concrete storage tanks have been integrated into the housing ensemble, positioned on a strip of land in the middle of the new housing development. The dwellings are clustered either immediately adjacent to or inside the concrete remains of the sewage plant. The rest of the strip of land is used to create an open public green space that is connected to Sloterpark, and thereby, with its wider surroundings.

The project consists of eighty-nine apartments. Apart from the seven units that have been accommodated in one of the three former water reservoirs, known as the Trommel, the apartments are situated in two volumes: a seven-storey building with a maisonette typology; and an eighteen-storey tower block at the end of the strip. The tower block has both single-floor apartments and interlocking two-storey units, avoiding any that have only a north-east orientation. Both blocks stand against and on concrete tanks, which function now as collective gardens for the residents of the apartments as well as providing parking and storage space.

Large openings in the concrete walls of the existing structures establish a relationship between the public space and that used collectively by residents. The seven units in the large concrete drum stand as a rectangular volume inside the perforated ring wall, with the top apartment emerging out of the concrete shell.

Tower and slab

Design	De Architectengroep, Dick van Gameren, and Bjarne Mastenbroek
Commission	1994
Construction	1996–1998
Client	Smit's Bouwbedrijf BV, Beverwijk
Contractor	Smit's Bouwbedrijf BV, Beverwijk
Structural engineer	Pieters Bouwtechniek BV, Haarlem

Trommel

Design	De Architectengroep, Dick van Gameren, and Bjarne Mastenbroek
Commission	1999
Construction	2000
Client	Bouwbedrijf M.J. de Nijs en Zonen BV, Warmenhuizen
Contractor	Bouwbedrijf M.J. de Nijs en Zonen BV, Warmenhuizen
Structural engineer	Pieters Bouwtechniek BV, Haarlem

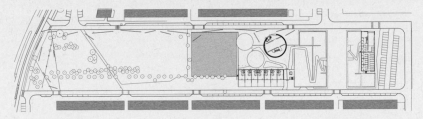

Site location plan

235 Apartments → 106, 109, 176, 177, 185, 197, 198, 206, 210, 221

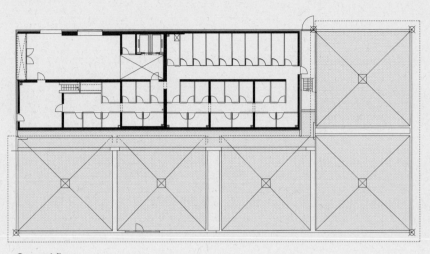

Ground floor

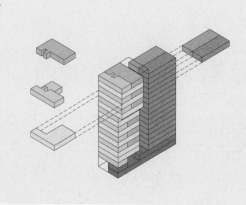

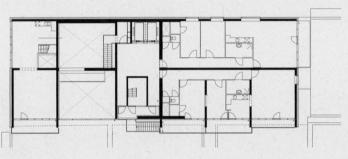

2nd floor

14th floor

4th floor

15th floor

5th floor

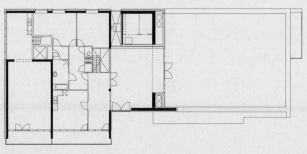

16th floor

236 D04 Zuiveringspark
Amsterdam

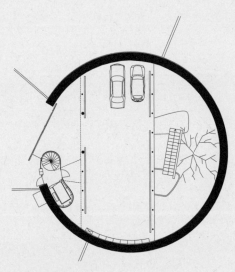
Ground floor

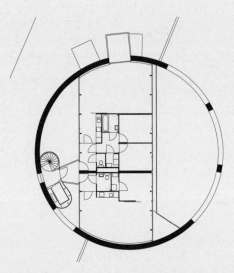
2nd floor

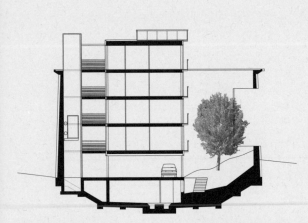
Section A

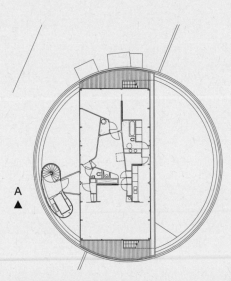
3rd floor

237 Apartments

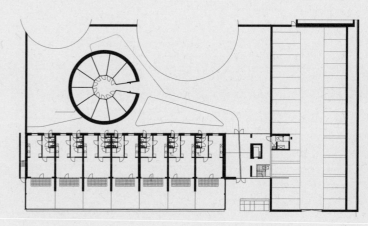

Ground floor

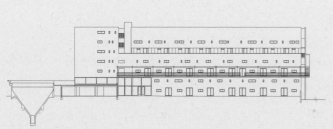

North facade

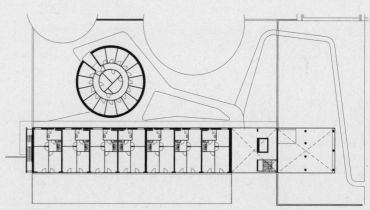

1st floor

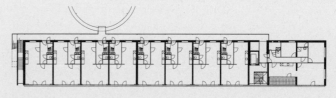

2nd floor

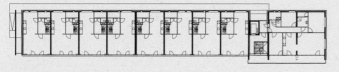

5th floor

3rd floor

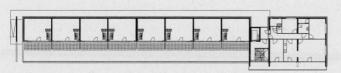

6th floor

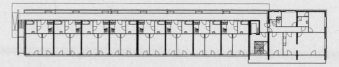

4th floor

Borneo Eiland
Amsterdam

The project consists of two parallel rows of three-storey townhouses with an internal parking street that is closed off on one side by three apartments. The apartments face the open water and escaped the strict formal stipulations of the West 8 urban plan for Borneo Eiland, part of the Amsterdam Eastern Docklands urban regeneration project.

The project had to be built with the contractor's standard formwork system for the load-bearing concrete partition walls and floors. Although built within the structure of 5.5-metre-wide concrete tunnel bays of the two rows of townhouses, the three apartments have very different internal layouts. After the tunnelling system was projected on the project's plot, half a tunnel was left over. This was used to make half a tunnel in exposed concrete to serve as an outside space for the three apartments. Cantilevering glass boxes in delicate balance reveal the space inside the project's concrete tunnels.

Architect	De Architectengroep, Dick van Gameren, and Bjarne Mastenbroek
Commission	1993
Realisation	1999
Construction	Stichting Boerhaave, Leiden
Client	Smit's Bouwbedrijf BV, Beverwijk
Contractor	Smit's Bouwbedrijf BV, Beverwijk
Structural engineer	Smit's Bouwbedrijf BV, Beverwijk

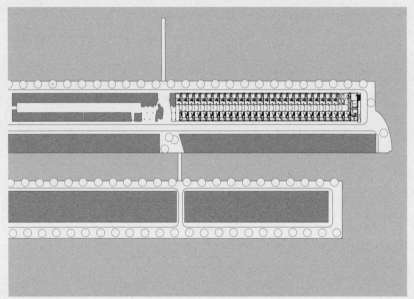

Site location plan

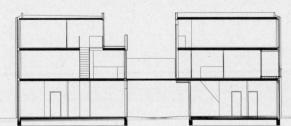

Section A

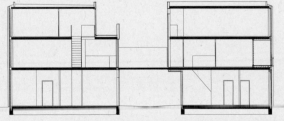

Section B

239 Apartments → 85, 86, 119, 124, 126, 197

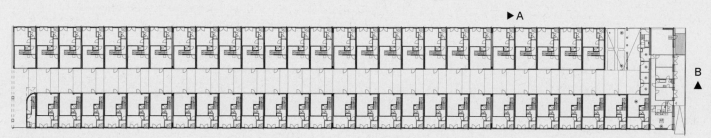

Ground floor

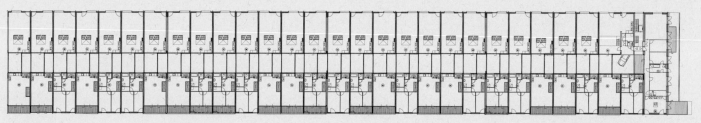

1st floor

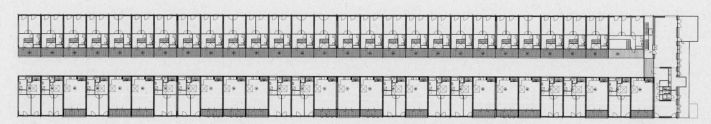

2nd floor

De Honingraat, Slotermeerlaan Amsterdam

The new community centre for Slotermeer is located at a corner of the Slotermeerlaan, opposite Plein 40–45, the central shopping and market area of this part of Amsterdam's Western Garden Cities. The building houses various social and cultural facilities for the local community. The vaulted main entrance has been carved out of the building's corner volume and provides access to the four-storey central communal hall. Daylight flows in from the tree-planted courtyard in the heart of the building.

The articulated volume connects to its surroundings: a seven-storey building along the main road and square, a five-storey side wing connecting to the existing postwar *portiekflats*, and a lower part that connects to the schools behind the building.

All facilities on the ground and first floors are accessible from the central hall. The building includes a branch of the Amsterdam Public Library, a community centre, a maternity centre, a youth centre, and a café. Together, the vaulted roofs and ceilings, the central patio, and large windows towards the street create light and open interior spaces. There are apartments for elderly people on top of the community centre. The glazed verandas of the apartments facing the main road act as sound buffers to protect the living spaces from traffic noise.

Architect	Dick van Gameren Architecten
Design	2008–2010
Construction	2011–2013
Client	Ymere Ontwikkeling B.V., Amsterdam
Contractor	Bouwbedrijf M.J. De Nijs en Zonen BV, Warmenhuizen
Structural engineer	Zonneveld inngenieurs BV, Rotterdam
MEPF engineer	Mabutec Installatie Advies, Utrecht

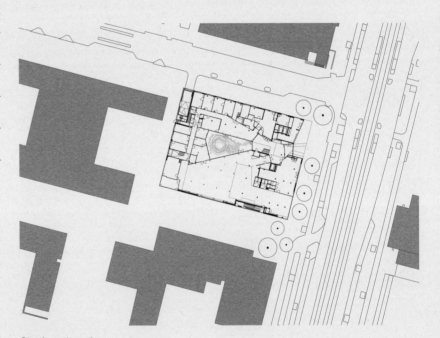

Site location plan

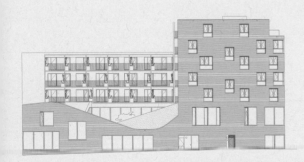

South facade

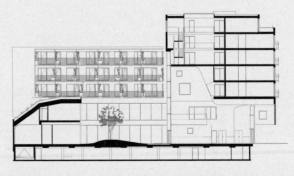

Section A

241   Apartments   → 136, 186, 187

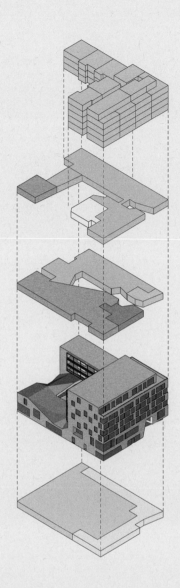

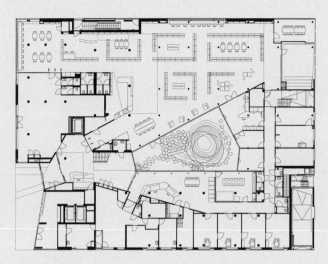

Ground floor

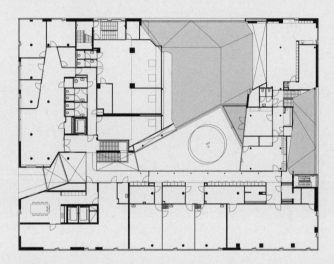

1st floor

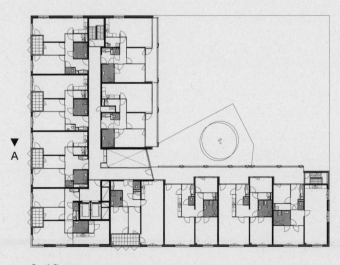

2nd floor

Noordstrook Delflandplein
Amsterdam

Setting into motion a large-scale reconstruction project for the Delflandplein neighbourhood in the Slotervaart part of Amsterdam's Western Garden Cities, the project was the first new building, tripling the original number of dwellings and preserving the number of social housing units after three *wooneenheden* were replaced with a mix of social and market housing.

The building combines 170 affordable housing units, a community centre, and commercial spaces in one volume. The U-shaped complex has a large variety of housing types and sizes, including small studios with common living rooms for people needing special care, two- and three-bedroom apartments for the elderly, and several three-, four-, and five-bedroom apartments and maisonettes for families.

A landscaped courtyard sits atop the parking garage, creating a green heart visible to and accessible for all residents. To block noise pollution, the facade facing the A10 ring road is predominantly closed. By contrast, the opposite side was opened as much as possible with large glazed frontages and balconies.

The large concrete facade panels clad with brickwork allude to the typical 1960s prefabricated brick assembly technique used in the neighbourhood, though they break with the monotonous, repetitive appearance of traditional prefab facades. By making the panels two storeys high, varying the brick patterns, staggering the vertical seams, and recessing the windows, the building takes on a more sculptural, powerful appearance.

Architect	Dick van Gameren Architecten
Design	2004–2007
Construction	2007–2009
Client	Far West/De Principaal, Amsterdam
Main contractor	BAM Woningbouw, Amsterdam
Structural engineer	Strackee Bouwadviesburo, Amsterdam
MEPF consultant	Huygen Installatie Adviseurs, Rotterdam

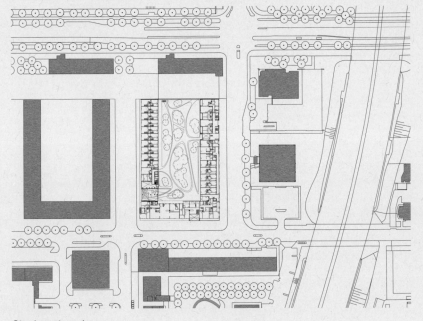

Site location plan

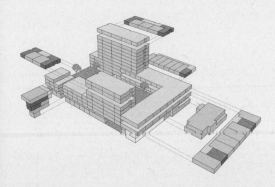

Section A

243 Apartments → 38, 40, 106, 109, 136, 137, 160, 184

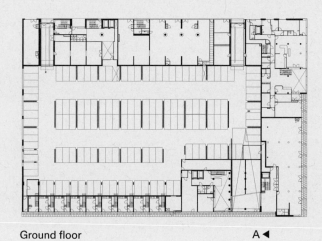
Ground floor　　　A ◀

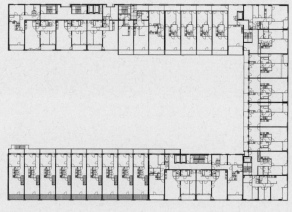
3rd floor

1st floor

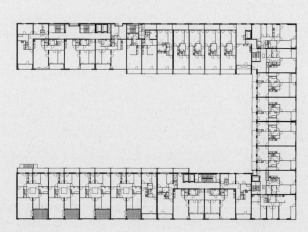
4th floor

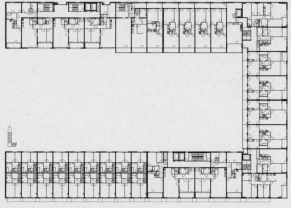
2nd floor

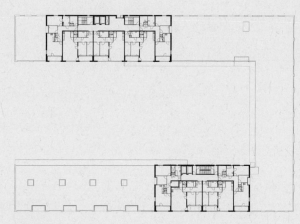
5th floor

De Bouwmeester
Amsterdam

De Bouwmeester is a series of linear and L-shaped clusters of elderly housing situated around a large central garden in a low-rise housing area of Slotervaart, part of Amsterdam's Western Garden Cities. Smaller enclosed patio gardens create a protected intermediary space for the often vulnerable residents. The remaining part of Herman Hertzberger's iconic and previously partly demolished project De Drie Hoven, a care home built in the 1970s, retains a dominant position in the ensemble of new and old buildings.

Architect	Dick van Gameren Architecten
Commission	2014
Construction	2016
Client	Woonzorg Nederland, Amstelveen
Contractor	Bouwbedrijf Berghege, Oss
Structural engineer	Pieters Bouwtechniek, Haarlem

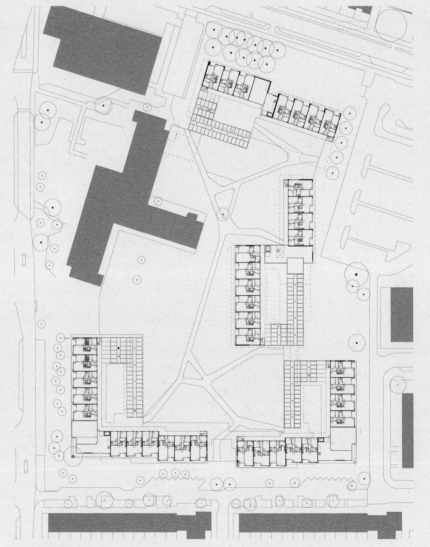

Site location plan

245 Apartments

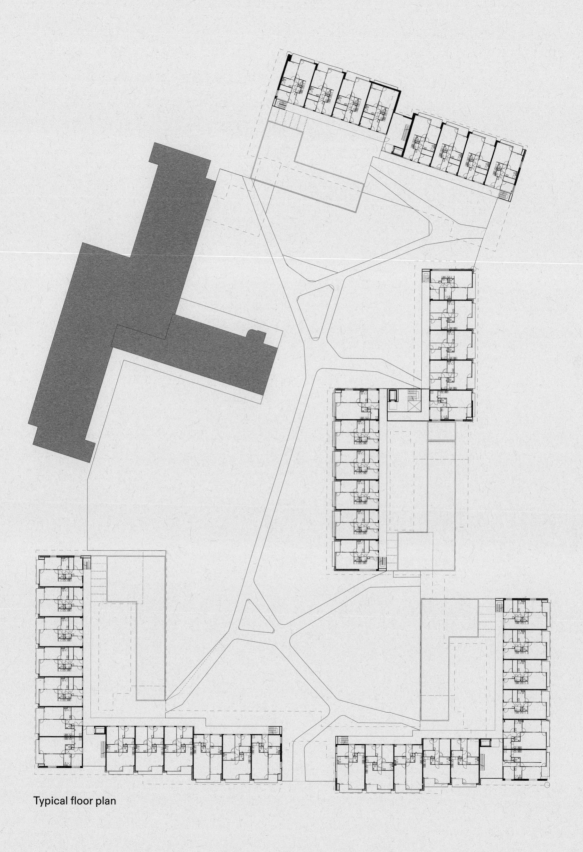

Typical floor plan

Oeverpad
Amsterdam

The Oeverpad project is located on the edge of the Sloterplas in Osdorp, the part of the Amsterdam Western Garden Cities furthest from the city centre. The assignment was to build 120 dwellings on an 80-by-80-metre plot in an unusual mix of categories: social housing units, market rental apartments, subsidised apartments for sale, and free market apartments, all in one building. The different categories all have their own entrance halls, situated next to large open gates that connect the surrounding public space with the collective inner courtyard. The apartments on the west side of the block were brought together in a taller corner volume, giving these units a view of the lake, and resulting in a U-shaped building that opens towards the west and the Oeverpad, the main pathway between the centre of Osdorp and the lake. Opening the block via the large gates, cut-outs, and the U-shape makes the green court a visible part of the lush green surroundings, following the original intentions of the AUP expansion plan.

Architect	De Architectengroep, Dick van Gameren, and Bjarne Mastenbroek
Commission	1994
Construction	1996–1998
Client	De Principaal, Amsterdam
Contractor	Bouwbedrijf M.J. de Nijs en Zonen BV, Warmenhuizen
Structural engineer	Pieters Bouwtechniek, Haarlem

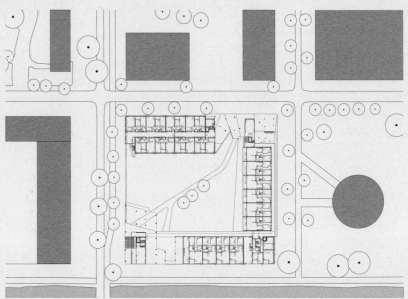

Site location plan

East facade

North facade

247 Apartments → 161, 162, 184

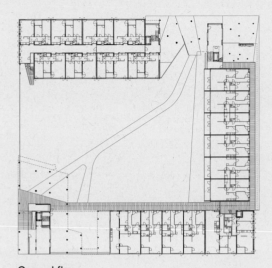
Ground floor

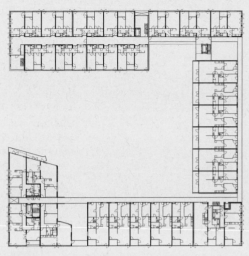
3rd floor

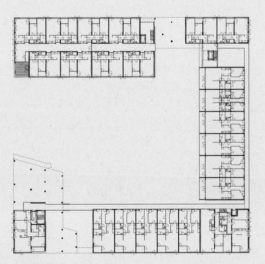
1st floor

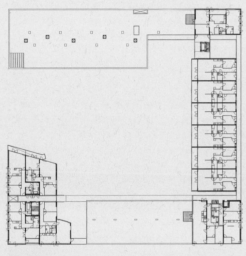
4th floor

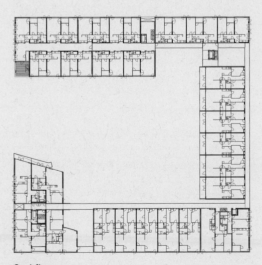
2nd floor

5th floor   6th floor   7th floor

Nierkerkecomplex Amsterdam

The project along the Nierkerkestraat in the Zuidwestkwadrant, a typical neighbourhood of Osdorp in the Amsterdam Western Garden Cities, replaces two long slabs of four storey *portiekflats*. The 1960s neighbourhood was rebuilt almost entirely in the period between 1990 and 2010. The Nierkerke project replaced the slab blocks with five compact five-storey apartment buildings on a half-sunken basement with storage and parking spaces. The five blocks are connected to each other with garden walls and fences.

Generous openings in the walls permit views from the surrounding streets into the collective courtyards. Level differences divide the courtyard into a number of individual compartments, connected to the buildings via the entrance halls. The five buildings all have wide and short internal corridors; two are designated as social housing, the other three as market housing for sale.

The layout of the blocks results in an economic way of building, avoiding the undesirable open gallery access. Most units have a corner position, allowing for an adaptable layout. The ground-floor units on the outside perimeter have split-level plans with high-ceilinged living rooms that are accessible from the street, allowing for use as independent workspaces.

Architect	Dick van Gameren Architecten
Commission	2006
Construction	2010
Client	Woningstichting Rochdale/Deltaforte
Contractor	Smit's Bouwbedrijf BV, Beverwijk
Structural engineer	ABT, Velp

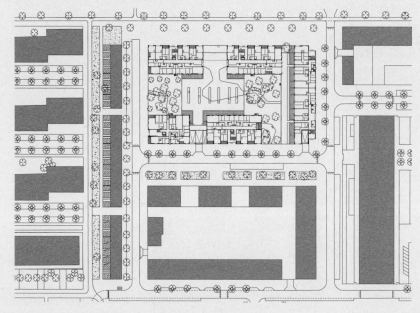

Site location plan

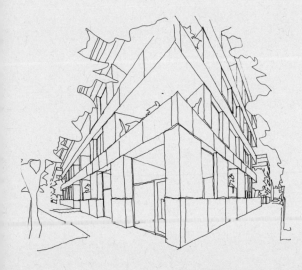

249 Apartments → 38, 40, 106, 108, 136, 160

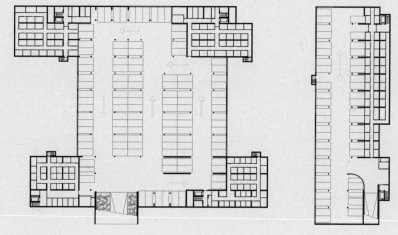

Basement

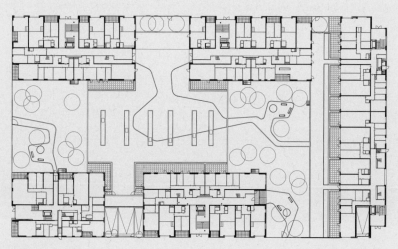

Ground floor

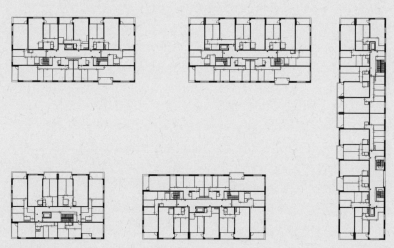

1st floor

Berkenstede
Diemen

The shape of the Berkenstede care home in Diemen, a village absorbed by Amsterdam, was largely defined by the urban master plan requiring four separate volumes. These volumes have been placed one behind the other, connected by a wide interior street that is publicly accessible, creating a shortcut for the surrounding neighbourhood. On the exterior, the complex appears like a miniature town with high and low buildings amid a hidden landscape of gardens, terraces, and patios.

From the interior street the different sections of the care home are visible and accessible. As a counterpart to the public interior street, a closed service corridor on the first floor connects all medical care and residential areas with one another. The patios and gardens provide connections between the inside and the outside and create constantly varying views from the inner street to the different parts of the care home and to the outside world. The completely glazed facades towards the patios and terraces bring in abundant daylight, thus avoiding the usual hermetic character of large care homes.

Architect	De Architectengroep, Dick van Gameren
Commission	1999
Construction	2005–2006
Client	De Principaal BV, Amsterdam, in collaboration with Stichting Amstelhuizen, Amsterdam
Contractor	Heijmerink Bouw Utrecht BV, Bunnik
Structural engineer	Zonneveld Ingenieurs BV, Rotterdam

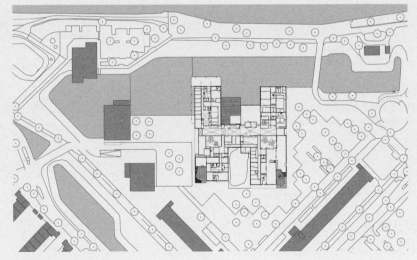

Site location plan

Section A

Section B

251 Apartments → 106, 108, 165, 185, 198

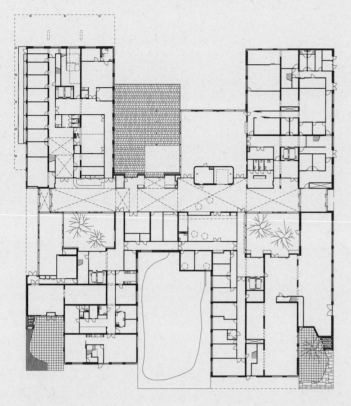

Ground floor

1st floor

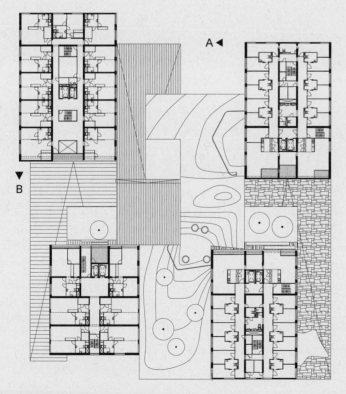

2nd floor

Blok 23B1, IJburg Amsterdam

Blok 23B1 was designed as the first social housing project on Haveneiland, the first phase of Amsterdam's new IJburg district. The project consists of a mix of townhouses, maisonettes, and apartments, with commercial spaces on the ground level facing the main arterial road that connects the island with the city. The project includes an underground parking garage.

The precisely stipulated building envelope, in combination with the mixed programme and the ambition to give as many units as possible a clear connection to the ground level, resulted in the introduction of a series of interior streets, some open, some covered. The inner streets intersect the block in different ways. One open street runs parallel to the main arterial road, providing access to the townhouses that open towards the collective courtyard, and to the maisonette units on top of the commercial spaces. The higher part of the volume has a double-height covered inner street on the ground level, giving access to the maisonettes. Between the second and fifth floors, the interior streets become wide corridors leading to single-level apartments. The units on the sixth floor are once again accessed from an open inner street on the rooftop that is flanked by detached and semi-detached two-storey maisonettes. A double system of stairs winds its way through the streets and links all the floors together.

Architect	De Architectengroep, Dick van Gameren
Commission	2000
Construction	2004–2005
Client	IJburgermaatschappij, Amsterdam
Contractor	Moes Bouwbedrijf West BV, Almere
Structural engineer	Adams Bouwadviesbureau BV, Druten

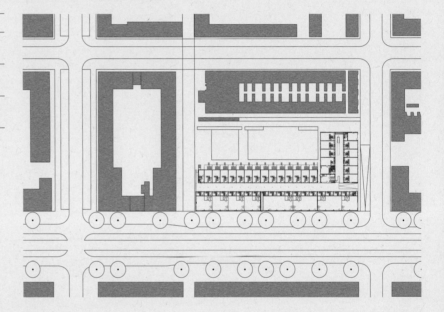

Site location plan

East facade

Section A

253 Apartments → 35, 37, 156, 157, 218

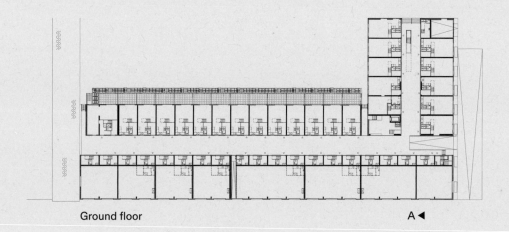

Ground floor   A ◀

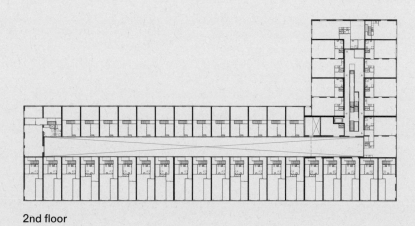

2nd floor

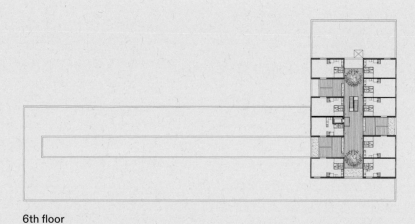

6th floor

Karspeldreef Blok AB
Amsterdam

Architect	Dick van Gameren Architecten
Commission	2004
Construction	2008–2009
Client	Woningstichting Rochdale/ Deltaforte
Contractor	KBK Bouw, Volendam
Structural engineer	Zonneveld Ingenieurs BV, Rotterdam

The Karspeldreef project is part of the radical transformation of Amsterdam South-East, formerly known as the Bijlmermeer, the large-scale housing district planned and built in the 1960s.

By bringing the elevated Karspeldreef road back to ground level, and by demolishing the large parking garage and ground-floor shopping centre Kraaiennest, space was created for a series of new buildings. Blok AB is the first of these buildings, which together constitute the new northern side of Karspeldreef, with space for businesses and shops at street level, and housing on the floors above.

Blok AB consists of four volumes that, connected to each other by gates and garden walls, form a closed perimeter block. All dwellings are built as social housing. The high volume on Karspeldreef contains a plinth with commercial spaces and six residential floors with three- and four-room dwellings. Similar housing types can also be found in the lower volume on the west side, along the Groesbeekdreef. On the east side is a building for the Salvation Army with one-room units that also accommodates a drop-in centre for the homeless with a second-hand shop on the Karspeldreef side.

The north side of the block consists of single-family terraced houses that are three storeys high and overlook the green space in the front, bordered on the other side by one of the few preserved honeycomb structures of the Bijlmermeer. The enclosed courtyard contains outside spaces for the various groups of residents: private gardens for the single-family houses, a closed garden for the Salvation Army, and a common green space for the apartments.

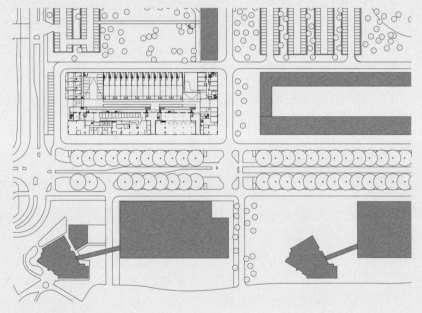

Site location plan

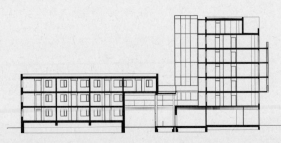

Section A

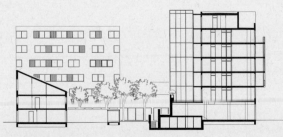

Section B

255 Apartments → 39, 41, 138, 139

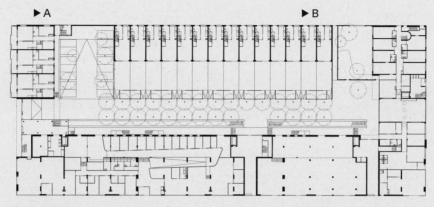
Ground floor

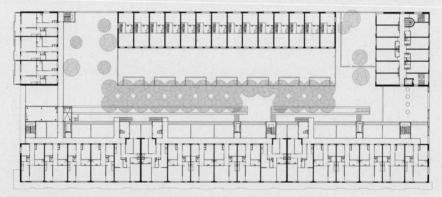
1st floor

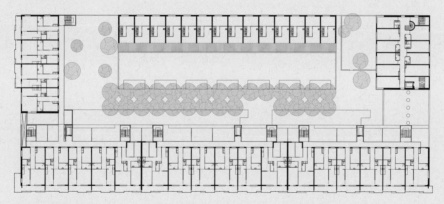
2nd floor

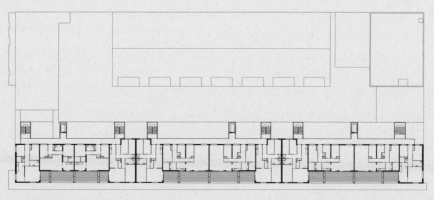
6th floor

Oeverlanden Purmerend

Bordered by a railway line, a river, and a major access road to the city centre, the Oeverlanden project is situated between Purmerend's small historic core and the extensive post-1960s housing areas that turned the tiny town into a sprawling satellite city of Amsterdam. The social housing project contains forty-three apartments for elderly people and two clusters of fifteen units for people with learning disabilities. On the ground floor a day centre and a restaurant run with the help of the residents face the main road.

The building is divided into four individual volumes, all narrow, but varying in length and height. Small, covered access galleries give access to four to six units on each floor. Seen from a distance, the building has a strong silhouette made by the clustering of the four volumes with identical pitched roofs. Up close, the building creates a quiet background to the rather noisy and chaotic surroundings. A 6-metre-high gate cuts the lower two levels in half, flanked by the two main entrance halls. The gate gives access to the open space behind the building, but also allows an underground water barrier to continue without interruption.

Architect	Dick van Gameren Architecten
Commission	2006
Construction	2010
Client	Bouwcompagnie, Hoorn
Contractor	HSB Bouw, Volendam
Structural engineer	Pieters Bouwtechniek, Haarlem

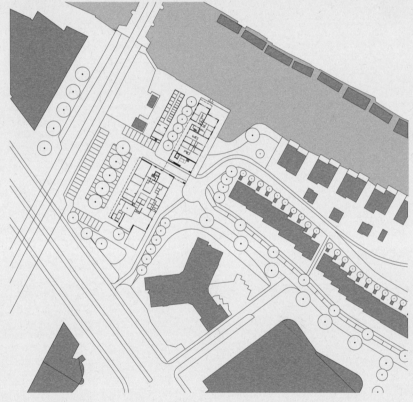

Site location plan

Section A

Section B

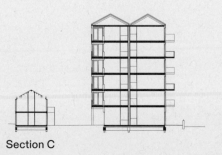

Section C

257 Apartments

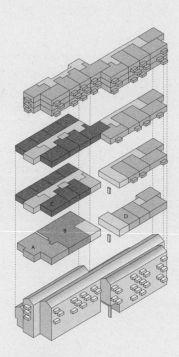

A Restaurant
B Day centre
C Residential care with common living room
D Apartments

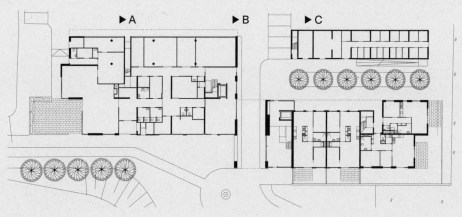

Ground floor

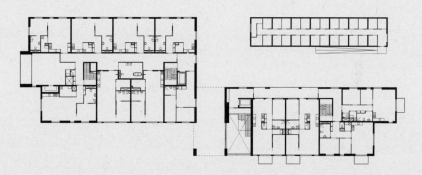

1st floor

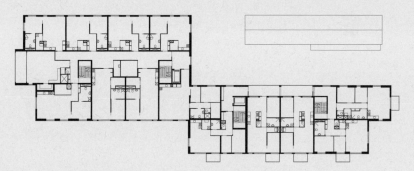

2nd floor

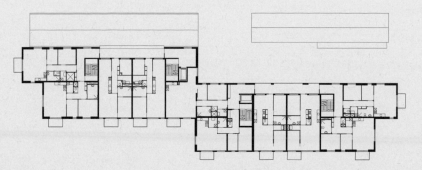

3rd floor

Vierde Kwadrant Huizen

The ensemble of three housing blocks is the final addition to a typical Vinex lowrise residential district next to the Gooimeer on the northern side of the former fishing village of Huizen, east of Amsterdam. The identical volumes are each composed of sixteen apartments and six terraced houses. Garden walls link the three volumes and combine them into one large building block. A parking facility is incorporated in each of the three blocks at ground level.

Three gateways in the garden walls provide access to the meandering path that connects all blocks and that is open by day and can be closed off at night. The open space between the three buildings acts as a series of connected collective gardens, designed by Michael van Gessel. Despite the limited building height of three storeys, a density of seventy housing units per hectare has been achieved, which is twice the average of Vinex districts.

Architect	Dick van Gameren Architecten
Commission	2002
Construction	2005–2006
Client	BPF Bouwinvest, Amsterdam
Contractor	Coen Hagedoorn Bouwgroep BV, Huizen
Structural engineer	Adams Bouwadviesbureau BV, Druten

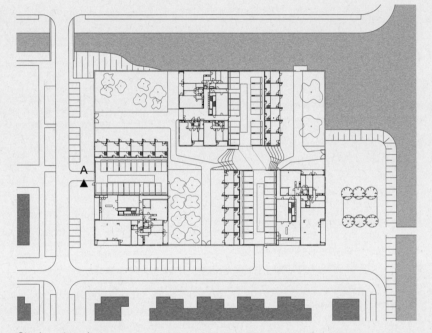

Site location plan

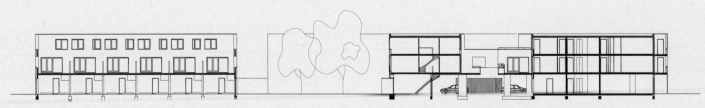

Section A

259 Apartments → 106, 109, 163, 205

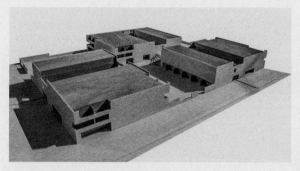

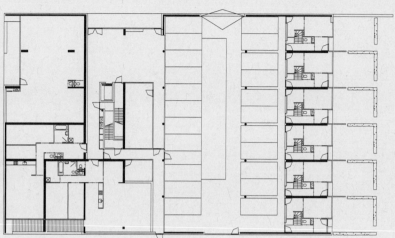
Ground floor

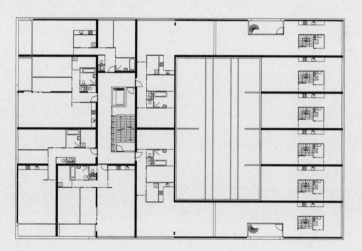
1st floor

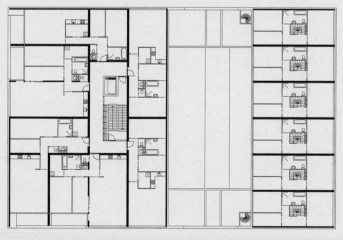
2nd floor

Casa Parana
Utrecht

The Casa Parana project is an assisted-living facility located in the post-war housing estate of Overvecht. It is surrounded by several twelve-storey apartment buildings and some later infill projects: a police station, elderly housing, and a travellers' site.

The main user of the building complex, Stichting De Tussenvoorziening, provides temporary accommodation for people who need help getting to a point where they can take care of themselves again. The residents in need of a shelter, often homeless or escaping a crisis situation at home, are supported by permanent tenants, most of them students, who serve as 'buddies'. The building has apartments of different sizes with varying degrees of independence. There are also communal spaces on each floor that are linked to outside terraces, created by two vertical incisions in the volume that also bring daylight deep into the building. The plinth has a staggered transparent facade that marks the collective programme. The central double-height corner space on the ground floor is used as a café, partly run by the residents. Additionally, other workspaces and amenities are situated on the ground level.

Architect	Dick van Gameren Architecten
Design	2010–2011
Construction	2013
Client	Portaal Woningcorporatie, Utrecht; Stichting De Tussenvoorziening, Utrecht
Contractor	Heilijgers Bouw, Utrecht
Structural engineer	Raadgevend Ingenieursbureau van Dijke bv., Alphen aan den Rijn

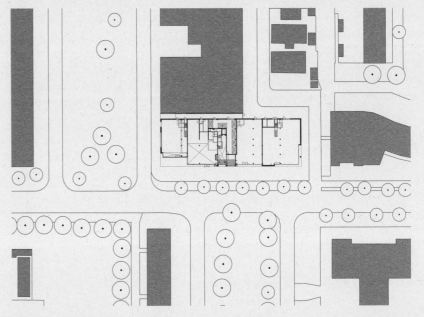

Site location plan

261 Apartments → 139, 186, 221

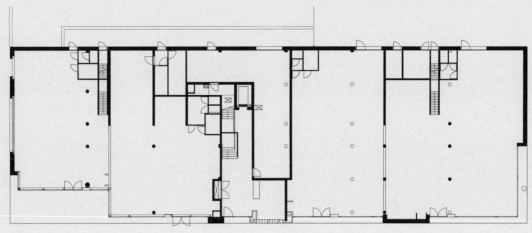
Ground floor

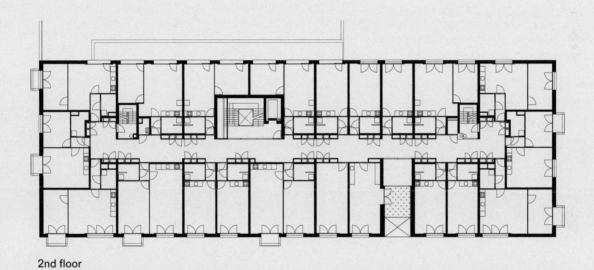
2nd floor

4th floor

Langebrug Student Housing
Leiden

The Langebrug project is situated in the heart of the historical centre of Leiden. The location experienced both fires and a disastrous gunpowder explosion, which had resulted in an almost complete disappearance of the original medieval urban fabric of alleyways and courtyards woven between two main streets. The redevelopment of the area into housing for 250 students has restored the medieval street patterns using existing and new garden walls to redefine the historical alleys. During the first phase, a preserved nineteenth-century corner building was redeveloped into thirty individual residences. Other student residences with shared facilities were subsequently built in five separate building volumes, preserving some parts of former structures.

The buildings have been designed to allow a possible future transformation from student housing to two- to three-bedroom apartments. Curving interior masonry walls guide the movement from the main entrances to the individual units. Green courtyards, visible through the gates and fenced openings in the garden walls, contrast with the red-brick pavements of the alleyways.

Architect	Dick van Gameren Architecten
Commission	2010–2012
Construction	2012–2016
Client	SLS/Stichting DUWO
Contractor	Van Rhijn Bouw, Katwijk
Structural engineer	Zonneveld Ingenieurs BV, Rotterdam

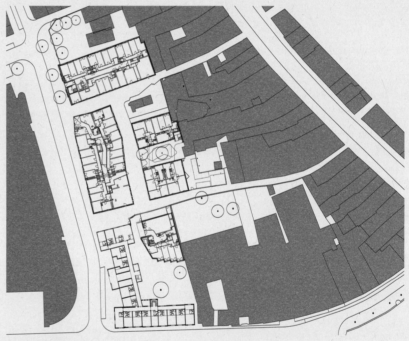

Site location plan

Walls

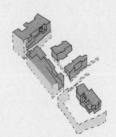

Back and side facades

Gardens

Street facade

263 Apartments → 146, 147, 209

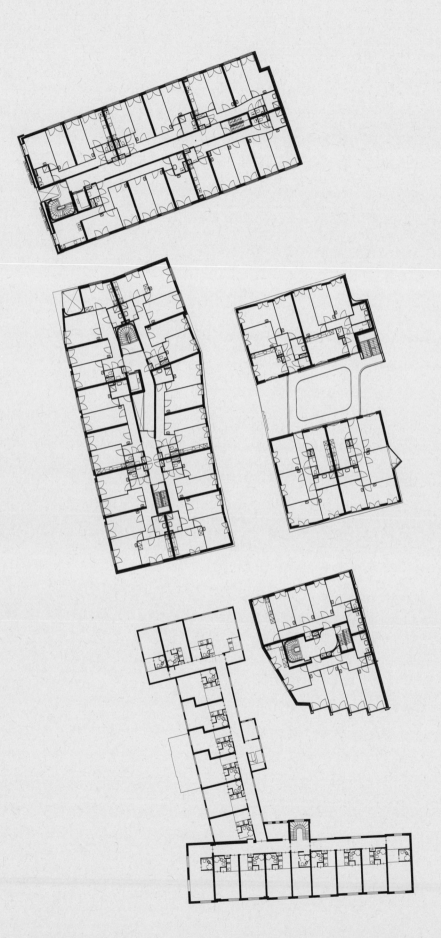

1st floor

Boerhaave University Housing Leiden

The Boerhaave tower offers accommodation for doctoral students and researchers at the University of Leiden. Located next to the early-twentieth-century former Anatomy Building, the scheme establishes a connection between old and new, and between the city and the university. The addition of the new tower at the end of the shorter wing of the U-shaped Anatomy Building creates a clearly defined entrance courtyard.

The brick facades and continuous stone plinth ensure that the existing building and the new tower form a coherent whole. The silhouette of the former Anatomy Building, with its staircase towers and steep slate roofs, resonates with the vertical articulation of the new tower and its crenellated parapet.

A gently sloping ramp leads visitors through the new courtyard towards the tower block entrance. Lifts and staircases give access to the twelve floors, each containing six independent apartments around a large central hall. The living area of each apartment has a corner window that provides panoramic views of the campus and the city of Leiden.

Architect	Dick van Gameren Architecten
Commission	2012–2013
Construction	2014–2015
Client	Stichting Boerhaave, Leiden
Contractor	Coen Hagedoorn Bouwgroep BV, Huizen
Structural engineer	Raadgevend Ingenieursbureau van Dijke, Alphen aan Den Rijn, the Netherlands

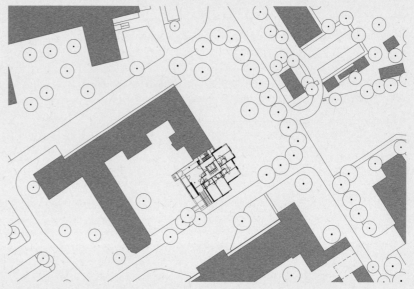

Site location plan

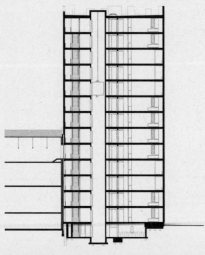

Section A

265 Apartments

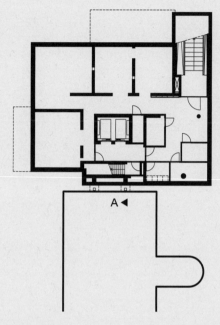

Basement

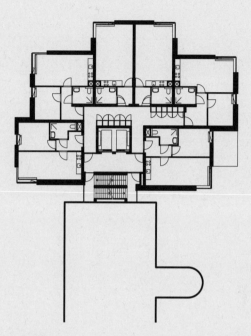

2nd floor

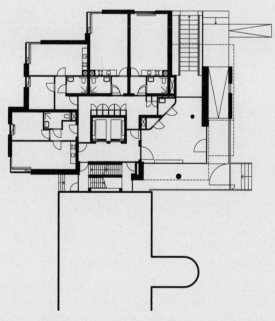

Ground floor

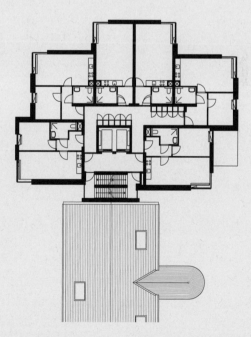

5th floor

Schokkererf
Nagele

The project is built on the site of a former restaurant and community hall called Schokkererf in Nagele. The village of Nagele is situated in the Noordoostpolder, the new land created in the former Zuiderzee, an inland sea that was closed off in 1933 and transformed into a lake, the IJsselmeer. Immediately after the Second World War, the new polder was planned as agricultural land, with one central town surrounded by ten new villages. Nagele became quite famous as the experimental village designed by the De 8 en Opbouw collective of architects. The design stands in sharp contrast with the traditional design of the other new villages in the polder.

Schokkererf is situated on the village square that connects the open land outside the village to the central green on which three schools and four churches were built in an open configuration. The site is bordered on the south by a cluster of five small buildings that each combine a shop with a family house. These free-standing units are placed on both sides of a small pedestrian path. Architect Jaap Bakema's original idea to cover the path and connect the buildings with an open pergola, never realised, was picked up in the design for a new Schokkererf. A pergola gives access to a number of commercial spaces and a doctor's practice on the ground floor. On top of the ground floor, several apartments are placed in a sculptural configuration, leaving space open for large private and collective roof terraces. Details and materials forge another connection between the new building and the Bakema project, creating a new ensemble that is respectful to the architectural heritage of Nagele.

Architect	Mecanoo Architecten
Commission	2016
Construction	2021
Client	Schokkererf BV
Contractor	Taurus Bouwgroep, Ommen
Structural engineer	De Boer Ingenieursbureau BV, Staphorst

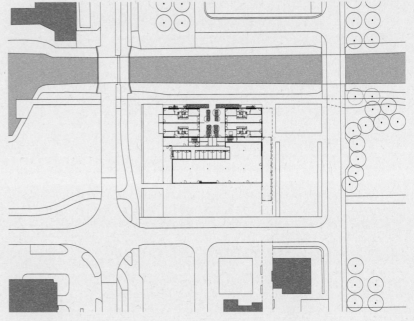

Site location plan

West facade

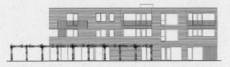

East facade

South facade

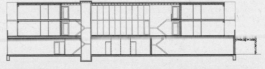

Section A

Apartments

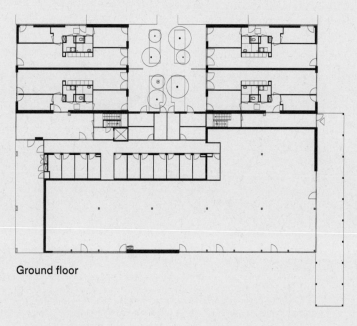

Ground floor

A ▲

1st floor

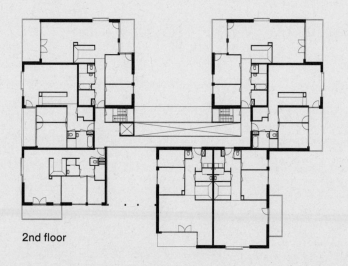

2nd floor

Canadian Club Apeldoorn

The Canadian Club project in the centre of Apeldoorn tries to make optimal use of the maximum building envelope. On top of a commercial ground floor, there are three floors with narrow, deep apartments, crowned by a roofscape with seven free-standing 'mini' bungalows.

The apartments receive daylight from both end facades, and by means of a light well in the heart of each unit, similar to the single-floor patio dwellings of the Oosterhout project (D30). The patio apartments are accessed via a wide gallery on the south side, combining the access with the individual outside spaces. The original village character of Apeldoorn is reflected in the street facade that is broken up into smaller parts by shifting the bays back and forth, and by the facade cladding of ceramic roof tiles.

Architect	De Architectengroep, Bjarne Mastenbroek, and Dick van Gameren
Commission	1993
Construction	2000
Client	Ontwikkelingsmaatschappij Apeldoorn
Contractor	Nijhuis Bouw BV, Rijssen
Structural engineer	ABT, Velp

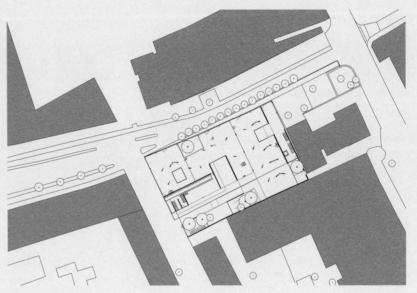

Site location plan

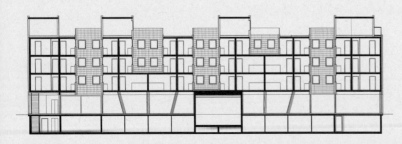

Section A

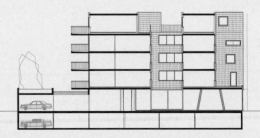

Section B

269 Apartments → 216, 217

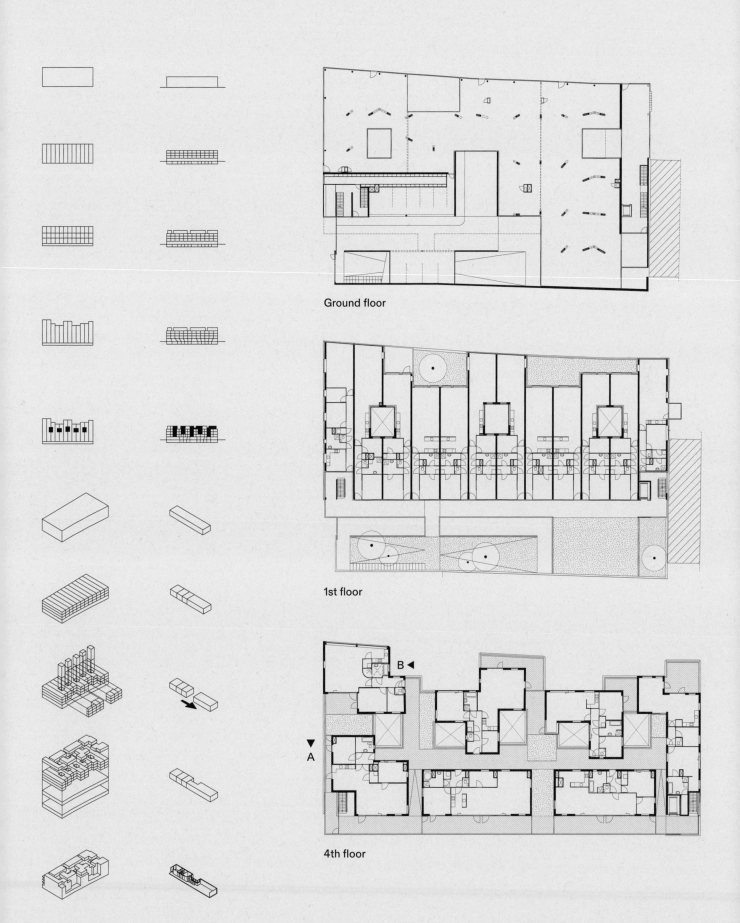

Ground floor

1st floor

4th floor

Gerard Noodtstraat
Nijmegen

The Gerard Noodtstraat apartment building in Nijmegen is situated between the inner city, largely reconstructed after the severe destruction of the Second World War; the preserved late-nineteenth-century ring around the centre; and the open green spaces of the Valkhof park and former castle grounds along the Waal river, the main connection between the Rhine and the North Sea.

The project is built on a long and shallow plot and consists of three segments that together follow the gentle curve of the Gerard Noodtstraat. A large collective garden is situated behind the building and is visible through the two main gates and entrance halls. To make this garden and to have space for shops and dwellings on the ground level, the car park was located on the roof, opening up the basement for storage spaces for each of the dwelling units. The parking platform, hovering like an aircraft carrier's deck over the building's main volumes, is constructed as an independent structure to prevent noise and vibration inside the residences.

Architect	Dick van Gameren and Bjarne Mastenbroek Architecten
Commission	1993
Construction	1995–1996
Client	Katholieke Woningvereniging Kolping, Nijmegen
Contractor	Tiemstra Nijmegen BV, Nijmegen
Structural engineer	Bouwadviesbureau Heijckmann, Huissen

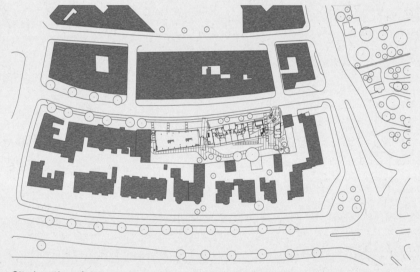

Site location plan

Section A

Street facade

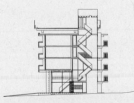

Section B

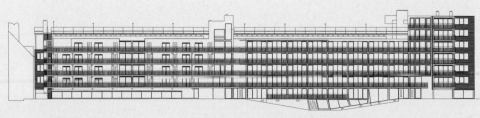

Garden facade

271 Apartments → 106, 108, 135, 175, 183, 216

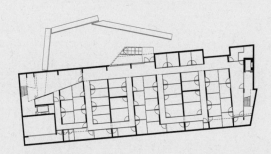

Basement

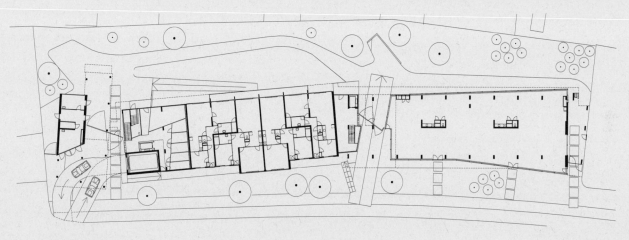

Ground floor

2nd floor

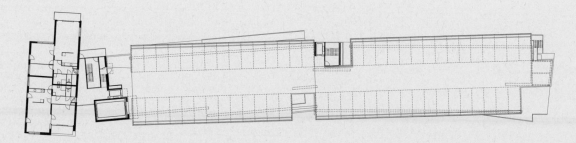

5th floor

Buigerij
Hengelo

The Buigerij project is part of a long-term development by the city of Hengelo to create a new residential neighbourhood on the site of the former Stork machine works. The Pijpenbuigerij, an industrial building of steel with brick infill from 1956, is typical of the former factory structures of the area. The large hall had been in use as a workspace for the bending of steel pipes. In reusing it as the shell of a new social housing building, the site's history remains visibly present and is further expressed by the large print of a photograph showing the original interior that has been applied to the cladding of the west facade.

A new building was positioned inside the shell, with only parts of the roof being removed and a new south facade added to make outside spaces for the dwellings. The access galleries are placed behind the preserved north facade, creating a collective outside courtyard space inside the former industrial building. A lower annex to the north has been converted into five long, narrow lofts.

Architect	Dick van Gameren Architecten
Commission	2004
Construction	2005–2009
Client	Van Wijnen Projectontwikkeling Oost, Arnhem; De Woonplaats, Enschede
Contractor	Van Wijnen, Eibergen
Structural engineer	Schreuders Bouwtechniek BV, Hengelo

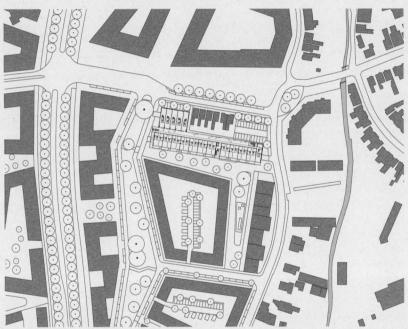

Site location plan

Section A

Section B

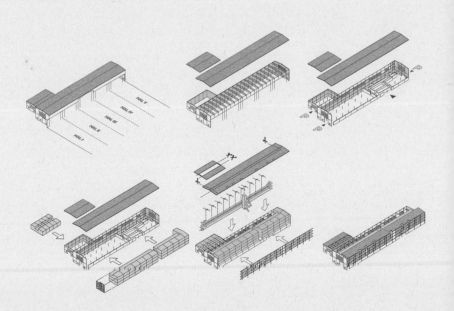

Apartments

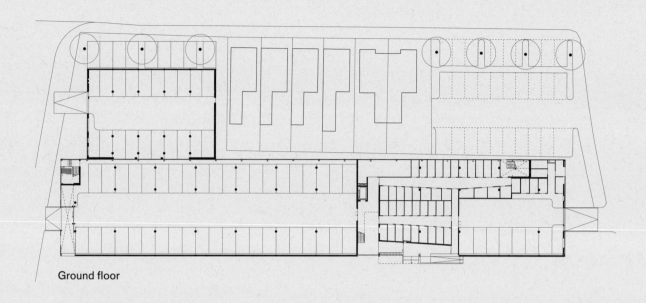

Ground floor

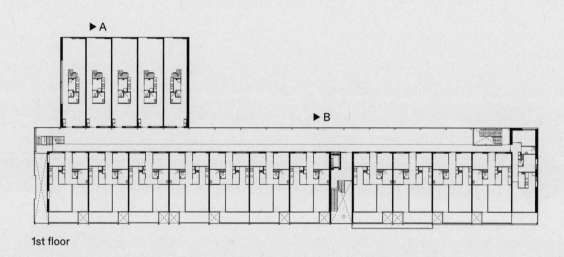

▶A

▶B

1st floor

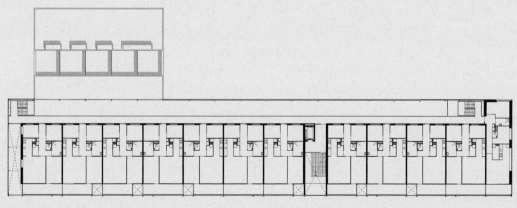

2nd floor

Marktplein
Emmen

The building brings order to the heterogeneous surroundings of the leafy village square of Emmen. It has a strongly articulated volume that unites the different building heights in the surrounding area. The curved lower part of the building follows the historic trajectory of the country road leading away from the square, while the apartments above it follow the noise contours of the post-war motorway to the west. The apartments are oriented towards the south and west for sunlight and views towards the square or the open landscape. Large terraces and glazed verandas form a screen between the apartments and the traffic noise. The top two storeys contain large penthouse apartments. The entrance to the apartments is via a generous forecourt, shielded from the streets by a wall, creating a green buffer between the building and the busy city centre surrounding it.

Architect	de Architectengroep, Dick van Gameren
Commission	1996
Construction	2001–2003
Client	Brands Bouwontwikkeling BV, Emmen
Contractor	Brands Bouwgroep BV, Emmen
Structural engineer	Ingenieurs Groep Emmen BV

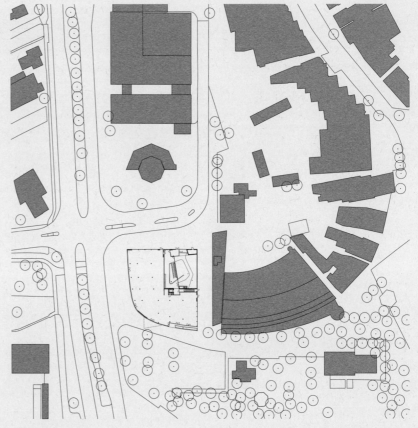

Site location plan

Section A

South facade

Apartments

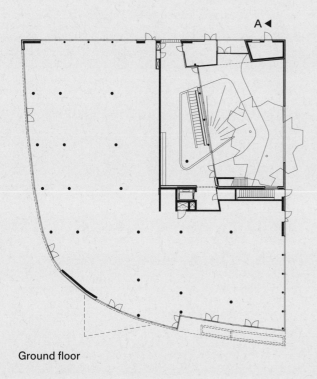

Ground floor

6th floor

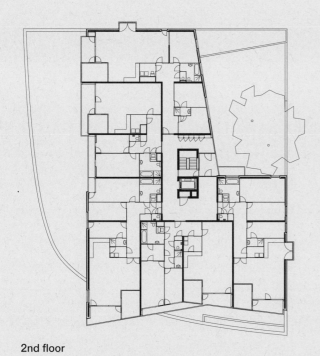

2nd floor

7th floor

Thamesmead South
London

The master plan for the regeneration of Thamesmead South intends to bring new connectivity, community, and character to the area. Thamesmead South was originally conceived in the late 1960s as the first phase of a highly ambitions scheme to create a new 'ideal' town on the south-eastern edge of London. The new project wants to bring some relief to the enormous need for affordable housing in London, and to bring new life to a housing estate that, only a few years after being built, started to have many problems, and a bad reputation.

This first phase of the regeneration of Thamesmead evolves along Southmere Lane, a new pedestrian route from the Abbey Wood Crossrail station in the south to Southmere Lake in the north, providing an enlivened sequence of streets and squares to create an improved sense of place. The master plan will provide over 1,500 housing units, around 10,000 square metres of commercial, retail, and leisure space, and a new public space.

A new central square on the edge of Southmere Lake will act as the focal point for residents and visitors and will restore community facilities. Active frontages for commercial, retail, and leisure space create a mixed-use area with a completely new public space, replacing the failed continuous raised pedestrian deck and the car-dominated ground-level spaces.

The master plan is based on a phased construction of ensembles: clusters of apartment buildings and terraced houses around raised shared courtyards. The first built clusters with around 235 new dwelling units allow for the inclusion of the original buildings that escaped demolition, as well as the buildings erected in an earlier but once more failed attempt to restructure the area.

Master plan	Mecanoo Architecten and Proctor and Matthews Architects
First phase housing project design	Mecanoo Architecten
Design	2015–2016
Construction	2017–2022
Client	Peabody Trust, London

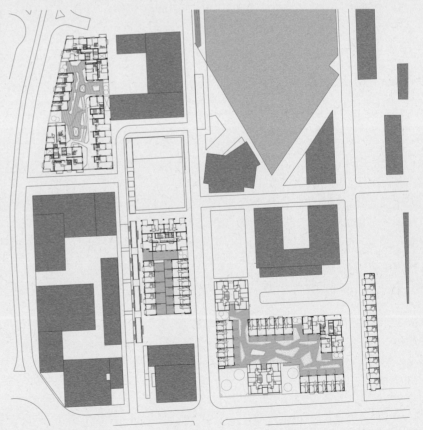

Site location plan

277 Apartments → 61, 63, 148, 149

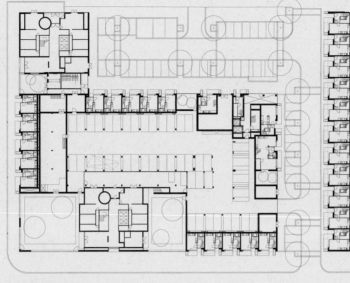

Ground floor

1st floor

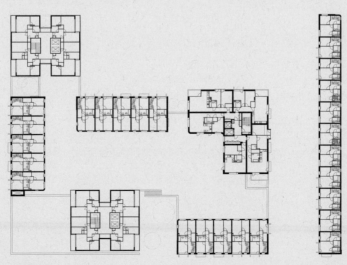

2nd floor

Leaf Street
Manchester

Architect	Mecanoo Architecten
Design	2014–2015
Construction	2016–2018
Client	One Manchester

The area around Leaf Street in Hulme, just outside Manchester city centre, has a complicated history of urban renewal. The typical Victorian terraced houses of the area were partly replaced in the 1930s, and further demolished after the Second World War to make room for the notorious Hulme Crescents, the largest social housing project in the United Kingdom at the time, a brutalist ensemble of crescent-shaped maisonette blocks. In the 1990s, the Crescents were demolished, and a large part of the neighbourhood redeveloped with cheaply built low-rise residential structures.

The new Leaf Street project is a fourth-generation urban-renewal housing development that combines apartments and single-family homes in a single snake-shaped volume. On the south-eastern side, the plot borders the main access road to the Hulme neighbourhood and a series of buildings of the Manchester Metropolitan University. Appropriate to this scale, the residential complex extends to five levels of apartments. The compact building volume meanders across the plot and gradually decreases in scale to the north. The three-storey townhouses on this northern side of the development are on par with the adjacent small blocks of flats from the 1930s.

The building acts as a connecting element between the various generations of housing bordering the plot. The shape of the building creates two semi-enclosed public green spaces and has allowed for the preservation of many existing trees on the plot. Cycling paths and footpaths across the carefully landscaped site make a clear connection to the surrounding city.

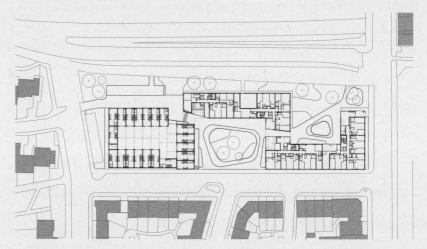

Site location plan

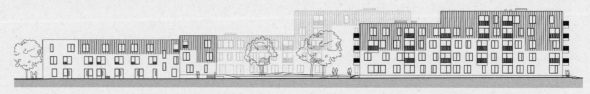

Leaf Street facade

Section A

Apartments

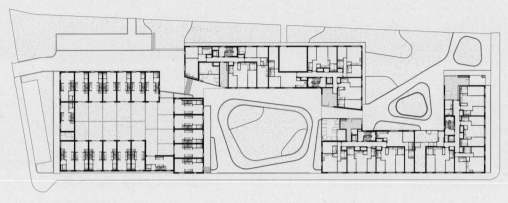

Ground floor

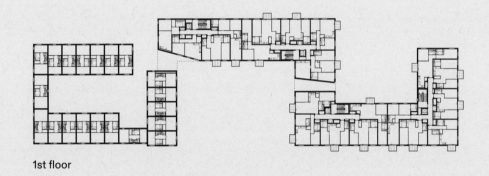

1st floor

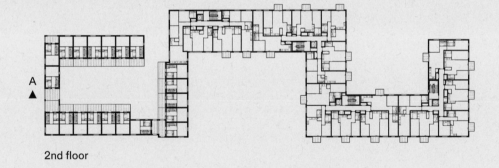

2nd floor

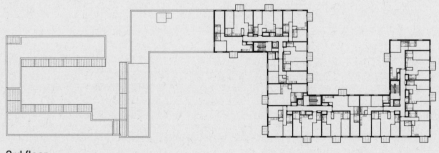

3rd floor

Blok 51C, IJburg Amsterdam

Blok 51C on IJburg's Haveneiland combines seventeen privately owned townhouses and twenty-eight social-housing units. The three-storey terrace of single-family dwellings is situated within the clear grid structure of Haveneiland, between a street and a canal. The block is divided into three zones: at each end a communal courtyard opens towards the public space, with the social housing forming linear clusters around the two collective courts. The seventeen large townhouses form the middle part of the block. A collective street runs at the back of these houses, giving access to the individual ground-floor garages. The living rooms are on the first floor, with an outside terrace built over the rear street, and connected with stairs to the gardens along the canal.

Architect	Dick van Gameren Architecten
Commission	2005
Construction	2009
Client	De Alliantie Ontwikkeling, Huizen
Contractor	Giesbers-Eemland Bouw BV, Bussum
Structural engineer	Adviesbureau Buizer BV, Wijk bij Duurstede

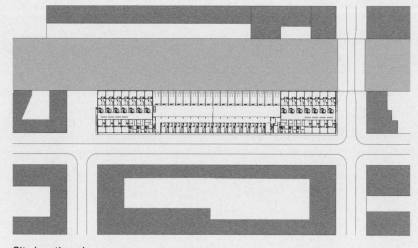

Site location plan

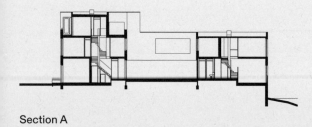

Section A

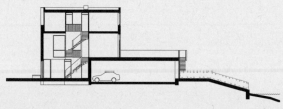

Section B

281 Terraced Housing → 81, 140

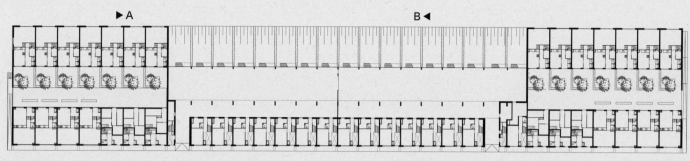
Ground floor

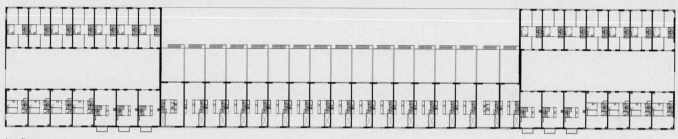
1st floor

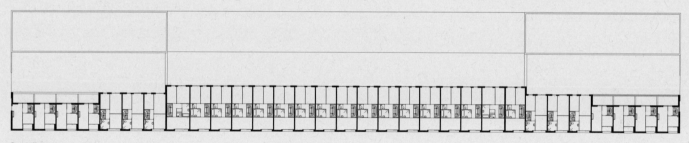
2nd floor

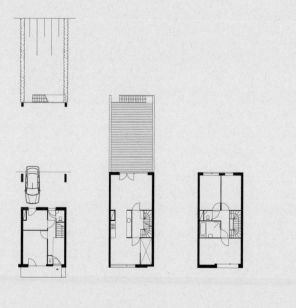
Type in central segment

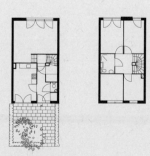
Courtyard type

Noorderplassen
Almere

The project is situated in the heart of the Noorderplassen area, a northern extension of Almere, the large new town east of Amsterdam. On a rectilinear plot of land, bordered on the west and north by the wide-open water of the Noorderplassen lake, a variety of terraced housing types have been designed around a collective inner court with car parking. Facing the lakeside, terraced houses of different sizes form an almost continuous front.

The eastern side of the ensemble is shaped by a linear repetition of patio dwellings. The patio units have an adaptable layout that allows for further extensions. The two corners of the plot along the main street on the south are closed with small three-storey townhouses on a minimal footprint. The south-western corner gradually slopes upwards, following the streets that rise to connect to the higher level of a bridge. The sloping rooflines and changing floor levels create in this corner a curious perspective distortion.

Architect	Dick van Gameren Architecten
Commission	2005
Construction	2008
Client	Blauwhoed Eurowoningen, Rotterdam
Contractor	Jorritsma Bouw BV, Almere

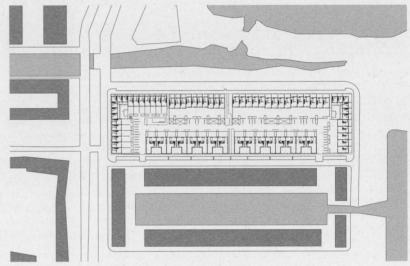

Site location plan

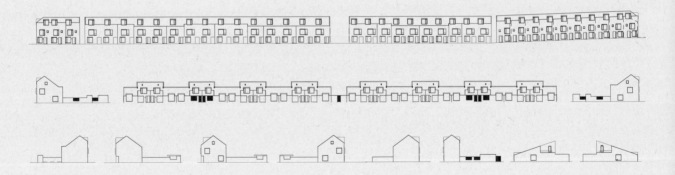

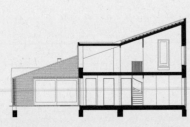

Section A

Section B

283 Terraced Housing → 143, 158

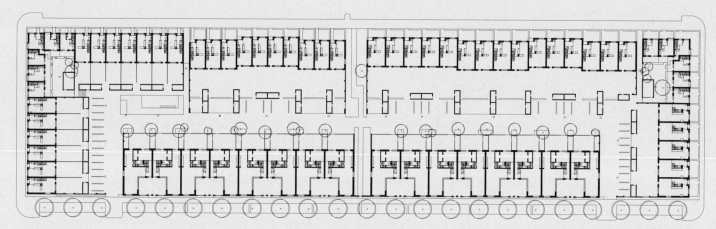
Ground floor

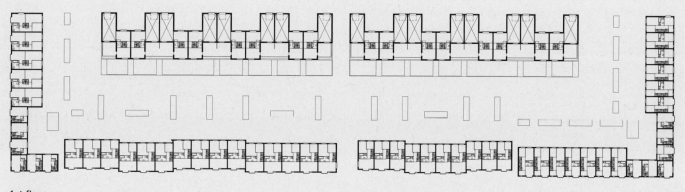
1st floor

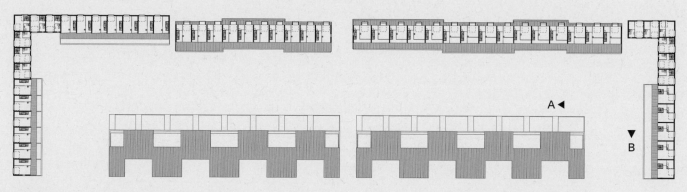
2nd floor

Talmalaan
Utrecht

The design for 173 dwellings at the Talmalaan in Utrecht is part of a master plan by Bolles+Wilson. The project is one element of an urban regeneration programme along a main road leading from Utrecht city centre to the Overvecht district, where Casa Parana (D16) is located. A series of 1950s apartment buildings along the Talmalaan have been demolished, and the road profile has been reduced in size.

The former buildings have been replaced by a low-rise, high-density cluster of townhouses. The project features several different types of rather compact terraced housing, varying in height and width. The design brief of the client is typical of the preference, even in a central urban location, to build terraced housing instead of apartments.

Ground-floor parking garages for all residents are situated behind the long blocks of terraced houses along the Talmalaan. These houses have the main living space on the first floor, with a bay window overlooking the Talmalaan, and an outside terrace built over the parking area at the back. In scale and use of materials, the new red-brick buildings with special brick-bond patterns respond to the nearby interbellum Tuinwijk-West.

Architect	Dick van Gameren Architecten
Commission	2006–2007
Construction	2009–2011
Client	Blauwhoed Eurowoningen, Rotterdam; Woningcorporatie Mitros, Utrecht
Contractor	Plegt-Vos, Utrecht
Structural engineer	Pieters Bouwtechniek, Utrecht

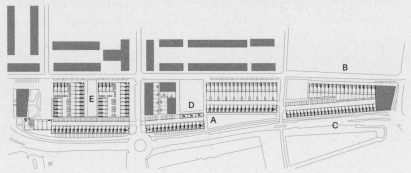

Site location plan

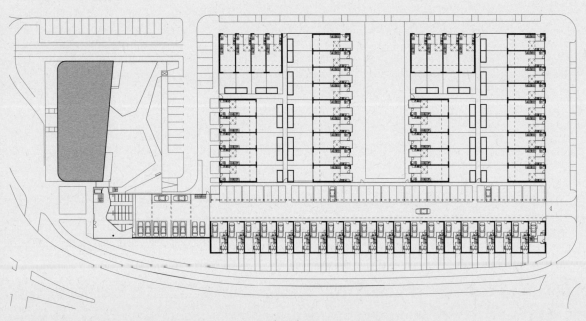

Northern block with types A, B, and C and a small five-floor apartment building

285 Terraced Housing → 6, 9, 81, 85, 140, 141

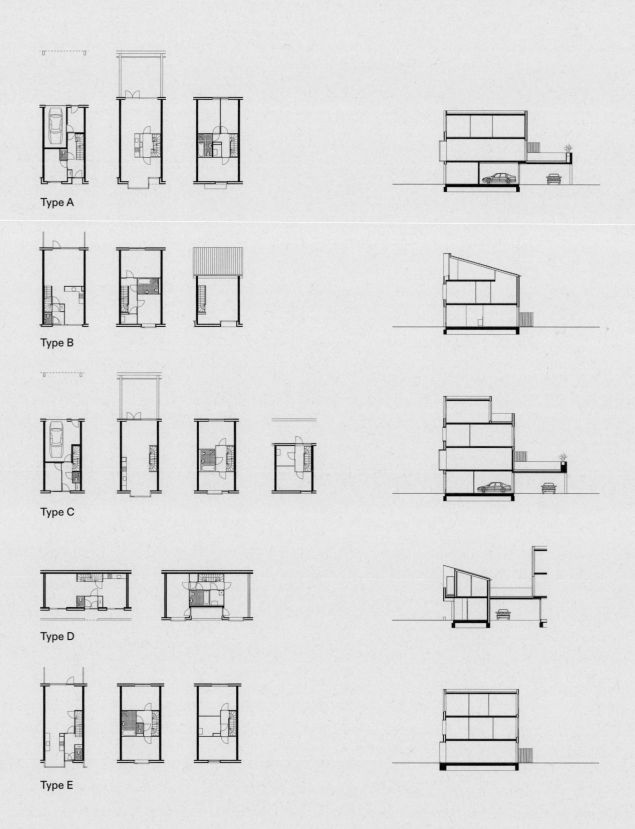

Type A

Type B

Type C

Type D

Type E

Deelplan 1, Ypenburg
The Hague

The basic principle of the master plan for 650 mostly terraced housing units is to make a clear connection between the new neighbourhood and its varied surroundings. The clusters of townhouses match the linearity of the adjoining neighbourhood, but fan out towards the large green park area at the other end, orienting as many homes as possible towards this public park and allowing the green space to penetrate far into the neighbourhood.

The tapering ridgelines of the roofs emphasise the accelerating meandering of the linear clusters towards the park, and bring unity to the different blocks, concealing a rich diversity of dwelling types. Streets are distinguished by the changing profiles, varying views to the green surrounding spaces, variation of trees, and the four different brick and roof tile colours.

Architect	De Architectengroep, Dick van Gameren
Commission	1997
Construction	1999–2002
Client	Heijmans IBC Vastgoed, Rotterdam
Contractor	Heijmans IBC Vastgoed, Rotterdam, Amersfoort
Structural engineer	Wijcon BV, Zwijndrecht

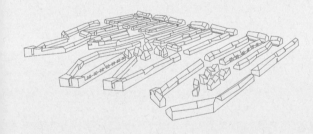

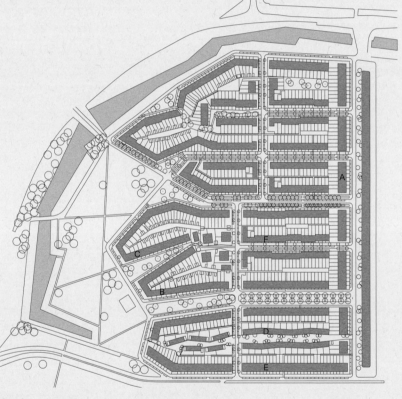

Site location plan

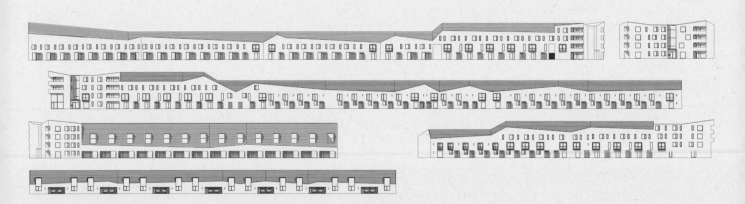

287 Terraced Housing → 34, 36, 81, 84, 144, 171, 172, 213

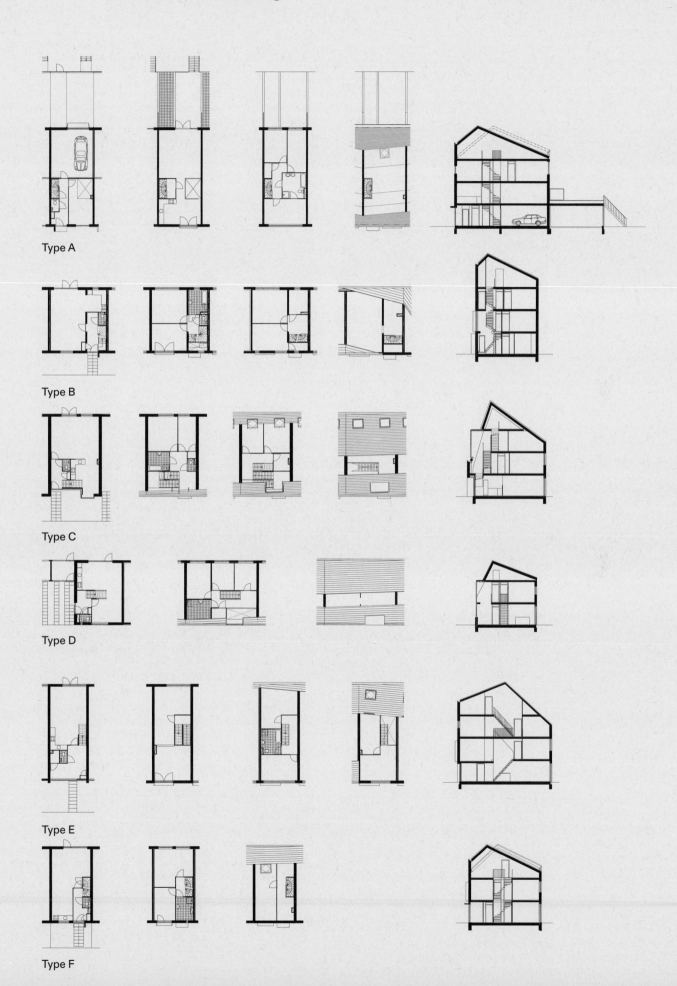

Type A

Type B

Type C

Type D

Type E

Type F

Park Oosterhout
Nijmegen

One hundred affordable rented and owner-occupied housing units were to be implemented on a Vinex housing estate full of traditional semi-detached houses north of Nijmegen. The client, a housing corporation, wanted to reduce the building costs as much as possible.

The location is divided in two by a wadi for rainwater collection. By making clusters of narrow (4 metres wide) but deep patio houses, it was possible to give each of them a view of the central green strip with the wadi, and the number of access roads could be reduced to a minimum. On the side facing the wadi, each house has a small terrace that looks onto the central green.

The interiors of the patio houses can be organised in a variety of ways, and there is potential for expansion on the roof. The clusters are quite unobtrusive because of the minimal width and height of the street fronts. This made it possible to argue convincingly that the design could ignore the prescribed aesthetics of retro 1930s pitched roofs.

Architect	De Architectengroep, Dick van Gameren
Commission	1997
Construction	2001
Client	Woningcorporatie Talis, Nijmegen
Contractor	Heijmans IBC Bouw
Structural engineer	Bouwtechnisch Adviesbureau Croes BV, Nijmegen

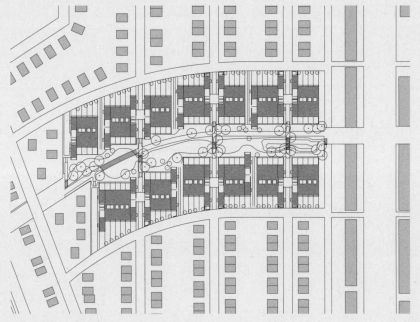

Site location plan

289 Terraced Housing → 81, 84, 166, 173, 204, 214

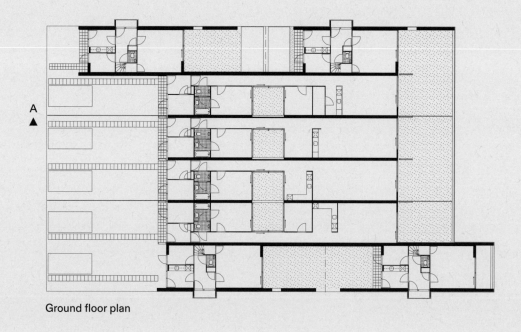
Ground floor plan

Section A

Grootstal
Nijmegen

The starting point for this project of 150 social-housing units is the design of the public space. The rigid linearity of the original municipal urban plan is modified by a series of shifts and inversions, creating a variety of green spaces in between the repetition of parallel terraced housing blocks. Perpendicular to these green areas are streets with parking zones running north–south. The car-free green spaces lead to the individual front doors, and finally end up at the large strip of parkland that runs through the larger neighbourhood as an ecological zone.

The housing itself forms a tranquil background for the green spaces. Private back gardens are enclosed by masonry walls. A concrete pavement zone, a *stoep*, creates a threshold between the front facades and the green space. Within a continuous pattern of houses 4.80 metres wide with single-pitch roofs, different dwelling types have been developed, each with its own interior spatial characteristics.

Architect	De Architectengroep, Dick van Gameren
Commission	1994
Construction	1995–1997
Client	Katholieke Woningvereniging Kolping, Nijmegen; Woningbouwvereniging Mr. C.J.A.M. ten Hagen, Nijmegen
Contractor	Heijmans IBC Bouw
Structural engineer	ABT, Velp

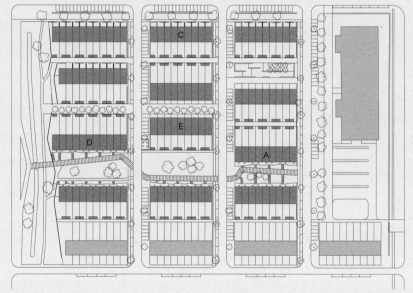

Site location plan

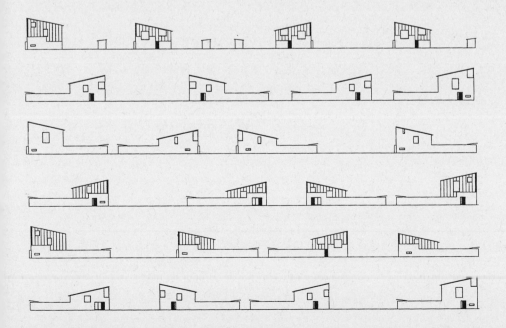

291 Terraced Housing → 81, 84, 173, 203, 214

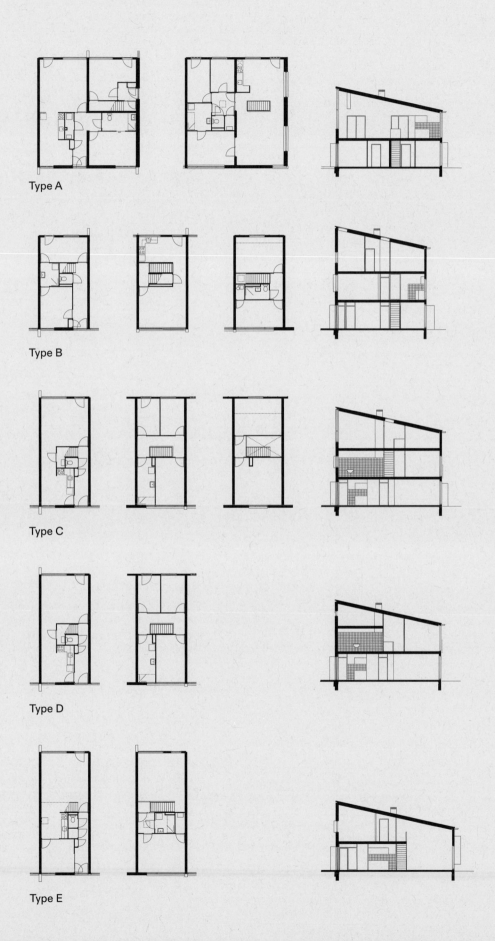

Type A

Type B

Type C

Type D

Type E

Canal House on Java Eiland
Amsterdam

This design for a canal house was built four times on both sides of two canals on Java Eiland in Amsterdam. Java Eiland is one of the former harbour piers in the Eastern Docklands that were transformed into residential areas in the 1990s. The Java master plan was designed by Sjoerd Soeters.

Within the prescribed structure of tunnels of reinforced concrete, an attempt has been made to create a maximum of spatial freedom to escape from the rigidity of this building system. This has resulted in a house in which all rooms vary in height in a complex split-level section. The rooms are connected by a continuous staircase whose position changes per level. A 6-metre-high living room is positioned on the first floor, while the top floor contains a 5-metre-high studio that receives light from the front and from the back via a roof-level patio.

Architect	De Architectengroep, Dick van Gameren
Commission	1993
Construction	2000
Client	Moes Bouwbedrijf West BV, Almere
Contractor	Moes Bouwbedrijf West BV, Almere
Structural engineer	Heijckman, Huissen

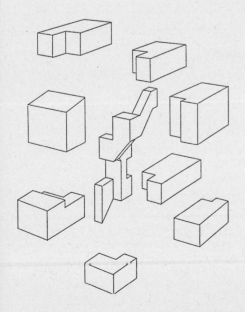

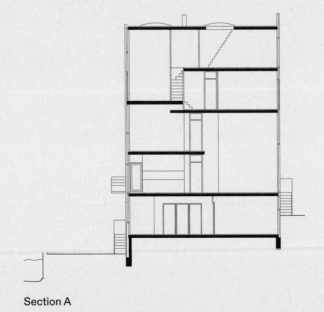

Section A

293 Individual Houses → 35, 37, 133

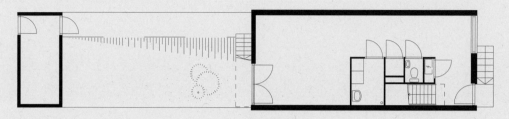
Ground floor

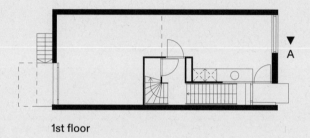
1st floor

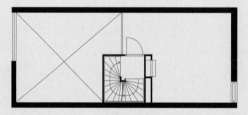
2nd floor

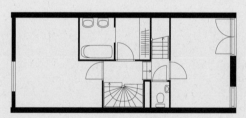
3rd floor

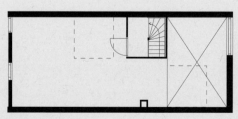
5th floor

Facade canal side

Townhouse Van Breestraat
Amsterdam

A typical townhouse in Amsterdam's Oud-Zuid neighbourhood, an upper-middle-class area dating to around 1900 west of the Concertgebouw, was in need of a drastic interior renovation. The necessity for a new concrete-pile foundation created an opportunity to add a basement level to the existing four levels above ground. The narrow and deep floors were opened up by removing partition walls. The major intervention took place in the heart of the house: the once cramped and dark stairs and internal corridors have been turned into a vertical hall full of daylight.

Architect	Dick van Gameren Architecten
Commission	2010
Construction	2012
Client	Private
Contractor	Bouwbedrijf Selie BV, Amsterdam
Structural engineer	Duyts Bouwconstructies BV, Amsterdam

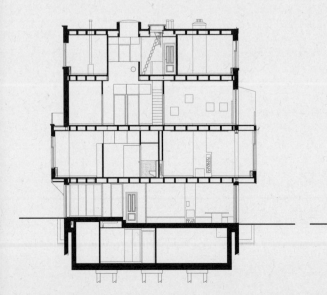

Section A

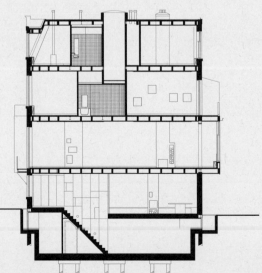

Section B

Individual Houses

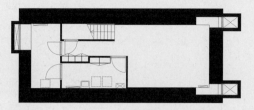
Basement

Ground floor

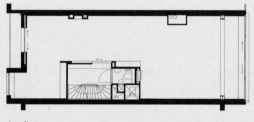
1st floor

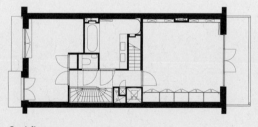
2nd floor

3rd floor

Benedenhuis Valeriusstraat
Amsterdam

In a typical Amsterdam Oud-Zuid townhouse, built around 1900, the lower part of a *boven-benedenhuis* has been redesigned. The characteristic narrow structure of the *benedenhuis*, consisting of two elongated bays separated by a supporting wall, has been maintained. The wider bay was originally divided into the main living rooms and bedrooms; the narrow bay houses the stairs connecting the three floor levels of the *benedenhuis*, the stairs to the *bovenhuis* unit, the corridors, and the kitchen. By taking out parts of the floors of the corridors, a 9-metre-high vertical hall, visually connecting all the rooms in the house, has been created in the narrow bay.

The wider bay has been left as open as possible. The bathroom on the first floor has been designed as a piece of furniture that separates the two bedrooms without marring the continuous space. All the lateral walls in the house have been removed, some replaced by glass partitions, so that the light can penetrate into the heart of the house from the front and the back.

Architect	De Architectengroep, Dick van Gameren
Commission	2001
Construction	2002
Client	Private
Contractor	Valk Bouwbedrijf, Lisserbroek
Structural engineer	Strackee BV Bouwadviesbureau, Amsterdam

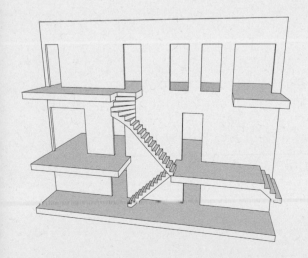

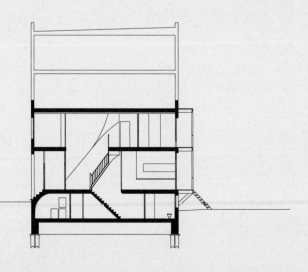

Section A

Individual Houses

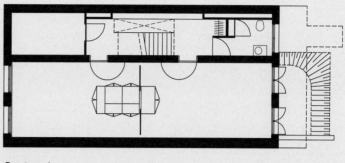

Souterrain

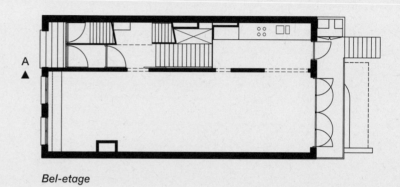

Bel-etage

1st floor

Former Corner Shop on Dufaystraat
Amsterdam

The house is a conversion of a former shop with an apartment at the back in the Oud-Zuid district of Amsterdam. It is situated on a typical corner plot, cut off at a 45-degree angle, resulting in a triangular floor plan. The old shop floor was located at street level, with the private side and back spaces on a higher level, 1 metre above the street.

The shop floor has been removed to create a large living hall that connects the half-sunken basement with the higher-level living spaces. A staircase with a landing at the front door on the street level connects the kitchen and bedroom in the basement with the other living spaces above.

Architect	Dick van Gameren Architecten
Commission	2005
Construction	2007
Client	Private
Contractor	Woonverrijking BV
Construction engineers	Pensera Ingenieursbureau, Amsterdam

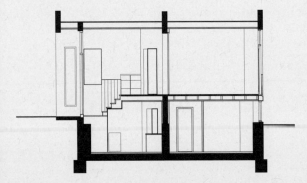

Section A

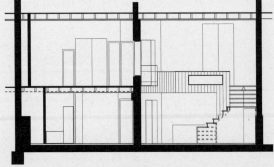

Section B

Individual Houses

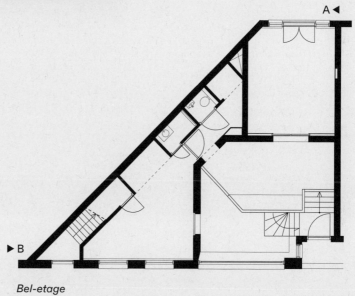

Bel-etage

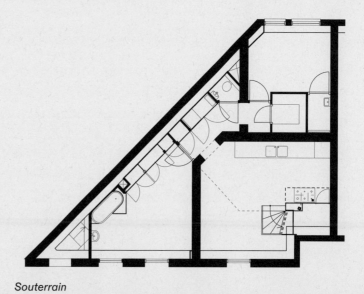

Souterrain

Scheepstimmermanstraat
Amsterdam

The house with studio on the Scheepstimmermanstraat is one of sixty individually developed and designed townhouses on Borneo Eiland, part of the regeneration project of the Eastern Docklands of Amsterdam. The narrow plot is wedged between its two neighbours, facing a street and backing onto a former dock. Within a mere 3.80-metre width, a large programme has been achieved with a low budget: a family house, a studio, and a parking space for one car that had to be incorporated inside the building envelope. The maximum permitted volume was needed to create enough floor area for all the functions required by the client's brief. The only empty space in the volume consists of two light wells – one with a ground surface area of 1 by 1 metres, the other with a ground surface area of 2 by 2 metres – to bring daylight into the centre of the 16-metre-deep interior. Two independent circulation systems have been created inside the volume. Continuous straight flights of stairs lead from the street to the studio on the top floor. The second route is a combination of a ramp, a spiral staircase, and a straight staircase that connect the private living spaces distributed over the three lower floors.

Architect	De Architectengroep, Dick van Gameren
Commission	1996
Construction	1999
Client	Private
Contractor	Bouwbedrijf M.J. de Nijs en Zonen BV, Warmenhuizen
Structural engineer	D3BN, Amsterdam

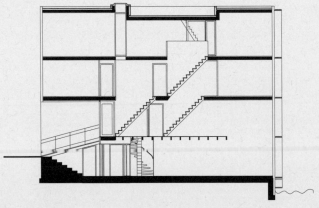

Section A

301 Individual Houses → 35, 37, 134, 135, 166

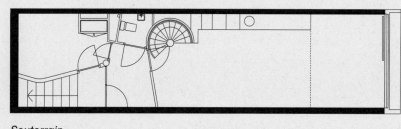

A

Souterrain

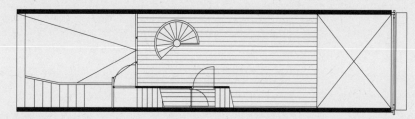

Bel-etage

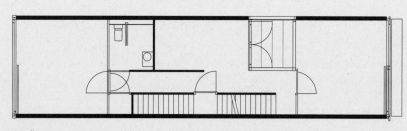

1st floor

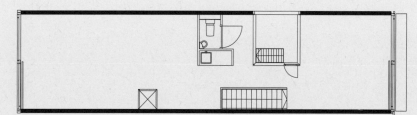

2nd floor

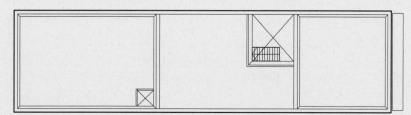

Roof

Villa 4.0
Naarden

A modest 1967 bungalow on a hexagonal ground plan had been modified and enlarged through the years to make an increasingly inward-looking house. The expanding wings were steadily enclosing the heart of the house, which contains the entrance hall and the living and dining rooms. Contact between the main living spaces and the surrounding garden was largely lost. The original 1960s detailing and material form were consistently applied during all the interventions, resulting in a house that was thoroughly outdated and of a poor technical quality.

The principal ideas of the new intervention were to create a house that is sustainable and to bring back a relationship between the interior and the outside landscape. The first step was to preserve as much as possible of the existing house, limiting both the amount of waste and the necessity of new materials. Outer walls and roofs were modernised by adding insulation; new and larger window frames replaced the existing ones. The walls of the central section were removed to create a new spatial heart for the house: a living hall giving access to all other areas. The physical bond between house and landscape has been consolidated by attaching an all-glass pavilion to the living hall that reaches out to the brook, creating a typical butterfly plan that embraces the gardens on all sides.

Three large skylights make a new roof for the central living hall, turning the original house's hexagonal plan into a three-dimensional sculpture. The skylights are an essential part of the carefully designed system of natural ventilation, the basis for the concept of keeping the house comfortable with minimal energy usage. A floor heating/cooling system is fed by an underground thermal storage unit. Extra heat sources in winter are a large wood burner in the kitchen and the new glass pavilion that accumulates warmth on sunny days. A solar heat collector on the roof provides warm water. Wastewater is purified and reused on site.

Design team	Dick van Gameren Architecten in collaboration with IDing Interior Design and Michael van Gessel Landscape
Design	2008–2009
Construction	2010–2011
Client	Private
Contractor	Bouwbedrijf L. Post en Zonen, Urk
Structural engineer	Breed Integrated Design, Den Haag

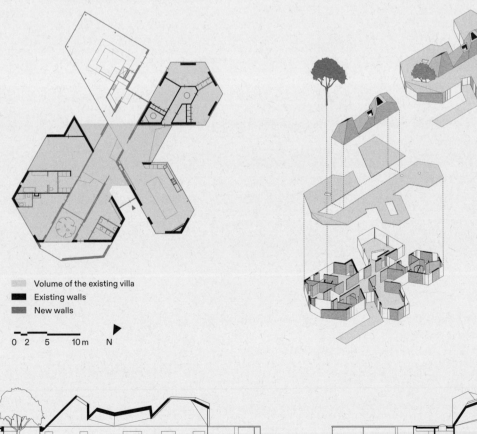

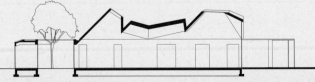

Section A

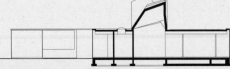

Section B

303 Individual Houses → 92, 94, 166, 167, 180, 190, 191, 200, 215

Floor plan

Achterhuis Oude Delft
Delft

At the back of a canal house on the Oude Delft, the main canal of Delft's well-preserved historic centre, a new garden-facing house, an *achterhuis*, was built, replacing a ruinous and unsalvageable nineteenth-century structure. Within the confines of the envelope of the former house, a new wooden structure was erected with a central 4-metre-high living hall, connected to lower side wings spreading out into the garden. A new staircase hall acts as an intermediary between the old front and the new back of the house. The old brick garden walls were preserved and connected to the new structure, creating a walled inner-city garden.

Architect	Dick van Gameren, Annenies Kraaij
Design	2017
Construction	2018
Client	Private
Contractor	Stramann Bouw BV, Waddinxveen
Structural engineer	LVD Ingenieurs BV, Rotterdam

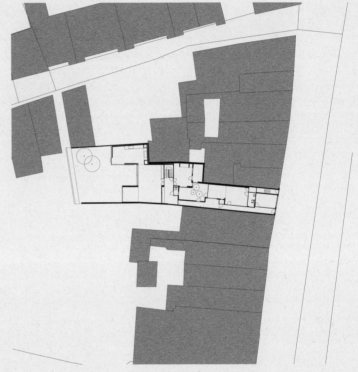

Site location plan

Section A

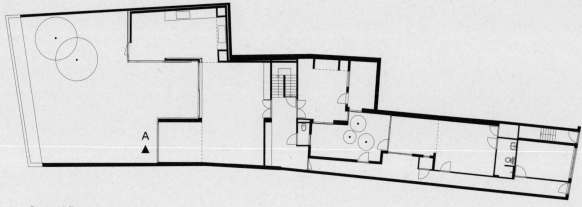
Ground floor

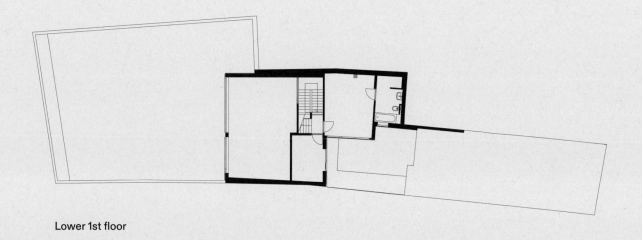
Lower 1st floor

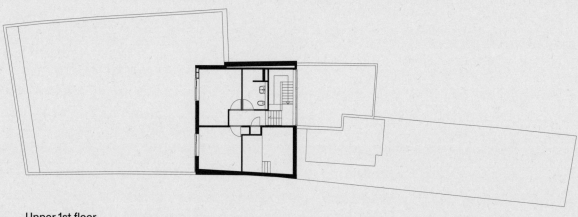
Upper 1st floor

House on the Lake
Lechlade, Gloucestershire, United Kingdom

The project is situated in a new development of free-standing villas around a series of lakes on the site of a former stone quarry in the Cotswolds, west of Oxford. The house stands on the edge of the water with wide views over the lake. The guiding design principle was to build a house that combines transparency with sustainability, forging a strong relationship between the house and the surrounding landscape.

The house is designed from the inside to the outside, creating uninterrupted views to nature outside, and at the same time providing shelter and intimacy by a careful landscaping of the area between the house and the access road.

In the heart of the house, a vertical open space connects all levels and creates a series of diagonal and vertical sight lines. The central void brings ample daylight into the sunken basement and connects the interior to the outside roof terrace. From the roof terrace one can enjoy wide panoramic views, as if floating quietly over the expanse of the lake.

Design and engineering team	Mecanoo, Arquitectura y Ordenación Urbana S.L. AOU SL, Boheme Development S.L.
Design	2015–2016
Construction	2016–2018
Client	Private

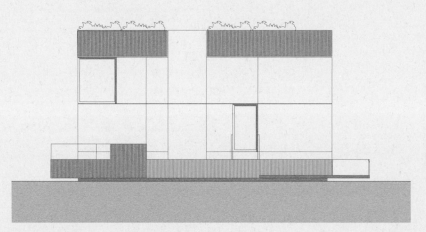

Entrance facade

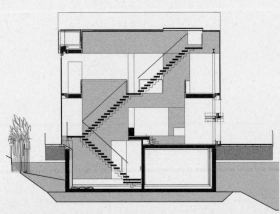

Section A

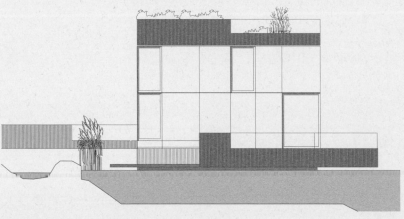

South facade

307 Individual Houses → 92, 95, 181, 199, 222

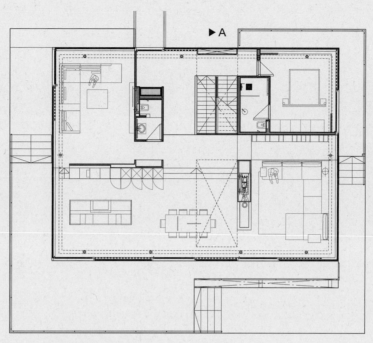

Ground floor

1st floor

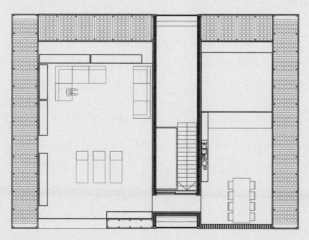

Roof

Residence and Staff Houses
Addis Ababa, Ethiopia

Architect	De Architectengroep, Dick van Gameren, and Bjarne Mastenbroek
Design	1998–2000
Construction	2002–2005
Client	Dutch Ministry of Foreign Affairs
Contractor	Elmi Olindo & CO, PLC, Addis Ababa
Structural engineer	Ove Arup & Partners, London, and ME Engineering, Addis Ababa
Local architect	Rahel Shawl, Raas Architects, Addis Ababa

The theme of uniting buildings with the surrounding landscape formed the starting point for the design of the Netherlands Embassy in Addis Ababa, capital city of Ethiopia. Located in the western part of the city, the site comprises 5 hectares of mostly endemic forest that descends steeply into a valley. A second guiding principle was the demand to create optimal privacy between the different buildings in the compound as required by the brief: a chancery, a residence for the ambassador, a second residence for the deputy ambassador, and three staff houses.

Situated centrally on the site is an elongated horizontal volume that houses the chancery and ambassador's residence. The new houses for staff are placed as terraces against the perimeter wall of the compound, all three with uninterrupted views of the landscape. An existing historic villa in the corner furthest from the compound's entrance gate is the deputy ambassador's residence and has been renovated and enlarged.

The two-storey residence of the ambassador comprises formal reception areas above and private spaces below, all connected via a series of voids and patios. Thanks to the height difference on the site, both floors can be accessed from ground level, which enables the spaces to be used independently.

Three concealed staircases connect the floors internally. The elongated volume evokes a traditional Ethiopian rock-hewn church carved from the landscape. The facades are made of concrete, cast in situ in rough wooden formwork, and pigmented in the red colour of the site's earth. The roof is designed as a shallow pond that fills itself during the rainy season, a subtle reference to water landscapes in the Netherlands.

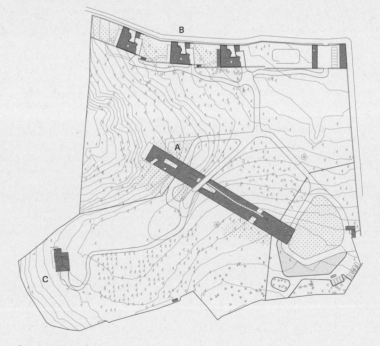

Site location plan

309 Individual Houses

→ 92, 95, 168, 169, 179, 194, 195, 201, 206, 207, 223

A: Residence

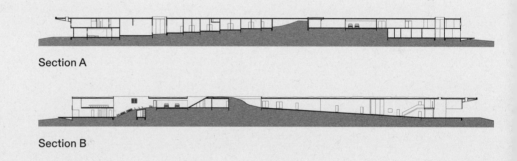

Section A

Section B

Lower level

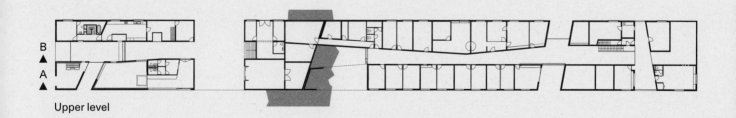

Upper level

Roof

310 D40 Residence and Staff Houses
Addis Ababa, Ethiopia

B: Staff houses

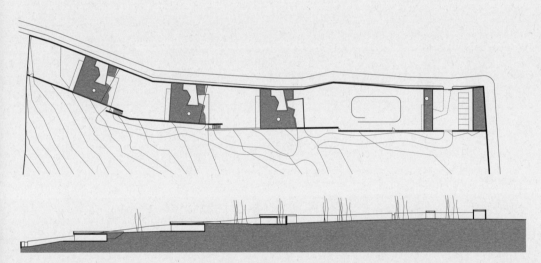

Cluster & section

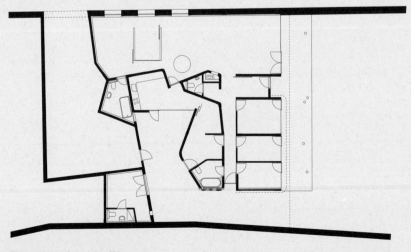

Floor plan of one staff house

311　Individual Houses

C: Deputy ambassador's house

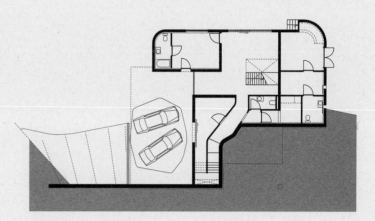

Lower garden level

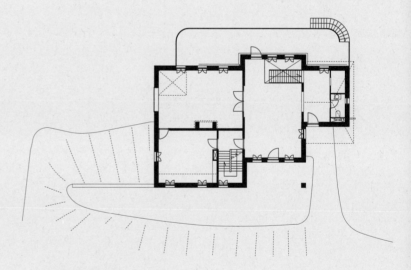

Ground floor

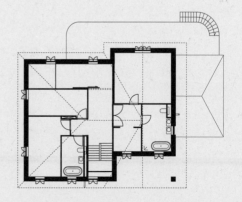

1st floor

Typological Studies for the Pampusbuurt, IJburg Strandeiland, Amsterdam

→ 125, 127, 145, 155

Design	Mecanoo Architecten
Commission	2018
Completion	2019–2020
Client	IJburg Atelier, Dienst Ruimte en Duurzaamheid, Gemeente Amsterdam

The municipal IJburg Atelier, responsible for the planning and design of the next phase of the Amsterdam IJburg development, asked for a typological study and a series of test designs for the new housing of the Pampusbuurt, part of Strandeiland, the latest addition to the new residential archipelago east of Amsterdam. The guiding ambition is to turn Strandeiland into a 'nature-inclusive', emission-free, and energy-generating sustainable neighbourhood.

The 150-hectare Strandeiland will be one of the largest residential neighbourhoods in Amsterdam and consists of two main parts that are separated by an inland body of water. The two parts, Pampusbuurt (north) and Muiderbuurt (south), will have distinct characters. The IJburg Atelier developed different urban planning and architectural strategies for each part.

The Pampusbuurt is characterised by streets that run east–west in straight lines and will have a more urban identity; the Muiderbuurt displays a more organic pattern and will have a more suburban character.

In the Pampusbuurt 5,000 dwelling units will be built, along with a number of schools, a commercial centre, and a large public beach. Strategies have been developed to define a design-and-construction process leading to a strong mix of housing types in order to create a neighbourhood where all people of Amsterdam, in all stages of life, can live together and feel at home. Studies on density, parcellation, architectural articulation, and variation have resulted in a series of rules and guidelines that will steer the design of the individual housing projects in the coming years.

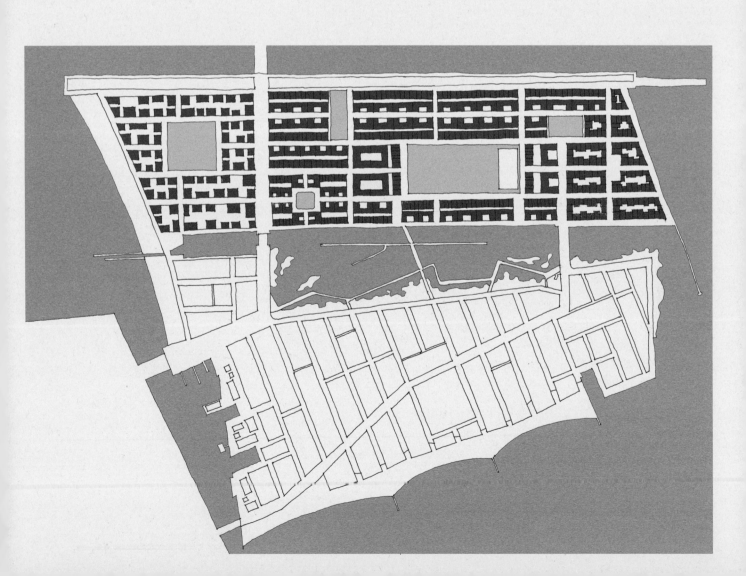

Maria Hilf Master Plan
Mönchengladbach, Germany

Design	Mecanoo Architecten
Commission	2017
Completion	2017
Client	City of Mönchengladbach

A study for the redevelopment of the Maria Hilf Hospital grounds in Monchengladbach, a German city near the Dutch border, was made on-site in a participatory process, involving the local citizens and the municipal council and government.

The site is on a hilltop north of the city centre. The project proposes to retain, as much as possible, the buildings of the former hospital. With new additions, the buildings will be transformed into a continuous structure around connected courtyards with apartments and collective workspaces and living spaces. Condensing the built fabric in this close-knit structure allows for the creation of a large public terrace in front of the complex, affording views towards the city. Ramps and stairs lead from the platform down to the surrounding neighbourhoods and the city centre.

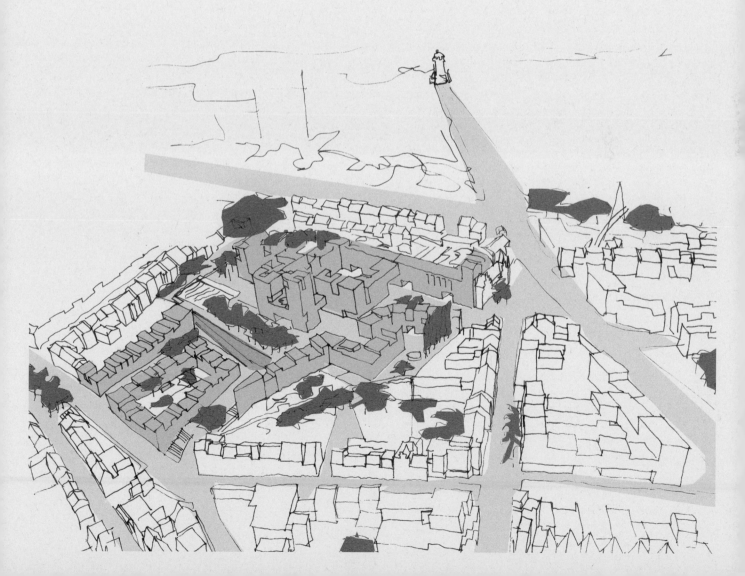

Lo Recabarren Master Plan
Santiago de Chile, Chile

Design	Mecanoo Architecten
Design	2014–2015
Realisation	2017–ongoing
Client	Tánica Group, Vitacura, Chile

The master plan for Lo Recabarren, north-east of the city centre of Santiago, will guide a mixed commercial and residential development on the site of a former plantation, now a beautiful natural area close to the Mapocho river, with the Andes foothills close by and the snow-capped Andes mountains in the distance.

The scheme makes use of existing characteristics, including views, landscape features, and buildings, to define the programming and the overall spatial layout. The master plan divides the land into sectors for living, working, and leisure. Commercial areas are located predominantly in the south; residential quarters are more prominent further north.

The master plan has in the centre a publicly accessible urban park, exceptional for this type of private development. The park is surrounded by a variety of housing types: apartment towers, smaller scale *palazzinas*, terraced houses, and free-standing villas. *Pircas*, crude masonry walls of river stones, are used to define the borders between public and private areas.

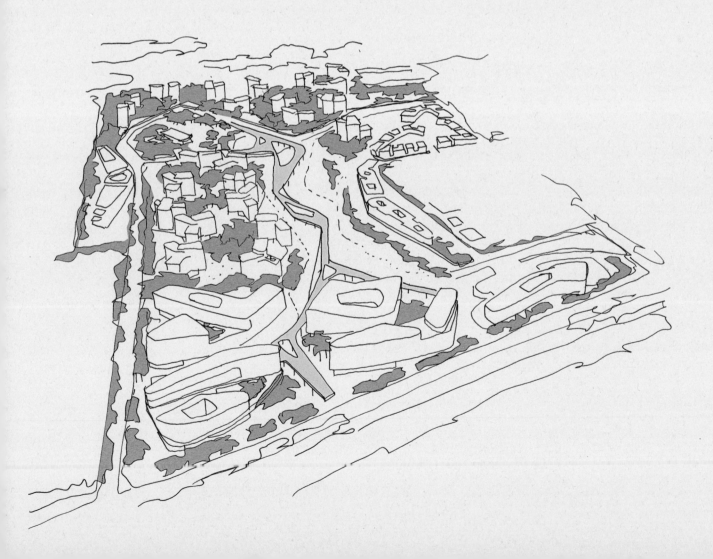

Eleven Facades

Eleven Facades

Detailed sections of ten projects together show the Dutch construction industry's most used building methods for housing projects. Since the introduction of the cavity wall as a principle for facade construction at the end of the 1920s, the outer shell of housing has been reduced to a cladding that can take many forms. As a counterpoint, the facade section of the Dutch ambassador's residence in Addis Ababa (D40) is added as an eleventh principle.

Brick

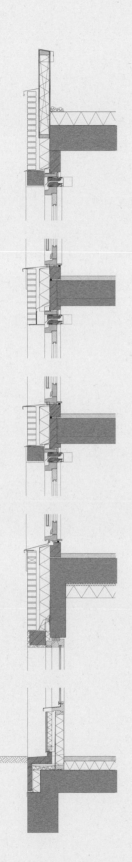

→ D01

While the Amsterdam School architects were accused of being shallow 20-centimetre-brick artists (the length of one brick determined the depth of a solid brick facade), the change to cavity walls further reduced the expressive possibilities of the facade to 10 centimetres. This 10-centimetre-thick brick shell is still the dominant facade option in Dutch housing construction, though it is being gradually replaced now with other, newer methods as the demands for thermal insulation and circularity of building materials increase.

The details of the Haarlemmerplein (D01) project and the Funenpark *palazzina* show the customary way of constructing brick facades. Steel profile supports or prefab concrete lintels clad with brick strips carry and connect the brick facade to the concrete load-bearing structure of the building.

Brick and Glass Facades

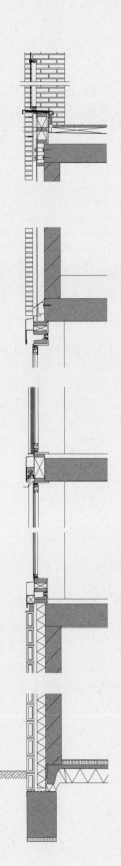

→ D03

The many masonry bond patterns possible in a solid brick facade have been reduced with only 10 centimetres of cladding. However, variations have been explored in the vertical bonds of the Funenpark building (D03), and in the vertical and horizontal relief patterns of projects such as the Talmalaan (D28) and Leaf Street (D25).

Stone

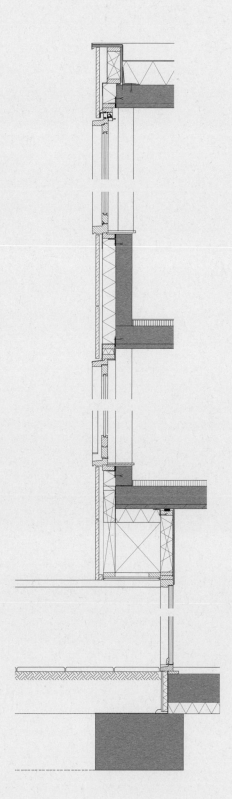

→ D15

An alternative to the brick skin is a cladding of stone. The Huizen project (D15) is an example of this. Stone cladding on stainless steel anchors makes lintels and other elements necessary to carry the load of a brick facade redundant. As stone cannot be found in the Netherlands, however, it is always necessary to import it.

Prefab Concrete

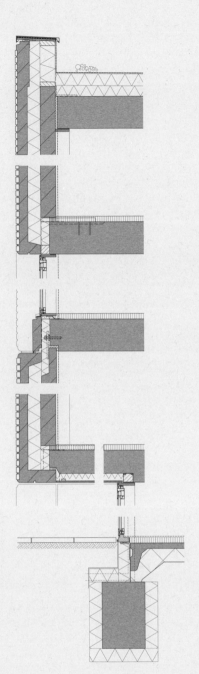

→ D07

Prefabricated concrete facade panels have been in use in housing construction since the start of the post-war reconstruction era. The repetitive and monotonous facades that were the result of the application of prefabricated methods in this period were not much liked, and still today are disparaged by many as 'Eastern Bloc' architecture, referring to the panel systems of the former Soviet Union and its satellite states. Prefabricated systems still have a number of advantages, such as a shorter period of on-site construction and better control of the (air-tight) connection between window frames and facade. The Noordstrook project (D07), using prefabricated systems to shorten the building time, tried to avoid the repetitive character of a prefab facade by shifting the position of the 6-metre-tall elements in such a way that the vertical joints are not in line with one another. The concrete elements were also decorated with brick strips in different colours and patterns to make the repetitive character even less apparent.

Glass Verandas

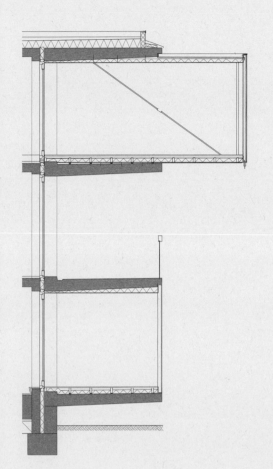

→ D05

Glass verandas have been applied in several projects to add variety and expression to the facade, and to create protected outside spaces and winter gardens. The apartments of the Borneo Eiland project (D05) have large glass verandas that cantilever from the prefab concrete balconies which run along the full length of the end facades. Other examples can be found on the facades of the tower at Zuiveringspark (D04) and of the Karspeldreef project (D13).

Metal Cladding

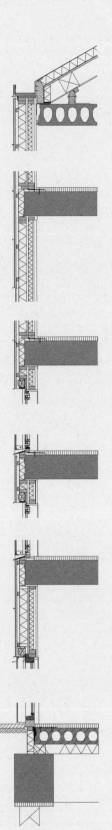

→ D14

Metal is another facade cladding option that, like stone cladding, avoids lintels, but has the extra advantage of adding very little weight to the building structure. The social housing in Purmerend (D14) has a dark-bronze-coloured metal cladding that wraps itself around the sculptural composition of a number of parallel linear volumes. The middle floors of the Funenpark *palazzina* (D03) have a metal facade as well; aluminium bands are mounted on all sides of the building with continuous aluminium window frames from floor to ceiling in between.

Existing Walls: Concrete

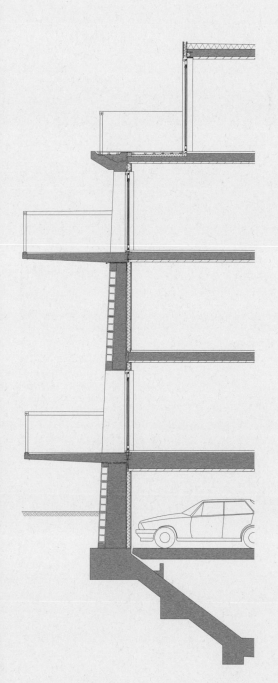

The apartments in the Trommel, the preserved water tank of the Zuiveringspark project (D04), have a facade completely composed of wooden window- and door-frames. The existing heavily steel-reinforced concrete shell serves as a foundation and provides stability to the inserted basic steel structure.

Existing Walls: Steel and Brick

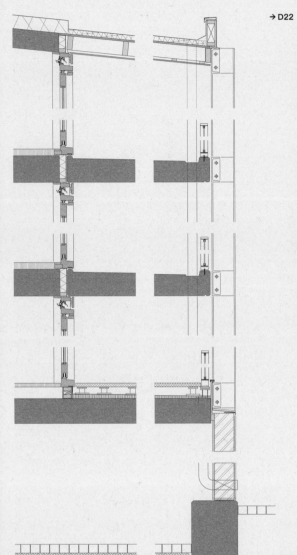

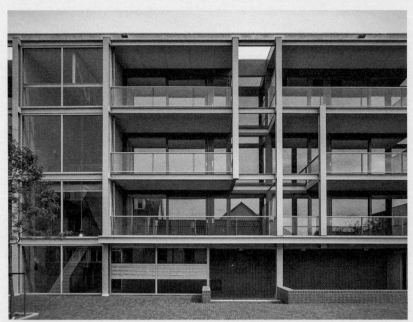

→ D22

Like the Trommel, the Buigerij project (D22) reuses the outer walls of the existing industrial structure as a screen between the new apartments and their surroundings. The existing building's structure of a steel frame with brick infill was repeated in the new south facade with balconies for the dwelling units. A similar structure of steel and brick infill was used in the two long street and quay facades of the Borneo Eiland building (D05), as a reference to the industrial past of the former docklands.

Plasterwork

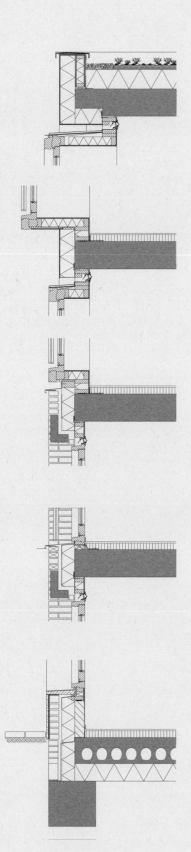

→ D17

Today's regulations regarding thermal insulation, as mentioned before, are now leading to other options and might make the 10-centimetre-thick brick skin of the cavity wall facades a thing of the past. Insulation is getting bigger and makes the structure to carry the brick skin more complex. The thermal insulation systems on the side and back facades of the Langebrug student housing (D17) are covered by a thin layer of mineral plasterwork. The facades of the Haarlemmerplein courtyards (D01) show a similar solution.

Wood

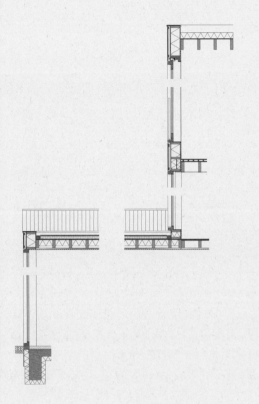

→ D38

Like thermal insulation, other aspects have become increasingly important, including carbon dioxide reduction during the building process, meaning that circular, renewable, and reusable building materials will likely take over from the still-dominant use of concrete. Wood appears to be a viable alternative. The *achterhuis* in Delft (D38) has both a wooden structure with a very thick layer of insulation and a wooden cladding.

Bringing these options to a larger scale in housing production is a clear challenge for the future.

In situ Concrete

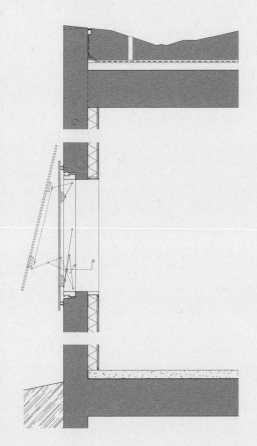

→ D40

In contrast with Dutch building practices and rules, in Ethiopia both climate and building regulations allow for an in situ concrete design that combines cladding and structure in one continuous monolithic system. The rough texture of the concrete facades is the result of formwork made by hand from irregular wooden boarding. A red pigment was added to give the concrete the colour of the site's soil. The openable windows are connected to a steel frame that is mounted on the concrete. This detail allows for a large tolerance between the precise window frame and the less accurate dimensions of the opening in the concrete wall.

Appendix

Glossary

Achterhuis
Literally the backhouse, the garden-facing part of the typical historic long and narrow Dutch townhouse. It is separated from the part facing the street, *het voorhuis*, by a small courtyard and connected to it via an internal corridor.

Bel-etage
The main level of a townhouse, raised above street level, on top of a half-sunken *souterrain* level, probably derived from the French *belle étage*.

Boven-benedenwoningen
Term used to describe the typology of two dwellings positioned on top of one another. The lower dwelling is the *benedenwoning*, the upper dwelling the *bovenwoning*. Both are directly accessed from the street. In larger cities, both dwellings are often maisonettes – units with two or three levels. In smaller cities one can find variations with a ground-floor unit of only one level, crowned by one or two maisonettes.

Doorzonwoning
Literally a sun-pierced dwelling. Term to indicate the ubiquitous post-war terraced house type with one main living room stretching uninterrupted from the front to the back of the house.

Drive-in woning
Term mostly used for *rijtjeshuizen*, or terraced housing, with an interior garage accessible from the front.

Eengezinswoning/eengezinshuis
Literally a one-family dwelling or house. Used mostly for terraced houses.

Etagehuis
The common term for an apartment building until approximately 1940.

Etagewoning
The common term for an individual apartment until approximately 1940. After the Second World War the term flat became more common. Apartment has only become the dominant term since the 1980s.

Flat
Term used to indicate an apartment building, or a single unit of one storey in such a building.

Galerijflat
An apartment building with an access system of open galleries or access decks. Also used for a single unit in such an apartment building.

Groeiwoning
Literally a growing house. Term from the post-war period for an incremental house.

Landhuis
A free-standing house in a rural or suburban environment, also often referred to as a villa.

Maisonnette
A duplex or maisonette unit; a dwelling of more than one storey, part of a larger apartment building. See *boven-benedenwoningen*.

Om en om woningen
Terraced houses with alternating front and rear facades. Introduced to avoid continuous closed-off rear facades facing a public space.

Portiekflat
An apartment building with a vertical access system of stairs that on each floor provide access to two dwellings via an internal hallway. Also used for a single unit in such an apartment building.

Rijtjeshuis/rijtjeswoning
A terraced house.

Souterrain
Half-sunken lower level of townhouses, mostly found in houses dating from between the seventeenth and nineteenth centuries. The *souterrain* used to hold service and storage spaces. By making it only half sunken, problems with the high groundwater levels in Dutch cities could be avoided.

Stadshuis
Townhouse.

Stoep
The privately owned and maintained strip of pavement, 1 to 2 metres wide, between a house and the public street.

Tuindorp/Tuinstad
Garden village, garden city. The difference between the two has never clearly been defined, and both terms are used in identical situations.

Vinex wijk
Typical, mostly suburban housing neighbourhoods built on the periphery of larger cities in the 1990s and 2000s. The name Vinex is derived from the acronym used for the national programme to build these new residential extension areas.

Voorhuis
Literally the front house, the street-facing part of the typical historic long and narrow Dutch townhouse, see also *achterhuis*.

Wilde Wonen
Wild dwelling or wild living, a term introduced in the 1990s to advocate self-built houses without the involvement of authorities, housing corporations, and project developers.

Winkelwoning
Literally a shop dwelling; a house or apartment with a street-facing commercial space.

Wisselbeuk
The structural bay in between two *portiekflats*, containing the access stairs and an extra bedroom for one of the units.

Woningcorporatie/woningbouwvereniging
Housing corporation or housing association. In the Dutch context, these are non-profit institutions that build, own, and maintain low-cost rental housing. Their housing stock can only be allocated to those with an income below a certain limit. This affordable rental housing is known as *sociale woningbouw*, or social housing.

Wooneenheid
Residential unit or visual unit; term introduced by Bakema and others to indicate a cluster of differentiated apartment buildings around a collective green space. The *wooneenheid* was the building block of many new residential neighbourhoods in the post-war period, for example in Amsterdam's Western Garden Cities and in the village of Nagele.

Woonerf
Literally living yard. The 1960s saw the introduction of the idea of structuring (mostly) terraced houses in often irregular clusters around informal streets and squares. In Dutch the resulting neighbourhoods are called by the slightly derogatory term *bloemkoolwijken* (cauliflower neighbourhoods). Also used as a term for the traffic structure developed for these neighbourhoods, based on the idea of a space where cars are only allowed at low speed as the streets serve as collective space for the residents and as play areas for children.

Woonwand
Literally a dwelling wall, a long linear housing block, often designed to form a protective wall between a major road or railway line and a housing neighbourhood.

Bibliography

Amsterdamsche Woningraad, ed. (1913) *De Verbetering der Volkshuisvesting te Amsterdam*. Amsterdam.

Amsterdamsche Woningbouwvereenigingen, ed. (1938) *Amsterdam Volkshuisvesting*. Amsterdam.

Artaria, P. (1947) *Ferien- und Landhäuser/ Weekend- and Country-Houses*. Erlenbach-Zürich: Verlag für Architektur.

Backström, S. and S. Ålund. (1950) *Fyrtiotalets Svenska Bostad*. Stockholm: Tidskriften Byggmästaren.

Baillie Scott, M. H. (1906) *Houses and Gardens*. London: George Newnes Ltd.

Baillie Scott, M. H. (1910) *Garden Suburbs; Town Planning and Modern Architecture*. London: T. Fisher Unwin.

Bakema, J. B. (1960–1961) 'Een huis in Spangen voor 270 families', *Forum, orgaan van het genootschap Architectura et Amicitia*, XV(5).

Bakema, J. B. (1962) 'De anonieme opdrachtgever', *Forum, orgaan van het genootschap Architectura et Amicitia*, XVI(2).

Bakema, J. B. (1964) 'Naar een Samenlevingsarchitectuur'. Introductory speech, Technische Hogeschool te Delft.

Bakema, J. B. (1964) *Van Stoel tot Stad; Een verhaal over mensen en ruimte*. Zeist: Uitgeversmaatschappij W. de Haan N. V.

Bakema, J. B. (1965) 'Stad op Pampus', *Forum, orgaan van het genootschap Architectura et Amicitia*, XIX(3).

Barzilay, M., R. Ferwerda and A. Blom. (2020) *Experimentele woningbouw in Nederland 1968-1980; 64 gerealiseerde woonbeloften*. Rotterdam: Nai010 Publishers.

Bazel, K. P. C. de. (1919) 'Onze tijd en het werk van M.de Klerk', *Wendingen, maandblad voor bouwen en sieren van Architectura et Amicitia*, 2(2).

Behrens, P. and H. de Fries. (1918) *Vom sparsamen Bauen. Ein Beitrag zur Siedlungsfrage*. Berlin: Verlag der Bauwelt.

Berlage, Dr. H. P. (1918) *Normalisatie in Woningbouw*. Rotterdam: W. L. & J. Brusse's Uitgevers-Maatschappij.

Berlage, Dr. H. P. (1922) *Studies over Bouwkunst, Stijl en Samenleving*. Rotterdam: W. L. & J. Brusse's Uitgevers-Maatschappij.

Berlage, Dr. H. P., W. M. Dudok, Ir. J. Gratama, Ir. A. R. Hulshoff, H. van der Kloot Meijburg, J. F. Staal and J. Luthman. (1933–1935) *Moderne Bouwkunst in Nederland, No 2 De Volkswoning; Hoogbouw, No 3 De Volkswoning; Laagbouw, No 4 De Middenstandswoning als Etage-huis en Flat, No 5 De Middenstandswoning; het Huis voor één Gezin*. Rotterdam: W. L. & J.Brusse N. V.

Berlage, Dr. H. P., Ing. A. Keppler, W. Kromhout and J. Wils. (1921) *Arbeiderswoningen in Nederland; Vijftig met rijkssteun, onder leiding van architecten uitgevoerde plannen, met de financieele gegevens*. Rotterdam: W. L. & J. Brusse's Uitgevers-Maatschappij.

Bernoulli, H. (1946) *Die Stadt und ihr Boden*. Erlenbach-Zürich: Verlag für Architektur.

Bock, M., S. Johanisse and V. Stissi. (1997) *Michel de Klerk, Bouwmeester en tekenaar van de Amsterdamse School 1884–1923*. Rotterdam: NAI Publishers.

Boeken, Ir. A. (1936) *Architectuur*. Amsterdam: Van Holkema en Warendorf N. V.

Bolton, A. T. (1922) *The Architecture of Robert & James Adam (1758–1794)*. London: Country Life Ltd.

Bosma, K., D. van Hoogstraten and M. Vos. (2000) *Housing for the Millions; John Habraken and the SAR (1960–2000)*. Rotterdam: NAI Publishers.

Brown, Theodore M. *The Work of G. Rietveld, Architect*. Utrecht: A.W. Bruna & Zoon, 1958.

Butler, A. S. G. *The Architecture of Sir Edwin Lutyens, Volume 1 Country Houses*. London, Country Life Ltd., 1950.

Cantacuzino, Sherban. (August 1973) 'Barbican built', *Architectural Review*, CLIV(918).

Chadwick, P. and B. Weaver, eds. (2019) *The Town of Tomorrow. 50 Years of Thamesmead*. London: Here Press.

Chermayeff, S. and C. Alexander. (1966) *Community and Privacy. Toward a New Architecture of Humanism*. Harmondsworth: Penguin Books Ltd.

City of London, Court of Common Council, Chamberlin, Powell and Bon, eds. (1959) *Barbican Redevelopment 1959, Report to the Court of Common Council of the Corporation of the City of London on residential development within the Barbican area, prepared on the instructions of the Barbican Committee by Chamberlin, Powell & Bon, Architects*. London.

Claus, F., F. van Dongen and T. Schaap. (2001) *IJburg Haveneiland en Rieteilanden*. Rotterdam: 010 Publishers.

Colenbrander, B. (2005) *Frans van Gool. Leven en werk*. Rotterdam: NAi Publishers.

Council for Research on Housing Construction, ed. (1934) *Slum Clearance and Rehousing*. London: P.S. Kings & Son Ltd.

Duiker, Ir. J. (1930) *Hoogbouw*. Rotterdam: W.L. & Brusse's uitgeversmaatschappij N. V.

Eberstadt, Prof. dr. R. (1914) *Städtebau und Wohnungswesen in Holland*. Jena: Verlag von Gustav Fischer.

Fraenkel, F. F. (1976) 'Het Plan Amsterdam-Zuid van H.P. Berlage', dissertation. Utrecht: Rijksuniversiteit Utrecht.

Feddes, F. (2012) *1000 jaar Amsterdam; Ruimtelijke geschiedenis van een wonderbaarlijke stad*. Bussum: Uitgeverij THOTH.

Feenstra, G. (1920) *Tuinsteden en Volkshuisvesting in Nederland en Buitenland*. Amsterdam: N. V. Uitgevers-Maatschappij v/h Van Mantgem & De Does.

Gameren, D. van, D. van den Heuvel, H. Mooij, P. van der Putt, O. Klijn and F. van Andel. (2010) *The Residential Floorplan. Delft Architectural Studies on Housing*. Rotterdam: NAi Publishers.

Gameren, D. van, D. van den Heuvel, H. Mooij, P. van der Putt, O. Klijn and F. van Andel. (2010) *The 'Woonerf' Today. Delft Architectural Studies on Housing*. Rotterdam: NAi Publishers.

Gameren, D. van, D. van den Heuvel, H. Mooij, P. van der Putt, O. Klijn and F. van Andel. (2011) *The Urban Enclave. Delft Architectural Studies on Housing*. Rotterdam: NAi Publishers.

Gameren, D. van, D. van den Heuvel, H. Mooij, P. van der Putt, O. Klijn and F. van Andel. (2012) *Living in a New Past. Delft Architectural Studies on Housing*. Rotterdam: NAi Publishers.

Gameren, D. van, D. van den Heuvel, H. Mooij, P. van der Putt, O. Klijn and F. van Andel. (2013) *Building Together. The Architecture of Collective Private Commissions, Delft Architectural Studies on Housing*. Rotterdam: NAi010 Publishers.

Bibliography

Gameren, D. van, D. van den Heuvel, A. Kraaij, H. Mooij, P. van der Putt, O. Klijn, F. van Andel, P. Kuitenbrouwer, J. Zeinstra and H. Teerds. (2015) *Global Housing. Delft Architectural Studies on Housing*. Rotterdam: NAi010 Publishers.

Gemeentebestuur 's-Gravenhage, ed. (1948) *Enige Grondslagen voor de Stedebouwkundige Ontwikkeling van 's-Gravenhage*. 's-Gravenhage.

Gemeentelijken Woningdienst, ed. (1920) *De Jordaan. Het tech nisch woningonderzoek en de systematische perceelbeschrijving van Amsterdam, eerste deel*. Amsterdam.

Graaf, W. A. (1934) Foreword to *Algemeen Uitbreidingsplan; Grondslagen voor de Stedebouwkundige Ontwikkeling van Amsterdam, Nota van Toelichting*. Amsterdam: Publieke Werken, Stadsdrukkerij van Amsterdam.

Habraken, N. J. (2000) *The Structure of the Ordinary; Form and Control in the Built Environment*. Cambridge, MA: The MIT Press.

Hårde, U. (1986) *Eric Sigfrid Persson. Skånsk funktionalist byggmästare och uppfinnare*. Stockholm: Byggförlaget.

Hertzberger, H. (1960–1961) 'Naar een verticale woonbuurt', *Forum, orgaan van het genootschap Architectura et Amicitia*, XV(8).

Heuvel, D. van den, ed. (2018) *Jaap Bakema and the Open Society*. Amsterdam: Archis.

Hoogstraten, D. van. (2013) *Koninklijke Haagse Woningvereniging van 1854. De bouwgeschiedenis van een kleine onafhankelijke vereniging*. Bussum: Uitgeverij THOTH.

Huygen, P. (1995) *Emmen, de bouw van een aangename stad in het groen*. Rotterdam: NAi Publishers.

Idsinga, T., J. Schilt. (1987) *Architect W. van Tijen 1894–1974*. 's-Gravenhage: Staatsuitgeverij.

Internationale Kongresse für Neues Bauen (CIAM), ed. (1931) *Rationelle Bebauungsweisen*. Frankfurt am Main: Verlag Englert und Schlosser.

Jelles, E. J., C. A. Alberts. (1972) 'Duiker 1890–1935', *Forum, orgaan van het genootschap Architectura et Amicitia*, XXII(5/6).

Joedicke, J. (1963) *Architektur und Städtebau; Das Werk van den Broek und Bakema*. Stuttgart: Karl Krämer Verlag.

Joedicke, J., ed. (1976) *Architektur-Urbanismus; Architectengemeenschap van den Broek und Bakema*. Stuttgart: Karl Krämer Verlag.

Kaa, Ir. H. van der. (1927) *Het Eengezinshuis en zijn Mogelijkheden in Nederland*. s-Gravenhage.

Kok, A. A. (1946) *Amsterdamsche Woonhuizen*. Amsterdam: Allert de Lange.

Komossa, S., H. Meyer, M. Risselada, S. Thomaes and N. Jutten. (2002) *Atlas van het Hollandse Bouwblok*. Amsterdam, THOTH.

Kohlenbach, B. (1994) *Pieter Lodewijk Kramer; Architect van de Amsterdamse School 1881–1961*. Naarden: V+K Publishing/Immerc.

Kramer, P. (1924) 'De bouwwerken van M. de Klerk', *Wendingen, maandblad voor bouwen en sieren van Architectura et Amicitia*, 6(9/10).

Langkilde, H. E. (1970) *Kollektivhuset, en Boligforms Udviklilng i Dansk Arkitektur*. Copenhagen: Dansk Videnskabs Forlag.

Le Corbusier. (1953) *The Marseilles Block*. London: The Harvill Press.

Le Corbusier. (1964) *La Ville Radieuse*, reprint. Paris: Editions Vincent, Fréal & Cie.

Leeuwen, E. van and E. Mattie. (2005) *Park Meerwijk Villapark te Bergen; Manifest van de Amsterdamse School*. Amsterdam: Uitgeverij SUN.

Leliman, J. H. W. (1924) *Het Stadswoonhuis in Nederland gedurende de laatste 25 jaren*. 's-Gravenhage: Martinus Nijhoff.

Loghem, Ir. J. B. van. (1932) *Bouwen, Bauen, Batir, Building; Holland*. Amsterdam: Kosmos.

Loosjes, Mr. A. (c. 1920) *Sprokkelingen in Nederland; Stadsgezichten en Woonhuizen in Amsterdam*. Amsterdam: Scheltema & Holkema's boekhandel, K. Groesbeek & Paul Nijhoff.

Meischke, Prof. dr. ir. R., Dr. Ing. H. J. Zantkuijl, Ing. W. Raue and Drs. P. T. E. E. Rosenberg. (1995) *Huizen in Nederland, Amsterdam; Architectuurhistorische verkenningen aan de hand van het bezit van de Vereniging Hendrick de Keyser*. Zwolle: Waanders Uitgevers.

Merkelbach, B. (1935) 'Landelijke Architectuur?', *De 8 en Opbouw, 14-daagsch tijdschrift van de architectengroep 'De 8' Amsterdam en 'Opbouw' Rotterdam*, 24.

Mieras, J. P. (1951) 'Woonhuis aan de Zwarteweg te Aerdenhout'. *Bouwkundig Weekblad*, 51.

Ministerie van Volkshuisvesting en Bouwnijverheid, ed. (1965) *Zestienduizend Gulden Woningen*. Den Haag: Staatsuitgeverij.

Molema, J. and S. Leemans. (2017) *Bernard Bijvoet (1889–1997). Cher Maître van de Nederlandse Architectuur*. Nijmegen: Uitgeverij Vantilt.

Museum Boymans-Van Beuningen, ed. (1962) *Bouwen voor een open samenleving; Brinkman Brinkman Van der Vlugt Van den Broek Bakema*, exh. cat. Rotterdam.

N. A. (1930) *N. V. De Nederlandsche Gist- en Spiritusfabriek Delft; De ontwikkeling der onderneming in zestig jaren 1870–1930*. Delft: N.V. Van Markens Drukkerij-Vennootschap.

N. A. (1937) '5 Herenhuizen, licht lucht zon hygiene komfort', *De 8 en Opbouw, 14-daagsch tijdschrift van de architectengroep 'De 8' Amsterdam en 'Opbouw' Rotterdam*, 13.

N. A. (1937) 'Verenigingsbouw op "Landlust"', *De 8 en Opbouw, 14-daagsch tijdschrift van de architectengroep 'De 8' Amsterdam en 'Opbouw' Rotterdam*, 17.

N. A. (1962) *Om de toekomst van 100.000 Amsterdammers; Brief van Burgemeester en Wethouders van Amsterdam aan de Tweede Kamer der Staten Generaal*. Amsterdam: Stadsdrukkerij van Amsterdam.

Nederlandsch Instituut voor Volkshuisvesting en Stedebouw, ed. (1930) *De Woningwet 1902–1929*. Amsterdam.

Nederlandsch Instituut voor Volkshuisvesting en Stedebouw, ed. (1932) *Pre-advies uitgebracht door de ver.arch.kern 'De 8' te Amsterdam en de ver. 'Opbouw' te Rotterdam over: Organische woonwijk in open bebouwing*. Amsterdam.

Nederlands Instituut voor Volkshuisvesting en Stedebouw ed. (1952) *50 Jaar Woningwet 1902–1952 Gedenkboek*. Alphen aan den Rijn: N. Samsom. N.V.

Newman, Oscar. (1961) *CIAM '59 in Otterlo. Group for the Research of Social and Visual Inter-Relationships*. Hilversum: Uitgeverij G. van Saane – Lectura Architectonica.

Bibliography

Nycolaas, F. (2015) 'Wenken voor een veranderbare stad; Een studie naar veranderingspatronen van Amsterdamse buurten en bouwblokken', dissertation. Delft: TU Delft, Architecture Faculty.

Orum-Nielsen, J. (1996) *Dwelling. At Home – In Community – On Earth.* Copenhagen: The Danish Architectural Press.

Ottenhof, F. (1936) *Goedkoope arbeiderswoningen; Afbeeldingen van 28 projecten ingezonden op de door de gemeente Amsterdam uitgeschreven prijsvraag.* Rotterdam: W. L. & J. Brusse's uitgeversmaatschappij N. V.

Rasmussen, St. E. (1940) *Nordische Baukunst. Beispiele und Gedanken zur Baukunst unserer Zeit.* Berlin: Wasmuth Verlag.

Rasmussen, St. E. (1953) *Fra Amsterdam og Delft. Studier over Huse og Malere.* Copenhagen: Foreningen Fremtiden.

Risselada, M., ed. (1997) *Functionalisme 1927–1961. Hans Scharoun versus de Opbouw.* Delft: Publicatiebureau Bouwkunde.

Roth, A. (1948) *La Nouvelle Architecture/ Die Neue Architektur/The New Architecture.* Erlenbach-Zürich: Verlag für Architektur.

Rowan, Alistair. (2007) *Vaulting Ambition. The Adam Brothers: Contractors to the Metropolis in the Reign of George III.* London: Sir John Soane's Museum.

Schwagenscheidt, Walter. (1957) *Ein Mensch wandert durch die Stadt.* Bad Godesberg-Mehlem: Verlag H. Müller-Wellborn – Die Planung.

Seitz, K., H. Breitner and A. Weber. (1992) *Die Wohnhausanlage der Gemeinde Wien auf dem Gelände der ehemaligen Krimskykaserne*, facsimile reprint. Vienna: Archiv Verlag.

Sennett, A. R. (1905) *Garden Cities in Theory and Practice. Being an Amplification of a Paper of the Potentialities of Applied Science in a Garden City.* London: Bemrose and Sons Ltd.

Slothouber, E. (2017) *Rietveld in Reeuwijk; Een onderzoek naar Rietvelds Reeuwijkse projecten 1957–1960.* Krommenie: Stichting erven Rietveld.

Staal, J. F. (1921) 'Bouwwerk van Vorkink en Wormser', *Wendingen, maandblad voor bouwen en sieren van Architectura et Amicitia*, 4(6).

Stissi, V. (2007) *Amsterdam het Mekka van de Volkshuisvesting. Sociale Woningbouw 1909–1942.* Rotterdam: 010 Publishers.

Teijmant, I., J. Versnel and B. Sorgedrager. (2001) *Goed Wonen in Nieuw-West.* Amsterdam: Uitgeverij Bas Lubberhuizen.

Tijen, van, & Maaskant and Brinkman & Van den Broek. (1941) *Woonmogelijkheden in het nieuwe Rotterdam.* Rotterdam: W. L. & J. Brusse N. V.

Unwin, R. (1911) *Town Planning in Practice. An Introduction to the Art of Designing Cities and Suburbs.* London: T. Fisher Unwin.

Velde, Mr. J. J. van der. (1968) *Stadsontwikkeling van Amsterdam 1939–1967.* Amsterdam: Scheltema & Holkema N. V.

Wagt, Wim de. (1995) *J.B. van Loghem 1881–1940. Landhuizen, Stadswoonhuizen en Woningbouwprojecten.* Haarlem: Schuyt & Co Uitgevers en Importeurs BV.

Wal, L. van der, J. Bommer, Mr. P. A. van der Drift, Ir. A. Keppler, Ir. F. B. J. M. Moubis and K. Limperg. (1938) *Beter Wonen. Gedenkboek gewijd aan het werk der woningbouwverenigingen in Nederland 1913–1938.* Amsterdam: N. V. De Arbeiderspers.

Wattjes, Prof. ir. J. G. (1923) *Nieuw-Nederlandsche Bouwkunst. Eerste en tweede bundel.* Amsterdam: Uitgevers-maatschappij Kosmos.

Wattjes, Prof. ir. J. G. (1931) *Moderne Nederlandsche villa's en landhuizen.* Amsterdam: Uitgevers-maatschappij Kosmos.

Wattjes, Prof. ir. J. G. and F. A. Warners. (1944) *Amsterdams Bouwkunst en Stadsschoon 1306–1942.* Amsterdam: C. V. Allert de Lange.

Weeber, C. (1998) *Het Wilde Wonen.* Rotterdam: 010 Publishers.

Wegerif, A. H. Gzn. (1919) *Bouw van middenstandswoningen.* Apeldoorn: N. V. Uitgeversmaatschappij De Zonnebloem.

Wijdeveld, H. Th. (1918) 'Het Park Meerwijk te Bergen', *Wendingen, maandblad voor bouwen en sieren van Architectura et Amicitia*, 1(8).

Wijdeveld, H. Th. (1920) *'Woningbouwnummer'*, *Wendingen, maandblad voor bouwen en sieren van Architectura et Amicitia*, 3(3/4).

Wils, J. (1922) *Het Woonhuis. 1. Zijn Bouw.* Amsterdam: Uitgeversmaatschappij Elsevier.

Wilms Floet, W. and E. Gramsbergen. (2001) *Zakboek voor de woonomgeving.* Rotterdam: 010 Publishers.

Woud, A. van der. (2010) *Koninkrijk vol Sloppen; Achterbuurten en vuil in de negentiende eeuw.* Amsterdam: Uitgeverij Bert Bakker.

Yerbury, F. R., ed. (1936) *Housing. A European Survey by the Building Centre Committee. Volume 1: England, France, Holland, Sweden, Denmark, Spain.* London: Rolls House Publishing Co., Ltd.

Zanstra, Giesen en Sijmons, Ir. A. Boeken, A. Komter, A. Staal and S. van Woerden. (1946) *Bouwen. Van Woning tot Stad.* Amsterdam: N. V. Uitgevers Maatschappij G. A. van Oorschot.

Zumpe, M. (1966) *Wohnhochhäuser. Band 2: Scheibenhäuser.* Berlin: VEB Verlag für Bauwesen.

Image credits

The numbers refer to the page and illustration number or position: a top left, b middle left, c bottom left, d top right, e middle right, f bottom right.

Book covers are not credited and can be found in the Bibliography. Illustrations taken from books are credited by the first author and where necessary the title, as listed in the Bibliography. Rights of all plans and drawings not credited here are held by the author.

Archives and collections

Stadsarchief Amsterdam: cover-a, 14-3, 15-6, 16-7, 18-9, 18-11, 18-12, 19-13, 24-24, 24-25, 25-28, 25-30, 32-42, 32-43, 33-45, 33-46, 33-47, 33-48, 36-52, 36-53, 37-57, 41-65, 47-10, 50-15, 50-16, 75-18, 96-76, 96-78, 97-80, 97-82, 97-83, 97-84, 105-106, 105-107

Collectie Haags Gemeentearchief: 23-23, 102-87, 102-89, 102-90, 102-91

Collectie Het Nieuwe Instituut Rotterdam: 22-19, 24-26, 47-9, 55-32, 74-15, 78-23, 78-25, 79-27, 97-81, 98-86, 108-110, 117-7, 121-16

London Metropolitan Archives: 59-39, 59-41

Architectural Press Archives/ RIBA Collections: 59-42

Stadsarchief Delft: 72-5, 73-9, 73-10

Magazines

Architectural Review: 58-35, 58-38, *Bouw*: 83-36, 105-108, 121-21, 121-22, 121-23, *Bouwkundig Weekblad*: 91-63, 91-64, 91-65, *DASH*: 36-49, 46-2, 46-6, 46-7, 51-21, 54-27, 58-36, 59-40, 62-45, 83-35, 117-8, 117-10, 120-13, 122-19, *De 8 en Opbouw*: 35-35, 85-50, 90-60, *Forum*: 54-28, 55-29, 55-30, 55-31, 78-21, 78-22, 88-57, 104-100, 105-105, *Wendingen*: 25-27, 42-1, 50-13, 50-14, 88-51, 88-52, 88-54, 89-55, 89-56, 89-58, 98-85

Books

Amsterdam Volkshuisvesting: 96-77, Artaria: 90-61, 90-62, Baillie Scott, *Houses and Gardens*: 88-53, *Barbican Redevelopment 1959*: 58-33, Behrens: 74-12, Berlage, *Normalisatie in Woningbouw*: 73-7, 73-8, 74-14, Berlage, *Moderne Bouwkunst in Nederland*: 35-37, 35-38, 74-16, 74-17, 103-92, 103-93, 103-94, 103-96, 103-97, Berlage, *Arbeiderswoningen in Nederland*: 22-18, Bernoulli: 58-34, Boeken: 25-31, Bosma: 108-109, *Bouwen voor een open samenleving*: 22-20, 22-21, Brown: 79-26, Butler: 94-68, Chermayeff: 84-40, 84-41, Claus: 37-56, *De Jordaan*: 19-16, *De Woningwet 1902–1929*: 19-15, 23-22, Duiker: 104-99, *Enige Grondslagen voor de Stedebouwkundige Ontwikkeling van 's-Gravenhage*: 102-88, Feenstra: 73-11, 96-74, Hårde: 79-28, 79-29, *Interbau Berlin 1957*: 105-103, 105-104, Joedicke, *Architektur und Städtebau*: 54-26, Joedicke, *Architektur-Urbanismus*: 121-15, 121-17, Kok: 72-6, Leliman: 82-30, Loosjes: 10-1, 16-8, 72-2, 117-6, Nycolaas: 40-61, Orum-Nielsen: 82-32, 82-33, Rasmussen, *Fra Amsterdam og Delft*: 8-4, Roth: 103-95, Schwagenscheidt: 83-37, Seitz: 51-17, 51-18, 51-19, 51-20, Sennett: 72-3, 72-4, *Slum Clearance and Rehousing*: 35-36, Tijen, van: 104-102, Unwin: 74-13, Velde, van der: 32-41, *Verbetering der Volkshuisvesting te Amsterdam*: 19-14, 22-17, 96-79, 97-80, Wal, van der: 14-2, Wattjes, *Moderne Nederlandsche villa's en landhuizen*: 94-69, Wattjes, *Amsterdams Bouwkunst en Stadsschoon 1306–1942*: 25-29, Wils: 89-59, Yerbury: 75-19, 75-20, Zanstra: 32-39, 32-40, Zumpe: 32-44

Photography and drawings

Marcel van der Burg: 6-1, 36-51, 40-62, 92-67, 132-a, 132-c, 136, 137, 138, 139, 140-a, 142, 143, 144-a, 152, 158, 159, 160-a, 160-b, 163, 166-d, 171, 172-d, 172-e, 174, 176-b, 176-c, 177, 178, 184-c, 186, 187, 192, 193, 205, 208-c, 210, 211-c, 213-a, 215-c, 220-b, 221, 226, 228, 233, 236, 237, 240, 242, 244, 248, 254, 256, 258, 260, 272, 282, 284, 304, 317, 318, 320, 326

Christian Richters: 37-54, 37-58, 85-48, 126-25, 126-26, 126-28, 133, 134, 135-a, 135-c, 144-c, 156, 157, 165-a, 166-c, 169, 179-a, 183, 184-a, 184-b, 185, 188, 194, 195-e, 195-f, 197-a, 198-b, 201, 207, 216-c, 217, 218-a, 219, 223, 230, 238, 246, 252, 268, 270, 280, 292, 297, 301, 309, 310, 311, 319, 324, 327

Dick van Gameren: 9-5, 37-55, 82-31, 85-49, 116-4, 117-9, 141, 153, 168, 173-a, 175, 179-c, 179-f, 195-a, 203, 204, 206, 211-a, 211-f, 216-a, 218-c, 220-a, 266, 290, 300, 308

Annenies Kraaij: cover-f, 41-66, 62-47, 65-52, 120-11, 121-14, 122-18, 122-20, 140-c, 162-b, 162-c, 176-a, 176-f

Machteld Schoep: 40-63, 41-64, 41-67, 146, 147, 165-b, 165-c, 209, 250, 262, 264, 325

Rohan Varma: 160-c, 161, 162-a, 184-f, 234-a, 294, 296, 298

Luuk Kramer: 173-b, 173-c, 185-d, 191-d, 191-e, 214-c, 299

Pedro Kok: 167, 180, 190, 191-c, 200, 215-a, 302

Greg Holmes: 73-70, 73-71, 154, 199-f, 278

Sebastiaan Kaal: 189, 198-e, 198-f, 295, 322

Nicholas Kane: 110-1, 126-27, 321, 323

Benedict Luxmoore: 63-50, 63-51, 148, 149, 276

Karel Tomeï: 166-a, 214-a, 288

Aerocamera BV–Michel Hofmeester: 172-c, 213-c, 286

Robert Adam: 46-3, Aerophoto-Schiphol: 62-46, Aerostockphoto: 116-5, Aviodrome: 66-1, 234-f, Eva Besnyö MAI: 78-24, Bernd Borchardt: 127-30, Blue Sky Images: 181-a, 181-c, Bureau Benno Stegeman: 36-50, William A. Clarke, National Monuments Record: 46-5, 46-8, Tjeerd Derkink: 220-c, Jan Derwig: 274, Richard Einzig, Arcaid Images: 58-37, Familie Archief Mieras: 120-12, Francesca Giovanelli: 197-f, 198-a, Alex Kirchstein: 47-11, Mariashot.photo: 181-b, 199-a, 222-c, 306, Harald Mooij: 83-34, Iskander Pané, Olivier van der Bogt, Otto Diesfeldt: 14-4, 14-5, Tony Ray-Jones/RIBA Collections: 59-42, 59-43, Sir John Soane's Museum: 46-4, Bart Sorgedrager: 40-60, Jan Versnel MAI: 40-59, Willemijn Wilms Floet: 50-12, Ad Windig MAI: 18-10, Thijs Wolzak: 213-f, The World's Most Secret Homes, video-still: 222-d, Wikimedia Commons: 7-2, 7-3, 53-24

Texts

Chapter 2 is a revised and extended version of a text previously published in French: Arpa, J. *Paris Habitat*. Paris: Editions du Pavillon de l' Arsenal, 2015. Chapter 4 is a revised text, previously published in: Gameren, D. van, D. van den Heuvel, H. Mooij, P. van der Putt, O. Klijn and F. van Andel. *Building Together, The Architecture of Collective Private Commissions, Delft Architectural Studies on Housing*. Rotterdam: NAi010 uitgevers, 2013.

Despite best efforts, we have not been able to identify the holders of copyright and printing rights for all the illustrations. Copyright holders not mentioned in the credits are asked to substantiate their claims, and recompense will be made according to standard practice.

Acknowledgements

This book would not have been possible without the contribution of many colleagues and friends.

First of all, I want to thank Bjarne Mastenbroek and Francine Houben, long-time partners in architecture and cherished friends without whom my professional life would have been very different. The three of us share a strong connection and gratitude to Max Risselada, our teacher at the Faculty of Architecture in Delft, who opened our eyes to the beauty and relevance of architecture, and the importance of housing design. I feel honoured that I could follow his footsteps when I was appointed as a professor in Delft.

The works documented in this book would not have existed without them, and without the contribution of all the wonderful and inspiring people who have worked with me to design and realise the buildings shown here. There are too many to mention, but I make an exception for three colleagues who have been over many years so loyal and resilient: Willmar Groenendijk, Maarten de Geus, and Sebastiaan Kaal. I also want to thank my colleagues during the Architectengroep years in Amsterdam, Ben Loerakker, Kees Rijnboutt, Hans Ruijssenaars, and Gert-Jan Hendriks, for all their support while I was getting started as a young architect.

To make this book, many people helped in collecting the material, making documentation drawings, and finding sources and images in libraries and archives. Here I want to mention Rohan Varma, Linda van Keeken, Robbert Guis, Giorgio Larcher, Manfredi Villarosa, Lada Hrsak, Gonzalo Zylberman, Omar El Hassan, and Sebastiaan Kaal. Many photographers contributed; a special mention is needed for Marcel van der Burg, who still surprises me with his striking and personal view of the projects. For the stimulating discussions on the history of Dutch housing, I thank my colleagues at the faculty, especially Aart Oxenaar and Harald Mooij.

Finally, I owe most to my partner Annenies and daughters Isa and Tessel for their support, patience, and interest in my work that took me from home too often. It is to them that I dedicate this book.

The author

Dick van Gameren is professor of housing design and dean of the Faculty of Architecture and the Built Environment at Delft University of Technology, and partner at Mecanoo Architecten. Combining his work as an architect with a professorship, Van Gameren maintains a critical approach to design by lecturing, researching, and publishing.

In his early career he received a first prize in the 1991 Europan Competition, and in 1995 the Charlotte Köhler Prize of the Prins Bernard Cultuurfonds. In 2007, he won the prestigious Aga Kahn Award for the design of the Netherlands Embassy in Ethiopia, and in 2012 the Best Building of the Year Award of the Dutch Association of Architects for the design of Villa 4.0.

The project for Thamesmead South in London won the English Housing Design Regeneration Award in 2017, and, in that same year, the Langebrug student housing in Leiden received the Rijnlandse Architectuurprijs.

At TU Delft, he leads the Global Housing Study Centre, an international education and research network which focusses on the issues related to designing and building affordable housing in the rapidly expanding cities of the Global South.

Main publications:
Revisions of Space: A Manual for Architecture, NAi uitgevers, Rotterdam, 2006.

DASH; Delft Architectural Studies on Housing, founding/chief editor of a book series (fifteen published volumes) on housing design for students, professionals, and academics; NAi010 uitgevers, Rotterdam, from 2008 onwards.

Living Ideals: Designs for Housing by Charles Correa, Charles Correa Foundation, Goa, 2018.

Global Housing, book series, founding editor, with Nelson Mota. First volume: *Dwelling in Addis Ababa*, Japsam Publishers, Prinsenbeek, 2020.

The projects documented in this book have been realised working in different constellations:

1991–1992	Van Gameren & Mastenbroek Architecten, Amsterdam
1992–2005	De Architectengroep, Amsterdam
2005–2013	Dick van Gameren Architecten, Amsterdam
2013–today	Mecanoo Architecten, Delft

The credits for each project are listed in the documentation.

Imprint

Concept and texts:
Dick van Gameren

Image research and editing:
Rohan Varma

Copy editing:
Christen Jamar

Proofreading:
Dean Drake

Design:
Bureau Sandra Doeller

Image processing:
Peter Schladoth

Printing, and binding:
DZA Druckerei zu Altenburg GmbH,
Thuringia

© 2023 Park Books AG, Zurich

© for the texts: Dick van Gameren
© for the images: see image credits

Park Books
Niederdorfstrasse 54
8001 Zurich
Switzerland
www.park-books.com

Park Books is being supported by the Federal Office of Culture with a general subsidy for the years 2021–2024.

All rights reserved; no part of this publication may be reproduced, stored in a retrieval system or transmitted in any form or by any means, electronic, mechanical, photocopying, recording, or otherwise, without the prior written consent of the publisher.

ISBN 978-3-03860-304-7

This book has been made possible with the support of:

Faculty of Architecture and the Built Environment
Delft University of Technology

Mecanoo Architecten, Delft

mecanoo